TRAINED TO SERVE JESUS

The Heart and History of Set Free Church and Its Founder Phil Aguilar

Foreword by Tim Storey
Interviews by David Trotter

Awaken Media

TRAINED TO SERVE JESUS: THE HEART AND HISTORY OF SET FREE CHURCH & ITS FOUNDER PHIL AGUILAR

Foreword by Tim Storey
Interviews by David Trotter

Cover photo by David Trotter.

Author photo by Waverly Trotter - www.waverlytrotter.com.

Interior photos courtesy of Set Free Church and the Aguilar family unless otherwise noted, and bio photos courtesy of individuals.

Designed by 8TRACKstudios - www.8trackstudios.com

ISBN: 978-1-935798-13-2

To the thousands of people
touched by Set Free churches around the globe
and the ministry of Pastor Phil Aguilar.

May you be inspired to continue
following in the footsteps of Jesus.

TABLE OF CONTENTS

TURNING SETBACKS INTO COMEBACKS

Phil Aguilar is a modern-day superhero. He was born to battle for the underdog. From the early struggles of his youth, he learned that life could get the best of you if you don't learn to fight back. 'Fight back' is what he has done. He is known as a pastor for the hurting, and he spends his days helping people turn there setbacks into comebacks.

In this book, you will learn the real story of a man sometimes in a state of recovery from his own pain, but at the same time bringing healing to so many. Phil Aguilar is a wounded healer who has helped change the lives of thousand of people. "The righteous will still bear fruit when they get older" is what the Bible states, and such is the case with Dr Phil. His latter days are now filled with purpose, gratitude, and hope - from changing lives in the recovery world to spending time with his children and his grandchildren. This book will challenge you to never give up on a God who said He is able.

Tim Storey
April 2017

TELLING THE STORY

During my freshman year at Southern California College (now Vanguard University), friends invited me along to a church service I've never forgotten. It would have been late 1991 or early 1992 when we drove to downtown Anaheim, fought for a parking place amidst rumbling motorcycles, and walked into a rugged warehouse at 320 North Anaheim Blvd.

I remember people swarming the streets surrounding this anything-but-traditional church building, and the only seats left were in wooden bleachers along the back. We squeezed in next to some rough-looking churchgoers, and thumping music consumed the crowd as everyone rose to their feet. Rock-n-roll, rap, hip-hop, country, and everything in between flowed throughout the service, and a sunglass-wearing pastor eventually stepped up to the mic to deliver a no-nonsense message.

I was experiencing Set Free Church.

I'm not too sure how much I paid attention to the message that day, because my eyes were scanning the room in awe of the motley crue of people assembled for this event that (in my mind) was a combination concert, sideshow, and Christian youth rally. As an 18-year-old Pastoral Ministries major at an Assemblies of God college, I was used to "basking in the presence of the Lord" while a praise band led us in the latest and greatest worship songs from Integrity, Maranatha, or Vineyard.

My discomfort with the experience was only matched by my intrigue of this man they called "Pastor Phil", so I moved in for a closer look after the service. People were pressing from every side trying to shake his hand or have him pray for their situation. He was charismatic, full of energy, and more than willing to take time to speak with each and every person.

As we stood at a distance and listened in on his interactions, I noticed a woman wearing a white lace dress and carrying bouquet of flowers, and she was being accompanied by a man in dark clothes. It was as if the Red Sea parted when people saw them coming toward Pastor Phil, and we all stepped forward again to watch the interaction unfold.

"Pastor Phil, we want you to renew our vows today!" the woman yelled.

"Alright, let's do it. Now's just as good a time as any," Phil responded.

What? They're renewing their vows in the middle of the street? Had they sent out invitations? Where was the photographer? How about a reception with cake?

My mind was rattled by the impromptu nature of this renewal ceremony followed by the hoots and hollers of the crowd. This...yes, *this*...was the thing I remember most about the one and only time I visited Set Free in Anaheim.

The passion of the couple. The confidence that Pastor Phil would say 'yes' to a spontaneous ministry moment. The willingness of the crowd to jump in on the celebration.

Frankly, the whole experience was a little too over the top for me at that stage of life, but I would never forget that day. In subsequent years, the Set Free Posse came to our college a couple of times, and I remember stopping to watch them in front of the library as they rapped and danced to their own beat. Throughout the years as I was a pastor in Orange County and eventually in Long Beach, I would hear something here or there about Set Free or Pastor Phil, but I didn't keep up with the ministry or his story until I stumbled across a Facebook post in 2010. Pastor Phil had written a book entitled *"Forgive Me Father For I Have Sinned"*, and I followed the link over to his website and purchased a copy.

A couple of weeks later, the book came to mind, and I realized that it had never arrived. I reached out via the email on his website, and Matthew Aguilar (his son) responded with an apology about the book not arriving. I wasn't sure if it got lost in the mail or it was never sent in the first place, so I offered to send my own book in exchange for a second copy of his. Within a matter of days, Phil's book arrived, and he ended up reaching out to me after reading mine - *"Lost + Found: Finding Myself by Getting Lost in an Affair"*. It was clear that both of us had walked down some dark and rocky roads, but his road was quite a bit longer than my own.

One night, Phil and his wife, Sandra, brought by their friend Chip Esajian for us to meet and talk about Chip's new book. When Phil walked in our front door, it was as if he owned the place. His charisma, confidence, and swag filled the room. I thought to myself...Who is this guy? Doesn't he realize he's just in my living room? While I absolutely loved connecting with a living legend, my kids were just happy when I took his book off the coffee table, because the cover emblazoned with his tattooed face was making them a wee bit uncomfortable.

Within a few months, we met for lunch at Chipotle, and my intrigue continued to grow. I was interested in what he had experienced throughout the ups, downs, twists, and turns of where his Harley had taken him over the years. I knew he had seen things I had never (and probably *would* never) experience in my lifetime. There were lessons to be learned from him for sure.

Fast forward to March 2016 when we sat down for breakfast, and I had one thing on my mind. Having produced two documentaries on social justice issues, I was hungry for another project that had a little different flavor - perhaps a little Tapatío. As we finished our food, I pitched Phil on the idea of producing a documentary on the history of Set Free and his ministry. To my surprise, he had been thinking something similar, but thought I was too busy to take on the project. We met a couple of more times to discuss the project and agreed to begin this year-long journey.

Producing the Set Free Documentary
For the past year, I have immersed myself in the story of Set Free Church and Pastor Phil Aguilar. I've read numerous articles, blog posts, cult buster message boards, and books on the subject. Phil and Sandra have given me the privilege of digging through boxes of old Set Free photos and bins of videotapes in their garage, and I've watched (and digitized) countless hours of services, ministry trips, and shows on Trinity Broadcasting Network.

With Phil's blessing, my team and I set out to interview all the key players from the start of Set Free Church along with numerous pastors and the Aguilar family themselves. In the process of reaching out to people, I quickly found out that many of them didn't want to be interviewed. Some people never responded, others politely declined, and one person even asked for $7,500 for a written interview. A list of declined interviewees includes Wayne Palmer, Bob Nixon, Lois Trader, Kid Ramos, Steve Schinhofen, Tom Daley, Oden Fong, Ron Enroth, Jackie Alnor, John Duncan, Jan Crouch, Tommy Barnett, Matthew Barnett, Stacee Bassett, and others. They all had their reasons for not wanting to participate, but it was rather frustrating for me as a documentary filmmaker to say the least. Whether they didn't want to be associated with the controversy or they feared retaliation for what they might say or simply wanted to forget painful experiences of the past, I had to take their "no" and move on to the next person. In some cases, I was able to have off-the-record phone calls or email exchanges to at least hear their unique perspective.

Throughout all the research and interviews, one thing became very clear in my mind - Phil Aguilar is a complex man. He has a deep passion for serving God, saving souls, loving black sheep, rehabilitating addicts, starting new ventures, and having fun with his wife, kids, and grandchildren. Yet, he also has the potential to be his own worst enemy, and I know that reality in my own life all too well.

While some might question the amount of time we've given in the film and this book to his upbringing, I believe it is critical to understand how it shaped him as a leader as well as the Set Free movement itself. Through the months I've spent digging into this story, I have come to admire all the people who were (and are) involved. Having started churches myself, I have a deep respect for anyone who invests their life in such a challenging and worthwhile cause. I also understand the messiness of planting a church and the potential for unmet expectations, broken relationships, and the dark side of leadership. Two people can experience the same events but have totally different perspectives on what, when, why, and how something happened. Throughout this process, I have wrestled with the facts as presented by multiple people, contemplated motives (including my own), and become enamored by the story itself. However you feel about Phil Aguilar and the Set Free movement, the reality is that he has touched thousands of lives, and his legacy lives on in former addicts, bikers, black sheep, leaders, pastors, and churches around the globe.

Assembling The Interviews

As with any documentary, there is far more left on the cutting room floor than actually appears in the film. There are many reasons, but oftentimes the content isn't the most interesting way to tell the story or it's simply too detailed for the average viewer. As a filmmaker, one of the most painful decisions is what *not* to include when you love the story so much. I wish everyone could watch every second of the interviews, but the film has to be crafted in a way that the viewer will stay engaged from beginning to end. Because I believe the full chorus of voices is worth being heard, I've gone to great lengths to transcribe every interview and edit them in such a way to tell the story in a linear fashion for you to explore in this book.

- The content contained in this book is derived from one-on-one video interviews conducted in 2016 during the making of *Set Free Posse*, a documentary on the heart and history of Set Free Church and its founder Pastor Phil Aguilar.

- Each chapter begins with a short introduction so you will have a framework to understand what each person is discussing.

- As best as possible, each interview has been cut into sections based on the linear nature of the story.

INTRODUCTION

- The interviewee's name and what they are speaking about is included at the beginning of their statement in order to help you immediately pick up on the conversation.

- **IMPORTANT NOTE:** For the most part, I have maintained the word-for-word transcriptions from the interviews to ensure the integrity of the person's thoughts and personality. *From time to time, this may result in a stream of consciousness more than a linear thought process, and I have inserted a dash (-) at the moment when the change of thought occurs.* In a few situations, a portion of a person's interview may not have been included in the book, because it was not connected to the history of Set Free or Phil Aguilar.

Please take a few moments to read the brief bios of the interviewees (and those referred to in the interviews) prior to jumping into the story, so you'll have a better sense of each individual's perspective.

May I also make a suggestion? It will serve you well to set aside judgments you bring to this material and hold off making more judgments along the way. Allow the magnitude of the events to permeate your mind and listen for how this story might speak to your heart as much as it has mine.

David Trotter
March 2017

Dr. Richie Cole, Pastor Phil Aguilar, David Trotter (Venice Beach, CA)

TRAINED TO SERVE JESUS

BRIEF BIOS

While most individuals in this section were interviewed for the documentary, some bios have been included for those not interviewed, because they are central characters in the story and will help you gain context. Bios are generally listed in the order of the person's appearance in the story.

GILBERT COTA AGUILAR was the father of Phil Aguilar. He was born on 5/30/1923 and passed away 2/27/2017.

CELIA KIMBLE BLANCO (SALAS) was the mother of Phil Aguilar. She was born on 8/26/27 and passed away 5/29/2012.

PASTOR PHIL AGUILAR (aka Pastor Phil, Dr. Phil, Pas, and Chief) is the founder of Set Free Church in Anaheim, California, and the co-founder of the Los Angeles International Church and Dream Center with Tommy Barnett and Matthew Barnett. As a motorcycle enthusiast, he is also the founder of Christ's Sons, Servants For Christ, and Set Free Soldiers motorcycle clubs. He has five children and 23 grandchildren. Currently, he and his daughter, Trina, operate So Cal Treatment Center (www.socaltreatment.org) and Black Sheep Recovery (www.blacksheeprecovery.com), residential drug treatment homes in Anaheim, California. He is also a pastor within the Church of God and oversees Set Free Burbank, pastored by his son, Philip "Chill" Aguilar. Pastor Phil (www.setfree.org) regularly at churches, outreaches, and conferences.

BILLY AGUILAR is a brother of Phil Aguilar, and he attended Set Free Anaheim for ten years. He served as the President of multiple motorcycle clubs over the years including Christ's Sons, Servants For Christ, Saints MC, Prophets MC, and Deacons MC. He and his wife, Frankie, live in Anaheim, California.

ELIZABETH AGUILAR BUCHANAN is the only sister of Phil Aguilar, and she married Phil's friend, Jim Buchanan. They served in multiple capacities of leadership at Set Free including the overseeing of a discipleship home. Elizabeth now lives with Jim in Porterville, California, and she is a professor at Porterville College.

JIM BUCHANAN is the husband of Elizabeth Aguilar, and he was a self-proclaimed "partner in crime" with Phil Aguilar in his youth. Jim served in leadership at Set Free in numerous ways including His Hands Extended ministry, and he is currently retired and living in Porterville, California.

PASTOR GLENN MORRISON founded Follow Up Prison Ministries (www.followupministries.org) in 1956 and spent thousands of hours in various prisons meeting with prisoners one-on-one and in group settings for Bible study and discipleship. Glenn led Phil Aguilar to Christ in Chino State Prison in 1977, and we had the privilege of interviewing Glenn and Phil together in Arizona prior to Glenn's passing on September 17, 2016.

PASTOR HERB SOKOL was a lay pastor and chaplain at Vacaville Penitentiary in Vacaville, California, who discipled Phil Aguilar during his time in prison, and he married Phil and Sandra in the prison itself.

PASTOR JOHN LYLE is Pastor Emeritus of Temple Baptist Church (www.tbcperris.com) in Perris, California, where he has served faithfully since 1958. John played a central role in helping Phil Aguilar go to Bible college and training him in Evangelism Explosion.

SANDRA AGUILAR (aka Saint Sandra) is the wife of Pastor Phil Aguilar, and she played an integral part in founding Set Free Church. In the early days, she was one of the first worship and children's ministry leaders as well as a confidante to Lois Trader, Phil's assistant. She is the mother of Christopher Runyan, Matthew "MJ" Aguilar, Philip "Chill" Aguilar, Trina Aguilar, and Hebrew "Roc" Aguilar as well as the stepmother to Geronimo Aguilar. She currently works with Phil and Trina at So Cal Treatment Center.

MATTHEW AGUILAR (aka MJ) is the son of Phil and Sandra Aguilar, and he grew up at Set Free Anaheim and the subsequent expressions of the ministry. Alongside his brothers Geronimo and Philip, MJ was known for his skills of songwriting, rapping, and dancing as well as producing multiple albums over the years. While currently serving as the Treatment Manager at So Cal Treatment Center, he is married to Renee, and they have six children.

INTRODUCTION

PHILIP AGUILAR (aka Chill) is the son of Phil and Sandra Aguilar, and he used his skills of songwriting, rapping, and dancing alongside his brother, MJ, to make a major mark on the ministry of Set Free over the years. Years later, he moved to Virginia to lead worship at Richmond Outreach Center with his brother, Pastor Geronimo Aguilar, until confronting him on issues of morality. Since then, Chill has traveled the world leading worship at churches both large and small and currently pastors Set Free Church in Burbank, California (www.facebook.com/setfreeburbank). He is married to Renae, and they have one child.

TRINA AGUILAR TIMANUS is the daughter of Phil and Sandra Aguilar, and she avoided the spotlight at Set Free as much as possible (although you can see her dancing and acting in several archive videos). She has a passion to help addicts gain freedom, and she operates So Cal Treatment Center with Pastor Phil and other family members. Trina is married to Michael "Turtle" Timanus, and they have four children (two sets of twins).

HEBREW AGUILAR (aka Roc) is the youngest child of Phil and Sandra Aguilar, and he currently operates Community Rehab (www.community-rehab.com) and Elevate Recovery Center (www.elevaterecoverycenter.com) in Orange, California. He is married to Dallas, and they have three children.

PASTOR WAYNE AND HOLLY PALMER hosted the first meeting of Set Free Church in their home, and Wayne was the assistant pastor working alongside Pastor Phil for many years. In December 1993 in the wake of Phil's departure, Wayne founded Freedom Bible Church (www.freedombiblechurch.org) in Anaheim, California, and he continues to serve as the Senior Pastor.

PASTOR BOB AND SHARON NIXON were key leaders at Set Free Church from early days, and Bob was an assistant pastor. As Pastor Phil transitioned out of leadership, Bob and a remnant from Set Free founded New Wine Church (www.new-wine.church) in September 1993, and he continues to serve at the Senior Pastor.

LOIS AND TIM TRADER were early members of Set Free Church, and she became Pastor Phil's long-time administrative assistant. According to Phil, she was the "mastermind" behind the church by keeping him organized as well as numerous ministries under the Set Free banner. Her husband, Tim, worked as a camera man for Trinity Broadcasting Network, and he shared about the Set Free discipleship homes with a TBN secretary. The resulting conversations with Paul and Jan Crouch paved the way for a tight relationship between TBN and Set Free Church.

PAUL AND JAN CROUCH founded Trinity Broadcasting Network in 1973, and it has grown to over thirty 24-hour global networks reaching every inhabited continent with Christian programming. TBN purchased and leased homes in Anaheim, California, for Set Free to use as discipleship homes, and the network hosted a Set Free television show at one time. Pastor Phil was on the TBN board for a season as well. Paul passed away on November 30, 2013, and Jan on May 31, 2016.

DAVID RAMOS (aka Kid Ramos) is professional guitarist, singer, and songwriter who has worked with James Harman, Roomful of Blues, the Big Rhythm Combo, The Fabulous Thunderbirds, The Mannish Boys, Bobby Jones and Los Fabulocos. He was a long-time band leader at Set Free, before leaving during the unraveling of the ministry.

GERONIMO AGUILAR (aka Pastor G) is the son of Phil Aguilar and his first wife, Karen (deceased). After not seeing his father for 14 years, Geronimo reunited with Pastor Phil while living with his grandparents in Anaheim. He made a significant mark on the trajectory of Set Free with the introduction of hip hop and dance to the church services and outreaches. He married Stacee Davis (now Stacee Bassett) and had two children before divorcing. After leaving Set Free, he eventually founded Richmond Outreach Center (ROC) in Richmond, Virginia, in 1999. He is married to Samantha, and they have three children together. Geronimo is currently serving 40 years in a Texas prison for multiple counts of sexual assault.

STACEE DAVIS BASSETT is the ex-wife of Geronimo Aguilar, and they have two children together. Her parents, Dave and Tobyann Davis, brought Stacee to Set Free for help during a time of crisis.

DAVE AND TOBYANN DAVIS are the parents of Stacee Davis who married Geronimo Aguilar. They initiated contact with Pastor Oden Fong at Calvary Chapel with allegations against Set Free Church and Pastor Phil Aguilar.

PASTOR ODEN FONG was the director of Calvary Chapel Outreach Fellowships (the overseeing office of Calvary Chapel church affiliation at that time) and was approached by Dave and Tobyann Davis to address allegations against Set Free and Pastor Phil Aguilar. Currently, he is the pastor of Poiema Christian Fellowship in Costa Mesa, CA.

PASTOR CHUCK SMITH founded Calvary Chapel in 1965 in Costa Mesa, CA, and what began as a small local church has now grown into an international ministry of over 1,500 fellowships throughout the world. Chuck Smith passed away on October 3, 2013.

DR. RONALD ENROTH was a Professor of Sociology at Westmont College in Santa Barbara, California, and a prominent evangelical Christian author of books concerning what he defines as "cults" and "new religious movements". His book *"Churches That Abuse"* included a chapter on Set Free Church. Currently, Ron is retired and living in Hawaii.

BILL AND JACKIE ALNOR published multiple articles about Set Free Church and Pastor Phil in their efforts to warn others about cults and dangerous movements. Although Bill passed away in 2011, Jackie has continued her work through her website (www.apostasyalert.org) and book entitled *"The Fleecing of Christianity"*.

FRED HUNTER served as the mayor of Anaheim, California, from 1988 to 1992, and he was a major supporter of Set Free Church. After Tom Daley became mayor in 1992, Fred served on the city council during the time in which Set Free was being evicted from their buildings. Currently, Fred is retired and living in Newport Beach, California.

TOM DALEY served as the mayor of Anaheim, California, from 1992 to 2002, and he took an active role in withdrawing the city's support of Set Free Church. Currently, he represents California's 69th Assembly District including the cities of Santa Ana, Anaheim, Garden Grove, and Orange.

TRAINED TO SERVE JESUS

KELLI MORENO gained freedom from a drug addiction at Set Free and lived in the discipleship homes for four years. She traveled with the ministry and performed as a dancer throughout that time. Currently, she owns a real estate company (www.kellimoreno.com) and lives with her husband, Mark, and their family in Beaumont, California.

ALEXA TEJEDA was a prominent singer at Set Free Church during its heyday, and she was extremely active in the day to day ministry in the evenings. After coming to the church in 1988, not only did she participate in outreaches, but she translated for the Spanish ministry and went to Israel with the church as well. Alexa has tremendous experience as a vocalist, show host, and actress on primetime Spanish television, and she is currently working in social services in southern California.

PASTOR TOMMY BARNETT is co-founder of the Los Angeles Dream Center (www.dreamcenter.org) and Phoenix Dream Center (www.phxdreamcenter.org) as well as the former senior pastor of Dream City Church (formerly Phoenix First Assembly of God).

PASTOR MATTHEW BARNETT is co-founder of the Los Angeles Dream Center (www.dreamcenter.org) and senior pastor of the Angelus Temple (www.angelustemple.org). The church grew from 39 members at its conception in September of 1994, to reaching more than 50,000 people each week in multiple services and over 200 ministries and outreaches today. The Dream Center houses over 600 people, and every week people receive food and many other services are offered to meet the spiritual and physical needs of the community.

PASTOR WILEY DRAKE (www.wileydrakeinbuenapark.com) is the pastor of First Southern Baptist Church of Buena Park, California (www.firstsouthernbaptistchurchofbuena-park.com), and he has been a supporter of Set Free since their challenges with the city of Anaheim. In 2002, the church opened its doors to Set Free to begin meeting on Saturday nights.

REGINALD ARIVIZU (aka Fieldy) is the bassist for the nu-metal band Korn (www.korn.com), and he followed Jesus and was baptized at Set Free - eventually inviting Pastor Phil on tour with Korn.

BRIEF BIOS

GEORGE NATZIC was a member of Servants For Christ and Set Free Soldiers motorcycle clubs while attending Set Free Church. Sensing the group was no longer serving its original ministry purpose, he chose to leave both the club and church. Currently, George is a businessman living in Corona, California, with his wife, Cheri, and their two children.

MICHAEL TIMANUS (aka Turtle) gained freedom from a drug addiction at Set Free and eventually married Trina Aguilar, daughter of Phil and Sandra Aguilar. He was a Set Free Soldier at the center of the Blackie's incident and subsequent raid at Set Free homes in Anaheim - resulting in a year in county jail. Currently, he partners with Trina to run So Cal Treatment Center, and he is the father of their four children.

JOHN "QUICKY" JUAREZ gained freedom from a drug addiction while living with Pastor Phil and has a unique perspective on Set Free as a member of the Vagos motorcycle club. Following the model of Pastor Phil, Quicky invites addicts to live in his own home as he helps them seek recovery.

PASTOR EDDIE BANALES is the pastor of So Cal Dream Center (www.facebook.com/SoCalDreamCenter) in Pomona, California. He was introduced to Set Free in 1991 and eventually affiliated with the movement and played a role in overseeing pastors after Phil's exit from leadership. He played a central role in connecting Phil Aguilar to Pastor Tommy Barnett and more recently to the Church of God. He is the author of *"From Gangs to Grace: The Story of Pomona's Eddie Banales"*.

PASTOR WILLIE DALGITY is the founding pastor of Set Free Church in Yucaipa, California (www.setfreerocks.com). After becoming aware of Set Free in 1991, his church affiliated with the movement in 1993. Under the leadership of Pastor Willie, Set Free Yucaipa has raised up numerous church planters who have started churches in California and as far as Massachusetts and Tennessee. The Set Free Ranch in Lake Elsinore, California, is a key aspect of the church's ministry to addicts and has helped hundreds of men and women gain freedom from addiction.

DR. RICHIE COLE worked with Pastor Phil Aguilar at Broadway Treatment Center in Anaheim, CA. Not only has Richie earned a Ph.D. in Clinical Psychology and has over 25 years of experience treating violent criminal offenders and addicts, but he is a member of the Mongols motorcycle club.

TRAINED TO SERVE JESUS

TIM STOREY (www.timstorey.com) is an author, speaker, and life coach who has served as a mentor to Pastor Phil Aguilar. Having traveled to over 75 nations, he is well known for inspiring and motivating people of all walks of life, from entertainment to executives, celebrities and athletes, to adults and children in the most deprived neighborhoods in the country.

CHAPTER ONE
LOOKING FOR LOVE

Every story has a beginning, and this is where the ministry of Phil Aguilar has its roots - Anaheim, California. By looking at Phil's elementary class photo, you'll quickly notice him as the only dark-skinned kid surrounded by rows of white children. Despite his love for the white-picket fence life-style he saw on TV, his father became violent toward his mother, and he left to be with another woman when Phil was an early teenager.

Phil's reaction to this experience set the trajectory of his life toward vi-olence, drugs, and a thirst for love. After being arrested for possession of marijuana, he began learning martial arts in jail, which was a skill that later served him well. Upon release, Phil connected with Karen who would become his first wife, and they had a baby boy named Geronimo. Despite getting married and trying to settle down, Phil eventually left them to open up karate studios down the East Coast, and he continued to fuel his drug addiction.

In an effort to get clean, Phil moved to Oregon to stay with relatives who were Jehovah's Witnesses, and he was baptized in their church in the pur-suit of a girl. After one date, her family wouldn't let him see her anymore, so he hitched a ride back to California.

PASTOR PHIL on growing up: I was born in Anaheim, California, in 1947 to a wonderful mom and dad. I grew up in a wonderful little neighborhood and ended up having five more siblings in my family. My dad was a bricklayer, and my mom was a housewife. I can remember watching *Leave it to Beaver* and *Father Knows Best*, just enjoying life. The area in Anaheim where I was from was predominantly Anglo, so here I was, a very dark kid in the mid-dle of a lot of white friends. They were from Oklahoma, Texas, and moved to California to seek gold or to seek a job at Disneyland - so my childhood was really cool.

Celia, Gilbert, and Phil Aguilar

Philip Aguilar (second row, second from the left) in 4th grade

My elementary school, Thomas Jefferson Elementary School, was right across the street from my house, kitty-corner, then right across the street was a big orange grove. I'm from Orange County, so there used to be orange groves everywhere. So there I am, playing in the orange grove with my friends - throwing oranges and playing kick the can. My childhood memories are nothing but wonderful. My dad would come home from work, but he wasn't real affectionate or anything like that. I really respected him, because in the TV shows, everybody respected their dads. I saw the white-picket fence at *Leave it to Beaver*'s house, and it was very attractive to me.

Phil (left) with siblings

LOOKING FOR LOVE

When I was getting close to 10, 11, 12, I could tell that there was turmoil at my house. I could tell that my dad was not caring for my mom very well. I could hear him scream at her, yell at her to the point of where I saw him grab her by the hair one night and throw her across the room. That just rocked my world, and I couldn't process it. The next thing I know, I see my dad with another woman, and that was a mind blower. One day, he took off with this woman that had 2 children, and he didn't move that far away. These kids happened to go to the same school I went to. I never heard of a dysfunctional family, never heard of divorce. I think we were the first ones on the block to have a messed up family, at least outwardly that everyone knew about. So I got kind of heartbroken about my dad being gone, and I looked for somebody to blame.

Aguilar siblings with Phil seated on the couch

BILLY AGUILAR on family life: I'm a middle child. You know there is 3 below me and 3 above me and growing up in Anaheim, still living here in Anaheim. Baptized in Anaheim in 1955. Raised six kids here in Anaheim, and it's been a tough road. Of course, I'm sure you know we came from a divorced family, so my upbringing was quick and fast, mean and strong. I had no choice. Luckily, I had two big brothers that were just amazing.

Phil is nine years older than me, so he got the dad part of him. I only got the father part of it. I think I was three when he went out for milk and never came back, you know? So Phil got the dad, the discipline. Plus, dad still came around with him and bought him a car for high school. Phil had all the fancy clothes, of course. He was a pretty spiffy guy in high school, I just always looked up to him for that part of him. I missed that whole boat with a father. Phil was actually the father figure at the house.

ELIZABETH AGUILAR BUCHAN-AN on early memories: Well, I'm the third child, the only daughter with six brothers. Life growing up with my mother was outstanding. She's a very liberal woman. She was a woman's liber before there was one. She loved her children unconditionally, and she was a working mom. We were latchkey children, but we were very happy. We adored my mother, and it was crazy. We lived in a very small three bedroom home right down the street from here. My mom lived there for over 60 years, and I love my brothers. I loved growing up with them. I always wanted a sister, but now that I look back at it, I'm glad I have just brothers.

Celia Aguilar with her six children and Phil in the center.

I remember my father leaving us. I was five, and I was very heartbroken even though I was very young. I felt like he divorced me, when he divorced my mother. I was very shy, having all those brothers, I resorted to books. I came home one day when I was in 2nd grade, and I opened one of Phil's literature books and I was hooked on reading, and I'm a reading professor today. I was very sad and very shy, not at home, but I became very shy outside of the home. My mother was very outspoken, and so I had her to do all my talking for me. But I looked up to my big brother always, my entire life. Even during the dark times, he was always my big brother. I remember one time a little boy next door was chasing after me, and I fell on the brick steps. My brother put me in my little red wagon, took me down to the corner where my mom was working with my grandfather at a cafe, and he took care of me. And he's still taking care of me.

PASTOR PHIL on the pain of divorce: The two people I blamed were God - I shook my fist at Him - and my mom. It had to be her fault, so I started playing the shame-on-you-mom game. I started playing the guilt game - "It's all your fault." I had a chip on my shoulder. I was just hating life. When I was 12 years old, I can remember going to the street corner and seeing the older guys and kind of sharing my problems. They said, "Why don't you drink this, smoke this, drop this", and the next thing you know, I started using drugs.

LOOKING FOR LOVE

I'm going into middle school, and I'm a heartbroken kid. I saw a group of guys beating up on this one guy one day and I go, "Yeah, that's what I call livin'." They didn't call them gangs back then. They called them crews. So me and the fellas from my neighborhood started a group called the Olive Street Crew. We would graffiti on walls in our neighborhood, "Olive Street Crew Rules," and stuff like that. We would jump people, steal, all that stuff.

Acting out all this broken-heartedness - now I have a victim mentality. My dad is gone, my mom is at work now every day, and I'm running the house. Nobody is telling me what to do. The older guys started showing me how to start sniffing glue, how to mix the pills together, reds and yellows. We had a freight train that ran down right the middle of Olive Street, and we'd hop that train and act like we are going to run away. I'd get to the L.A. County line, and they'd kick us off the train. I just had no supervision. My mom was great and wonderful, but she was always working. She couldn't take care of us, so all my brothers and my sister, we were just there. We had a good grandfather that helped out in the mix, but by the time I got to high school, I was getting high all the time.

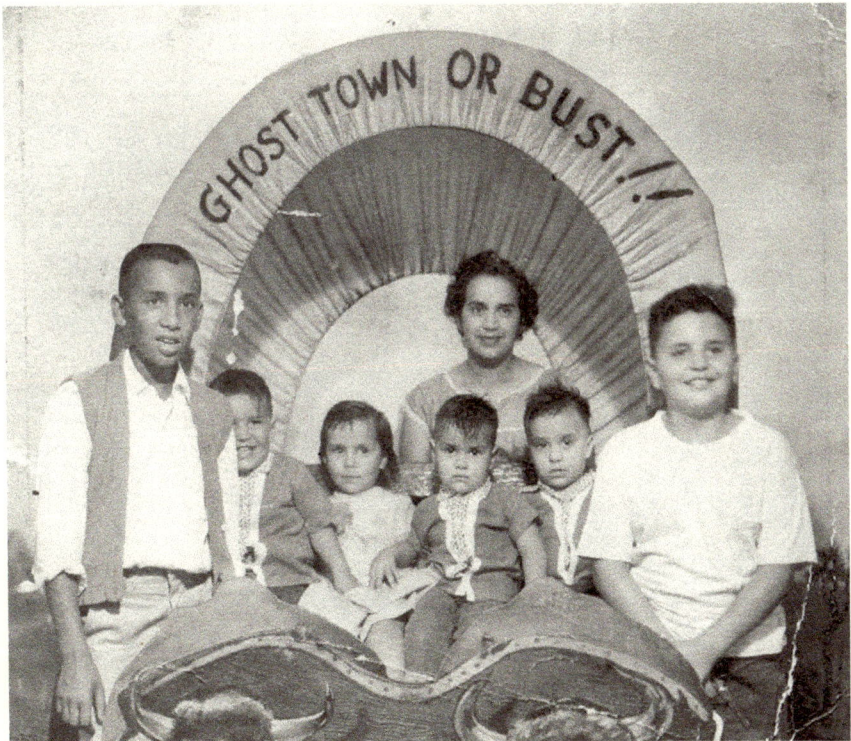

Celia Aguilar with her six children and Phil on the left

27

TRAINED TO SERVE JESUS

I found this girl that I fell in love with, a little redheaded girl named Annie. She started showing love for me, and I talked my mom into helping me buy a friendship ring. I had puppy love, but the cool part about that puppy love was it kind of renewed my spirit, and I was happy. I used to sneak out to go see her, because she lived on the other side of the tracks.

I liked that feeling of being sneaky, scandalous. It was exciting. I'd take a few beers over to her brother's house while she was babysitting her brother's kids, and we'd get a little bit buzzed. I loved the feeling of knowing that she said she loved me. We'd be on the phone until midnight, and I'd tell her, "You hang up." She says, "No, you hang up." "No, you hang up." Then we did another half hour of foreplay on the phone. It was all good, and I was feeling whole again.

One day, I see Annie riding down the street in front of Tastee-Freez where we all hung out. She was sitting in the front seat, right next to one of my good friends, Max. So I said, "Okay God, one time. My dad broke my heart and left, that was plenty, but now my girl broke my heart and she's left." I said to myself, "I will never trust another woman again. I will never trust anybody again." I made a declaration that day, "Nobody ever better get in my way - man, woman, or child." I said it just like that.

Celia Aguilar with her six children and Phil in the lower left.

LOOKING FOR LOVE

ELIZABETH AGUILAR BUCHANAN on challenges with her brothers:
Life was chaotic. It wasn't just Phil, it was also my brother Bert that was doing all kinds of crazy things. Like Phil would start the trouble, and Bert would have to end it for him. Bert was much bigger and stronger and so he'd have to step in for Phil, and it was scary for me. Sometimes they would be fighting with people in the street, and I would go to the corner liquor store where there was a telephone and call the cops on them. I didn't want to call from my phone so they didn't know it was me, but I would call the cops on them.

There would be times where people would be banging on the door wanting to see him, because there was something going on or the cops would be at our door as well. So it was very chaotic. I didn't like him at the time. I didn't like either one of my older brothers. I mean I loved them in my heart of hearts, but I was very disappointed that they were going down the wrong road, and I didn't like it.

PASTOR PHIL on drugs: I just went on a roller coaster ride of drugs and alcohol and women and violence. I can remember at 19 years old, I was a hippie at that time up at Haight-Ashbury, growing my hair out, just a rebel, smoking weed every day, taking LSD every weekend.

One day I got busted for selling $10 worth of marijuana. Back in those days, marijuana was compared to heroin and everything. So I'm a flower child, I get locked up, and they send me to the county jail for a year.

So what does a flower child do when he goes to jail? All of a sudden he comes down and realizes, this is thug life in here. Met a Samoan guy named David Saignow, real cool guy, and he started teaching me martial arts.

JIM BUCHANAN on being friends with Phil: Oh, we were friends in high school. I don't even remember it was so long ago, but we did many bad things. We were horrible. We were crime partners. My Bible says it's a shame to even speak of those things that were done in darkness, but for the edification, I will. So we were very bad. Just check any box you want, guilty. Before he went to prison, he was in jail, and we were in the same tier. He was a couple of cells down when we were up in high tower in Orange County Main.

BILLY AGUILAR on Phil's skills: My brother Phil was a second degree black belt when I was in high school and had a karate studio down the street from the school. Of course, I ended up in juvenile hall for knocking the guy's eye out. I was a great student. I fought in one of his tournaments that Mike Stone and Chuck Norris put on, their first one. And I learned to defend myself real quick, because brother Phil wasn't always around. He left an aura around people that didn't like it, because he would beat the crap out of them. Phil was very abrasive with people. Very dangerous man, very dangerous man. You know, you see him today, and they'll talk about him or say things

Phil Aguilar

about him, but they don't realize who this guy was back in the day.

PASTOR PHIL on Karen and Geronimo: So a year later, I get out of there, and I got a girl waiting for me. She's been writing me while I was in jail. She was a high school girl that loved me. Her name was Karen, a beautiful Jewish girl. At that time, anybody that would love me, I was happy to be loved. So, she waited for me until I got out of jail, and then we hooked up together. The next thing you know she gets pregnant.

Back in those days you get a girl pregnant, to do the right thing you got married, so I was going, "Wow, this will be heavy." To make a long story short, she moved to New York City to hide from the people that she knew. Her family sent her out there to the Jewish relatives in the Bronx to go have this child and put it up for adoption. Well, during this time I said, "No, that's my kid. I want a little mini-me."

I hitchhiked out to New York. I talked to the medical staff at the hospital, because they had already put the baby up for adoption and gave him the name Scott. I promised to be a good

Karen, Phil's first wife and Geronimo's mother

dad, and they asked, "Will you raise him Jewish?" I said, "I'll raise him anything you guys want me to. I don't care, Buddhist, Jewish, it doesn't matter to me." So I went there, saved my kid, named him Geronimo, and he was my firstborn son.

Phil and Geronimo

Then Karen and my baby moved back to California. The parents paid for us to go to Las Vegas, and there we are in Las Vegas doing the "I do's," and I was going, "I don't believe I'm doing an 'I do', because I don't really want to do this." But, for the sake of making everything right, the kid having a legal name, we got married, and she got an apartment. Her parents helped her out and I tried to do the straight life.

I'm a young guy, and I was riding my Harley, and I liked to get out in the wind with my partners and go party. I loved to party. I loved getting high. I was a sex addict, and I loved girls. I can remember when my son was three years old, I pulled up on my Harley. "I love you, but son I got to get in the wind. Karen, you are a great lady, but this isn't for me." I took off, and I didn't see my son Geronimo for 14 years. I was back out doing my life.

I had a little stint there where I thought I'd get straightened out. One of my cousins. Jerry Pittington, was a big national star in the karate circuit, kick boxing, so I started training with him. I became one of the top 20 lightweight fighters in America so we opened up studios from Baltimore, Maryland, and Virginia. I traveled around the United States fighting, but I got bored and came back to California.

Next thing you know, I meet this girl, and we start doing cocaine together. I'm smuggling cocaine, I'm selling drugs, and I'm living the high-life now.

I've got all kinds of toys, bikes, cars, this and that, I'm just a high-class cocaine addict. Then, one day this girl that I kind of had the hots for, she asked me, "Hey, you ever did heroin?"

I can remember growing up - everybody I ever met that did heroin was a loser, and their life was jacked up. They stole from their moms, grandma - they were just a wreck. So I told myself, "I'll never do that drug." But this girl was my angel of life. She was so pretty, and she said, "Let's try it one time." I had a little voice in my head saying, "Hey, don't go there, hey stupid, slow down, stop, don't do it", but she just looked so good. She happened to have a house in Laguna overlooking the ocean and was a psychiatrist, so that made it

Phil (left)

sound even a little bit better. I go, "Okay, let's do it one time", so I scored a little heroin for us.

I can remember turning my head and putting my arm out. She came in with her smock from work, and when she stuck that needle in my arm, I'm telling you, that was Nirvana, that was bliss, that was heaven. No more problems, no more worries, no more woes. I was so happy.

Little did I know that this was addicting to the point where I had no ability to stop. I was living in a penthouse suite, and within 6 months, I had sold everything I owned for this heroin. From a penthouse, I ended up in a garage with Hepatitis B, all yellow skinned, and went down to about 120-something pounds. I had a few other people, and we were all sharing the same needle. We had never heard of HIV and all these other diseases at the time. I'm strung out like a dog, and now I'm stealing and doing whatever I need to do to get my dope. I'm getting locked up for under the influence - just sick as can be. I went from rehab to rehab trying to detox, and then I get back out, trying to do right.

Now I'm about 27 years old, and finally no place would take me but I have some beautiful relatives. They were Jehovah's Witnesses and had all moved to Road River, Oregon. My mom asked her sister and brothers and all of them, "Would you take my son in? He's a heroin addict and needs help. Nobody else will take him."

My nickname at that time was King Cobra. I was a snake. I'd rob from mom, dad, grandfather, steal their cars, wreck their car. I cared about nobody except for myself. I was a hope-to-die dope-fiend, but they took me in. I moved up to Road River, and here I am in a little country town now. While I'm up there, they told me that I had to go to five JW meetings a week.

I'm going to these meetings, and sure enough, I fell in love with one of the hot ladies there in the church. She happened to be one of the special kids that all the dads and everybody watched over, because her dad had died not too long before I got there. I was like the traveling salesman coming to meet the farmer's daughter. They said, "You can't date this girl unless you become a baptized Jehovah's Witness."

I got into the book *Paradise Lost*, and I was going to work for this girl because she is a fox. Got baptized six months later in Medford, Oregon, and I got to take her out on a date. One date is all it lasted. I ruined that one, because she was not about to put up with my BS and all that stuff going on. So the family said, "You aren't going to see her anymore." Next thing you know, I'm out of this town. I stole some rifles and meds from people I knew and talked some other girl into giving me a ride back to California.

Phil (aka King Cobra) with his dog

TRAINED TO SERVE JESUS

CHAPTER TWO

MEETING SAINT SANDRA & JESUS

After returning to California, Phil meets Sandra DeFalco and eventually moves in with her. Despite her best efforts to help him get a job, Phil turned to drugs once again, and life began to spiral out of control for both of them. This resulted in Phil's arrest for child abuse after Christopher, Sandra's son, was hurt while being watched by Phil. During his time in Chino State Prison, Phil met Pastor Glenn Morrison and chose to follow Jesus. Sandra joined him in this newfound faith, and they ended up getting married at a prison wedding ceremony.

After Phil was released, he sensed a calling into ministry, and they moved to Perris, California, and served at Temple Baptist Church with Phil eventually attending Pacific Coast Baptist Bible College. A professor invited him to join the staff of Anaheim Bible Church, so Phil and Sandra moved back to Anaheim to join the ministry. After finding the church to be restricting, they began to contemplate starting something new.

PASTOR PHIL on meeting Sandra: After I got back to California, I found a friend named John Bowling, he said, "You can come and stay with me for a while." I spent the night and was feeling kind of healthy. I didn't have any clothes, so I asked my brother for something, and he gave me this Hawaiian shirt. I put it on, and I went with my partner John to this restaurant called DeFalco's Italian Restaurant.

Now, I'm not into Italian food, but I saw some good looking things on the menu there. One was this lady, Sandra, who is now my beautiful wife. She had a younger sister there, so I started talking to her and said, "Hey, hook me up with your sister. Let's go out on a date." At the time, I didn't realize it, but she is from back east, so she didn't know what a Mexican was.

When Sandra sees me in the Hawaiian shirt and with long hair, she thinks I am a Hawaiian guy - didn't know that I'm a hope-to-die dope-fiend. I had just been clean for the last six months, so I just happened to be looking good. I invite her out on a date and she says, "Yes." I'm digging this. She is as straight as can be. A normie, goes to college, plays volleyball with her friends, does barbecues and has a beer here and there, but nothing like my lifestyle.

She invites me over to a little picnic at her house, and I meet up with some of my old biker partners. We come riding up with some bikes with sleeping bags up front and she goes, "What are you doing with sleeping bags?" And I said, "We're moving in." She'd never met somebody quite like me, and she was like – I want to help the little puppy dog. She didn't really know about my life, but she had a heart, a big heart. She was attracted to me for whatever reason. She saw something somewhere deep between all those layers. So we started dating, and before you know it, I moved in and her roommate moved out.

SANDRA DEFALCO AGUILAR on meeting Phil: It was a crazy time. Actually, I had just moved back to California from Chicago. I did one of those big Italian weddings to make everybody happy except for myself and married an Italian man who wasn't exactly anything that I thought he would be. We had a son together. He agreed to go to counseling, but as time went on, it wasn't working out. So I came back to California, and my parents had opened up a restaurant. My mom always had Italian restaurants. So they opened up a restaurant in Anaheim, and prior to that, I had worked at some other places in Fullerton and other places. I just always worked in the restaurant business. I was brought up in it. So they opened up this place in Anaheim, and it was in the section of Anaheim - I never was in Orange County really. So it was a section - we didn't know the difference between one section and another. And also, we didn't know at the time, it was in a redevelopment area.

So my parents opened this restaurant and adjacent to it was this Irish pub. It was on this cool little street in Anaheim which actually is still there even after the renovation. So I worked still at my other job, I was a cocktail waitress. I worked at my other job and then I helped my mom there. So there was a guy who had a place for rent down the street and I found out that whole street was college students. So I rented this place from him so I could be closer to the restaurant and became great friends with everybody on the block.

Phil surrounded by friends

36

MEETING SAINT SANDRA AND JESUS

So one of my times when I was in the restaurant, he came in with a friend of his - an older man. I was delivering sandwiches to the pub side. So my little sister worked there also. She worked there all the time. So later my little sister told me there was this guy in here and he was asking about you. I'm like, "Really?" She's like, "'Yeah." I'm like, "Well, let him know I'm not interested." I was engaged at the time to another person.

It was kind of like at this point in my life, I need to figure out what I'm going to do. I had been dating people. I'm a young single mom, working really hard. So it was time for me to maybe think about settling down again. Nice guy, however he had never had children before. There was a lot of issues there too. So I told my sister I'm not interested. Well then, he asked again. He kind of pursued it. So I'm like, "You know what? I think I'm just going to say, 'Yes'." I said, "Tell him, okay. I'll go out with him."

Because in my mind I'm thinking, if you are going to accept this invitation, you shouldn't be engaged. It was kind of giving me confirmation that I shouldn't be engaged to this guy, it wasn't the right person. Anyways it was so funny because here it is after I said, 'No' three times, I finally said, 'Yes'.

He was supposed to pick me up, and we were supposed to go some-where. So anyways, he ends up telling my sister - this was the days before cell phones, telling my sister to tell me he forgot he had a pool tourna-ment that he had to go to, and he had to be there. Remember I knew nothing about this guy at all, right? So I end up telling my girlfriend who lived with me at the time, "Okay, we are going to go by there and see if he's really at a pool tournament. Because if he isn't, then I'm never going to accept a date with him again."

We were going to go out afterwards and go dancing. So we got all dressed. So in Anaheim down that street where our church ended up being, there was bar after bar. That was one of the reasons they were ren-ovating. They wanted to get rid of all these bars. So we went into this one bar - you have to walk down these steps to get to it. So we are walking down the steps and whole place reeks of beer and smoke and everything else. We are all dressed up, everybody in the place looking at us like, "What are they doing here?" And there he was - really playing pool. I was shocked. Let's get out of here, because he's playing pool.

Of course his story is, he knew he had me then, because I went to go check to make sure. After that I told him, "Forget it. Pool tournament is more important." So then we played the cat and mouse game I guess you call it. So one night it was like midnight, he knew where I lived, and he stopped by and he said, "Hey, I need some water. Can I use your hose for my radiator?" So it just kind went from there. We ended up just starting to date and nobody liked him that knew him. Because they knew of his reputation in Anaheim. I had no idea. My friends on the street didn't like him, because he came from a different cut.

So I was having a party and I said, "I'm having a party tonight, if you'd like to come that would be great." So he's like, "Sure, can I bring some friends?" I'm like, "Yeah, of course you can bring some friends." So here my quiet little college street, and all of a sudden we hear all these motorcycles. And all these motorcycles pull up with either a chick on the back or backpacks on the back. Something on the back, whatever. They actually pull up on my lawn. We are like, "What the heck?" Had no idea. Some of them had backpacks and stuff like that. I'm like, "What are you doing? Are you on a trip? Are you going somewhere?" He goes, "No, we always bring backpacks. We are spending the night." I'm like, "What?" So it kind of started off like that.

Okay, this is completely out of my league. I'm not a drug addict. I'm not a motorcycle person at all. Not even a thrill seeker in any way whatsoever. It's very hard to explain to people, but there was a part of him that I admired. Because he was the host and took care of everybody. He made sure everybody had what they needed. He just had that personality that was just very warm and welcoming. We just kind of went from there.

PASTOR PHIL on Sandra's help: She tried to help me. She said, "We need to get you a job." I tried the job thing, that lasted 2 days. That didn't work. I'm living there, and I really respected her for being a real woman, a great woman. She had a three year old son that she was raising on her own. She was great with her parents. Everybody disliked me being around, because everybody could tell this guy is a loser. I got nothing, and I liked to party all the time.

Life was going okay, and then one day one of my brothers who was a big drug dealer said, "Hey, I'd like you to make a shipment for me. A delivery from Ojai, California, to Orange County. I'll pay you some big money to deliver it, but you got to make sure it gets to the point of delivery. I'm working with this cartel, some big guys, and if you take their stuff, they'll harm you." I told him, of course yes, because I'd been clean for a few months. I got it, no problem, and I drove up to Ojai.

I put this kilo of Peruvian flake cocaine, at that time valued at a couple of hundred thousand dollars, I put it in the trunk of a car that I borrowed from my girlfriend. I started getting ready to deliver it all the way back to Orange County, which is a couple hours' drive. When I'm driving, I know

MEETING SAINT SANDRA AND JESUS

I'm going to get paid some money. I'm going to be doing alright. I'm not thinking about getting busted or anything like that.

As I'm driving back, I can hear something from the trunk calling my name. It knew my first name, my middle name, my nicknames, everything like that you can think of. It says, "Pinch me, pinch me", which in the drug world means, take a little bit off the top, and then deliver the rest, but just take a little bit. In my mind, I started thinking I'm going to take an ounce, and I'll put a little lactose or something to fill it up. Then, I'll deliver it and it'll be alright. By the time I got to the house, I started a ministry. I didn't call it ministry back in the days, but here was my ministry - "catch me if you can ministry".

I already had a self-fulfilling prophecy. Nobody - I'll never trust nobody. If I think you're going to hurt me 10 years from now, I'm going to go take care of you now and get it over with. That became my life. I spoke my negative, hateful world into existence. So I said, "No, I'm going to take it all." I called up my brother, "Come find me." I called another one of my brothers and said, "Come on over."

I start gramming up cocaine. We are snorting it up. Then we are shooting it up, and we went on a run for a couple of weeks. Eight balls, heroin, cocaine. My mind started going crazy. Remember, earlier I said "man, woman, or child, you get in my way there is trouble"? Well, let me tell you, I went on to fulfill all those negative prophecies in my life. Now I know "as a man thinketh, so is he", but in those days, I had no clue.

I never had a dad who hugged me or told me "I love you" or asked "how you doing kid?" I had a mom that loved me, but enabled me. She didn't know how to say 'no' to me. I had all this going on in my life, and I'm just jacked up. I'm full of drugs, full of hate, full of no life. I got a beautiful lady, but I don't know how to treat her. So, I'm on this run with all these drugs, and I went out to the bars. Bartender lady, I can remember just like it was yesterday, saying something I didn't like. Boom - hit her just like that. I went back to the house a few hours later, because we got people coming over to pick up drugs.

My girlfriend at the time, Sandra - her nerves, her stomach, she got so sick she had to go to the hospital, and she asked me to watch her son. I'm the last guy you want watching your son. I don't have time for any of that stuff. I'm full of all that heroin, but it's my sick head that caused it all. Her son started coming around in the room, and I just started smacking him around. Then, a bunch of people came over buying drugs and making a whole scene.

Phil and Sandra

SANDRA on asking Phil to watch her son, Christopher: When he lived there most of the time, he chased out my girlfriend, my roommate. She's done, she didn't want to be there anymore. So I worked and my little sister would watch my son when she didn't work. It kind of worked out good. So his dad who had not seen him for like 2 years decided he wanted to visit with him. So I said, "Okay, I'm working so you can take him while I'm working," and my sister was supposed to be at the house for when he came back.

Well my sister wasn't there and so when he left him, Phil was there and he said, "Yeah, I'll just keep him." Not knowing at the time, he had been using drugs again. So being naive to drugs, I didn't know a lot of the symptoms and things.

So what happened is I had a bed and you know how when your mattress is not too firm and you put a sheet wood underneath it? It stuck out about this far. So the story I had heard was that he was running, and he ran into that after he took a bath. He ran into that. Well if I go back I realize, first of all, Phil was too out of it to know really what happened. Because he was doing heroin at the time.

When I got there, he was passed out. So there is no real witness to what happened. However the police had been wanting to get him because he was a nuisance in the community. He was always getting in trouble for this or that. He had been in trouble before. He was a violent person. On the natch, when he is loaded, he is not violent at all. But because of his karate skills, all these different things, he ended up where he had this reputation of being a bad person. So to them, when I took my son to the hospital to get check to make sure everything is okay, the attending physician at the time said, "What happened?" Not sure - this is what I found out.

They were following me all the time, the police. Everything that I did. So they were at the hospital too, and I didn't even know it. So boom, that was it, we got him now. We are going to get him on this child abuse. And that's how the whole story started. Which is why he ended up just saying, "Okay, plea deal." So the abuse really didn't happen, but that was the story for him to get a deal. So it was a very sad situation.

SANDRA on whether Phil hurt her son: He never did, and that was the part that is so hard for me. It was hard for me with my son, because as time went on, which is a whole other story, this is what he's told over and over and over again. Then other things had happened where his dad ended up getting custody of him. It just turned into a big mess. So as time went on and my son got older, he doesn't remember anything like that. So it was kind of like put into everybody's - and because of the whole situation, it was really more of a drug deal that they were trying to get him on. Because he had been delivering drugs for some really bad people, and they just wanted to catch him on something. So the lawyers said, "Do a plea deal," and that's what he did.

PASTOR PHIL on his arrest: Next thing you know, "Aguilar, come out with your hands up." It was the Anaheim Police surrounding the house. I'm taking the rest of the stash, and I'm going to the bathroom to flush it all down. I pull on that toilet, and I can remember flushing. My brother and people inside the house were scrambling. Police were all over the place with guns drawn. Then, I felt a cold pistol right at the temple of my head and a voice said, "Make a move Aguilar. We'd like to kill you." Boom, I'm arrested. They take me down to Anaheim Police Department sick as a dog, because I'm full of drugs. About 24 hours went by and who shows up to visit me at the Anaheim city jail but my girlfriend, or my ex-girlfriend at that time, Sandra.

SANDRA on Phil's arrest: So the police came to my door, the detectives and asked, "Is he here?" Then all of a sudden before you know it, I hear flushing of the toilet and scrambling. That was my first raid. They came through the ceilings, the windows, everything. It was just horrible. They ended up shackling him. So they take him away and they sit there with me and they are like, "Do you realize how dangerous this person is? Do you realize who you are with?"

Remember I saw the whole other side of him. I didn't see this dangerous person. I didn't see anything but a guy who became clean - went back to his drugs. Because when I met him, he was clean. He had been clean for over a year because he had studied with the Jehovah Witnesses. His mom sent him there to go get clean.

So anyways, it ended up where the detectives are telling me, "Here's the deal. You need to move out of this house tonight, or we will take your son and put him in child protection place," the place where they put children. It was a couple of days before Christmas. Of course I'll do anything if you are going to take my son away from me.

So at the door was all this stuff sitting there, packed boxes and they started going through all the stuff. I'm sure they were looking for drugs. And as they were going through the stuff, they are finding my checkbook, anything that was of any value was in this box and Jim Buchanan, who is now my brother in law, he was supposed to pick him up, but he never got there in time to pick him up so the police picked him up instead because he was going out of town for good. He was going to try to get away, it didn't work out. So he went to jail and his mother said to me, "Whatever you do, do not send him money." She said, "That is a mistake I made all those years, sending him money."

I moved out immediately and moved in with my sister. The detectives came and told me that I had to go and see him at the county jail. Actually, it was the Anaheim Police department. I had to go see him and find out where the drugs are. Because they are still looking for all these drugs, and they know they are somewhere. They searched my house and never found them. So I had to go there and start asking him questions, and then as I'm there I'm like, "Did you take my this and that?" anything of any value. My gold silverware that I had. Things that were sentimental. "No, are you kidding I would never do that." Just lying the whole time.

So I was like, "Okay, I'm done. This is great. This is how God took him away. Now I don't have to think about him anymore." Because I kept trying to get rid of him, but I couldn't because he kept coming back. I couldn't get rid of him. So I just felt like this is it now, he's gone. Basically that was what I thought was going to be the end of the chapter.

PASTOR PHIL on talking to Sandra while he's in jail: She's on the phone looking through the glass and just asked me a few questions. She goes, "Did you take all my stuff? Did you hurt my son like the police said you did? Did you do all these terrible things to me?" Just like it was yesterday, I can remember looking at her straight in the eyes going, "I can't believe that you would think that I would ever do something like that. I'm ashamed of you. Get out of here." That's how full of hate, bitterness, demons, whatever you want to call it, I was.

I can remember being so happy that they locked me up. I was a threat to society. I was a threat to everybody, and I hurt everybody that I said I loved. There was a part of me deep inside that said, "It sure is good you are off the streets." My mom was happy, but I called her for bail, "Mom, bail me out. It's a big bail so you are going to have to put up your house. But I'm going to be a good boy, I'm going to change." Here I am about 28 years old. For the first time I can ever remember in my life, my mother said, "No."

Like I said, this big ole baby boy was always extorting money from his mom. She finally said the best thing that she could have ever done for me. I didn't take it as good at the time. But she said, "No," and there I was in jail, and she was happy I was there. She did help me get a lawyer, and I told him, "You know what? Just plea bargain me out. I don't care what they give me, how long they give me." I really didn't care. I didn't want to get out. I knew it was horrible. I didn't want to get out.

PASTOR PHIL on meeting Pastor Glenn Morrison: They gave me a one to ten year sentence in state prison, and this was the beginning of a new life as I started to sober up and clean up and dry out. My emotions came back, and I decided I was going to start writing Sandra. She says, "I don't want to see you again. I don't want to hear from you." I got the 'Dear Phil' letter big time as I'm on the way to state prison. A lot of people used to talk about going to colleges like USC or Stanford or Penn State. I had no interest in going to Penn State, because I was going to the state pen. It was like a badge of honor.

I'm there with all the other black sheep, with all the other rebels, the 1%. When I got to Chino State Prison, I had a wakeup call, because now I'm sober and clean. I realized I've been stupid in my life, but I'm not totally crazy. I realized I had to make a choice here.

One of the guards says, "Hey, any of you boys want religion? Walk on down the hall." So I said, "I'll go on down there and check it out." Get out of my cell, go on down the hall, go into a room where there is about 50 men. And I'm expecting maybe some young girls or somebody to come in and do some Christian music I heard they did. The next thing I know there is kind of a short portly looking bald headed white fellow who comes in the room, and I'm going, "Wow, who is this guy?" He introduces himself and says, "My name is Glenn Morrison from Follow Up

Prison Ministries." This was in early 1977, and they just changed one of the criminal laws where they took away the death penalty. So people like Charlie Manson and others were released back onto the mainland with myself and everybody else.

Pastor Glenn Morrison speaking to inmates (photo courtesy of the Morrison family)

PASTOR GLENN MORRISON on his work in prison ministry: When I go into a prison I do a variety of things. Sometimes I'm speaker at chaplain services. I walked death row in San Quentin prison where I served as an acting chaplain for a number of years. I met a lot of men in what they call the adjustment center. And believe it or not, the men in the adjustment center were more violent than the people on death row. So people misunderstand that. But at any rate, I walked the cell blocks. I'd teach seminars in Christian discipleship. I lead Bible study groups. I also have a group of workers to work with me, and they are known as the God Squad.

I find working with the hardcore criminal to be the easiest type of person to work with. Because they are tired, burnt out, and they are looking for some kind of relief, some kind of answer. I know the man that was labeled the worst criminal in the system officially became a Christian because of that. I found him to be a man who was open and searching, and he accepted the living Bible from me and things went from there until he confessed his faith in Christ.

PASTOR PHIL on following Jesus: I can remember distinctly that day, and I can remember Glenn, this preacher guy, standing up in front. He'd see different men, and he'd give them a hug, and I thought that was weird as can be. What's he doing hugging? What are men doing hugging anyway? And then as we got ready to start this meeting, he got up, and it was just like it was yesterday. I can remember him talking about this Jesus who was all about forgiveness, about love, about peace. That he'd give you another chance. I was sober and clean enough now that I was listening. I knew I hurt everybody that I said that I loved. Nobody wanted to see me. In fact, everybody thought I was in the best place I needed to be.

My life was basically over. I had no hope, no plans for the future. I knew one thing though, I didn't want to ever go back out in the streets just to come back in again. So as I sat through that day, I listened to this Reverend Glenn share about the love of Jesus. It was all good. I was taking it in. But then near the end of his little message, he kind of pulled one on me. He kind of shocked me. And he said, "If any of you here want to give your lives to Jesus today, I'd like you to stand up."

Now that did not sound cool to me. I might be doing the next 10 years with these men in here, and I'd never known Christians as anything but weak. So the last thing I wanted to do was be associated, affiliated with these people. I had a reputation I thought that I had to be a certain thing.

Then I can remember asking the question, I go, "Will God take anybody no matter what they did?" And he says, "Yeah, it doesn't matter. He will forgive any sin there is." And then I can remember the preacher going that day, "You tried drugs. You've tried sex. You've tried everything else, why don't you just try God?" And once again he said, "If you'd like to give your life to God, stand up. Be bold."

And inside of me, there was a battle. It seemed like hours, but it was only moments, because my pride was in the way. I just didn't want to let anybody know that I was weak, and I needed this crutch called Jesus. That I couldn't do it on my own. Then I started thinking in my head, "Man, I just can't do this." And then as I continued in my thoughts I realized, "What have I got to lose? I can try God, and if it doesn't work, I just go back to my old ways." So I didn't understand then. I do understand now, that it was the power of God, but I stood up that day and I was one of two people that prayed that prayer to give Jesus a chance in my life. And I knew when I prayed that something had happened inside of me. I couldn't describe it. I still can't describe it. Wasn't any wild and crazy thing, but I knew in my knower that something had changed. Not that God could read lips, but he could read hearts and that he read my heart.

My heart was, "Man, I'm done with that lifestyle. I will do anything to change. I don't care what it is. I don't want to get out in the streets. I don't need my lady, and I don't need anything. I want to see what this God has to offer." So there I stand up, and one other fellow stood up. The preacher prayed a closing prayer for us, and then everybody started to go back to their cell.

And the preacher hugged me - first time I'd been embraced by a man in my life. My dad never hugged me so I never knew what that was like. I started walking down the main line, and I saw a lot of inmates go up to the other guy that stood up and ask him, "Hey, were you serious about what you prayed with that preacher?" And he told everybody, "Nah, I was just jiving the preacher. I didn't mean it." Then they came and hit me up, "Hey were you serious man with that preacher when you stood up?" And all of sudden that same kind of power came inside of me again, and I said, "Yeah, I was serious and I'm going to follow Jesus the rest of my life." I didn't even know what I was saying. I was brand new. I was raw.

I didn't even know what that meant at the time. But sure enough, I can remember saying that, and then I headed on back to my cell. That was the beginning of a brand spanking new life for me. All of a sudden as I started cracking open the Word of God and started reading the Bible, the cell bars kind of started looking attractive.

PASTOR GLENN MORRISON on leading Phil to Christ: First of all, he was being held in the reception center, which is a state prison where they studied the men and determined what prison to place them in. And occasionally, they will release a man, but not very often. The day that I met Phil, it was only a matter of a few days before the Supreme Court of California overturned the death penalty. So there was a half a dozen or so men that were sent back to this particular reception center, and they showed up before the chapel service, and we had a reunion. Because

Pastor Glenn Morrison and Pastor Phil Aguilar (many years later)

I had been working with them on death row, alright? And then I realized we were holding up the chapel services. So I apologized to the men in the chapel, and we went into the chapel service.

At that time, I gave the Gospel message and an invitation for people to make a decision to follow Christ the rest of the their lives. Well, there were a few that made that commitment, stood to their feet, and we counseled and so on. And then as chapel was over, these men went back to

their units. Well Phil was one of those men, and he went back along with another man to their unit that they came out of and they met a group of men who were there to intimidate them. The first man caved in. He said, "Yeah, I just wanted to make that preacher feel good. That's why I did what I did." Phil said, "Yes, I have determined to follow Christ." That not being his exact words, but that's what he did. That took guts. That took courage. But that was what Phil did. And that was the beginning of a real miracle in Phil Aguilar's life.

My life has been one marked just basically by availability to God for Him to work through. He has opened doors. He has closed doors. But the doors that he's opened have just been so marvelous, and the lives that have been touched is beyond anything I can begin to dream. I've thanked God for the privilege of just being a servant.

BILLY AGUILAR on Phil finding Christ: There was a guy in there with him named Greg Gumpher, and this guy was probably one of the baddest boxing dudes you ever ran into. Him and Phil gave their life to Christ. So you know, I know a lot of people locked up, but my brother Phil, you find religion or you find Christ. There is a big difference, and Phil found Christ. I heard about it. My brother Bert, we talked about it. We said, "Well, we'll have to see when he gets out. See if the proof is in the pudding." If he's going to come out and start terrorizing everybody again or he's going to come out and be a completely different man. And sure enough, he was a different man.

PASTOR PHIL on experiencing the Holy Spirit: Going to the chow hall to eat food, I was thankful for the food that I had, and I wasn't complaining about liver or this or that. I started feeling this transformation happening in my life. It wasn't about the circumstances or the situation in my life, but understanding that the Kingdom of Heaven was in me. I realized that I could do something about it right where I was at. I didn't need to wait until I got out. I didn't need to wait until I got married or had kids. Right then or there, I started experiencing that Jesus feeling, feeling this Holy Ghost thing, this Holy Spirit thing. But I didn't want to be religious - I didn't like all that stuff.

I'm locked up for one to ten years in a state prison. The way they did it back in those days is called the "Indeterminate Sentence Law" - so every year you go before the parole board to see whether you are going to do one year or ten years. I got transferred around from Tracy to San Quentin to Vacaville, and I meet this volunteer chaplain who comes in named Herb Sokol. This guy started mentoring and discipling me.

TRAINED TO SERVE JESUS

ELIZABETH AGUILAR BUCHANAN on Phil's faith: He came to know the Lord pretty quick after he went to prison. Just a few months after he went, my first child passed away at 11 months old. I had been a Jehovah's Witness at the time. My mother as I said was very liberal. She told us to try this out, whatever we wanted, all roads led to God, that was her idea. So I had a lot of relatives that were Jehovah's Witnesses, so I became one. I was happy that Phil came to know the Lord, but I wasn't really sure if he was for real. He's such a leader, and when he does something, he does it all the way. He was into the Maharishi. Back in the 70's, he was really into it, and all of his friends were into it. When he grew pot, all of his friends were into growing pot. So when he went to prison, I actually was relieved. I remember now being relieved, because he was no longer getting into trouble. He was in a safe place as far as I was concerned. '

SANDRA on learning about Phil's newfound faith: He started writing me. Every day I would get a letter from him. Every day. Telling me how sorry he was. Just the whole thing. Then of course his brother and other people would tell me, "That's just jail house talk. That's all it is. He just wants you to come visit." I ignored his letters. Eventually he got sent to Chino. Then he started writing me from there.

When he started writing from Chino, his letters were different. I didn't throw them out. I started reading them because they had so much in them. You could tell there was something that happened to him. Something different. He started sharing the Lord. He started sharing about what God has done in his life. He started sharing about all the things that he wants to do if he even spends the rest of his life in prison to make up for all the bad that he did. Just things like that I was just amazed at these letters he was sending me.

I never wrote him back. Because I never wanted him to think I was ever going to have contact with him. I never wrote him back, because I never wanted to have any communication with him or even let him think I would have communication with him because he had ruined my life. He had basically ruined my life. So I ended up reading the letters.

I was brought up very Catholic. The difference between him and I, I was brought up Catholic and I would go to confession and make up stuff that I did bad. Because I thought I had to say something. He would go to confession and steal the offering on his way out. That was the difference between the two of us. So we were very different.

48

MEETING SAINT SANDRA AND JESUS

When he started talking about the Lord, I never heard God presented that way. The Lord Jesus, salvation. I had never heard any of that. So after reading all his letters, this one day after about six months I decided I'm going to read the scriptures in the Bible that he sending me. Through that, I ended up asking and accepting Christ as my savior, because as a Catholic I never had learned that before.

So after reading the scriptures and everything he sent me, I'm like, "This is what I want." Because all he kept writing about was the peace that he had. "This is what I want, I want peace too." I wanted to move on with my life. I wanted to put everything in the past. So after I gave my life to the Lord and started getting closer to the Lord, I felt compelled. I have to go see this person. I have to see this changed person for myself.

Somebody else could be writing these letters. I have to see him. So at this time, he was still at Chino waiting to be transferred. So I went to go see him. He was shocked. If you've ever been to prison, it's a process. So I didn't know what to expect. They have you talk on the phone through the glass. When I saw him I couldn't even believe it was him. The transformation was unbelievable. When he got arrested, he was probably about 115 pounds at the most. Just thrashed from the heroin. Just sickly looking.

Now I'm looking at this person who is so healthy, so radiant, so full of joy and peace. I was like, "Wow, this is amazing. You are not the same person at all." So it was my first experience of a transformed person in the Lord, absolutely. So when I saw him and we were talking, I just knew I finally saw for myself. Well he said to me, "Did you get my last letter?" And I said, "What last letter?" And he goes, "Well I wrote you a 25 page letter." I'm like, "Really?" He said, "Yes, my chaplain told me that I need to put you on the altar and just pray whatever God wants for you and for your life and for me to stop writing you. So it was the last letter." He said, "Isn't that why you are here?" I said, "No, I never got that last letter." He said, "Yeah, I sent it to you, because I just felt like my time ministering to you was done."

Well that was amazing in itself and guess what? When I got home, there was that letter that he was never going to write again, because he knew that he needs to let me go and do what I need to do. So of course after I saw him and I saw the transformation, I saw this was the person that was always inside of him that I would see little sneak peeks of it. That's what I was drawn to. So a chaplain came to visit me that he asked to come visit me. He prayed with me and I as you would say publicly accepted Christ as my savior. He started sharing with me a lot of different things that just really struck me as I think God wants me in the ministry.

SANDRA on visiting Phil in prison:
He had gone to San Quentin and several different prisons before they finally had put him in Vacaville. Now Vacaville is a medical facility prison. So you can volunteer to go there if you have done violent crimes, you can volunteer to go there because they do a lot of testing on you there. You are like guinea pigs. So he accepted to go there. The wonderful man there, Herb - Herb Sokol. He is a godsend. He just had a small group of guys, and they were like truly born again Christians. So Herb was what you would call a lay pastor. He wasn't paid to go there, because he wasn't going to be all things to all men. He was just a born again Christian. So he had this group of guys, and he took

Phil and Sandra

Philip under his wing. He was very hard on him, but very loving. So Phil had told him about me and he said, "'Oh no, you don't need any worldly people in your life." So we began writing each other. I started writing him now. Not sending him anything, but just writing him. He never asked for anything. It just became very pleasant and very wonderful.

I decided to go, because Herb said, "If you ever want to come here, there is place for you to stay. Someone can pick you up from the airport." So I decided, "Okay, I'm going to go visit him." It was a weekend. I took my older sister, had my son and I'm like, "Okay, this is perfect."' So I didn't know what the heck I was doing. I flew out to Sacramento, took a taxi all the way to Vacaville which is a good 25, 30 miles. I got to the prison to go visit and finally went through the whole thing and they told me, "You can't go in with that on." I'm like, "What?" So I had this blue jumpsuit. You can't wear anything that resembles blue Levis.

So a girl in line tells me, "Don't worry honey, there is place down the street for prisoners' families, and they help you. They have a thrift store, and they will get your clothes and everything." So I went back in a taxi, changed. So time is flying, right? I know you only have a certain time to visit. So then I finally get in the place, and they kept calling his name, he didn't come out. So I thought, "Okay, this is the wrong thing. I shouldn't have done this. I'm just going to go back home." Then all of a sudden they said, "Okay, visitor for Aguilar." So they have you walk down this yellow line, and here I'm thinking, "Okay, I'm going to be on the phone," because that's how it was at Chino. I'm not experienced with prisons, right? No, you just walk through this door, and there you are with all these other inmates and their families.

So you are visiting in the flesh. And once I saw him again and actually saw him in the flesh, of course we hugged and embraced. We kind of both knew by that time that this is it. This is really it. Even though I didn't want it to be, I thought, "Yeah, this is where I need to be."

Then I met Herb who is just wonderful. He is like a breath of fresh air. Amazing man, big old man, burly man, but so loving. So he had said to me, "Well, I'll tell you what, I'll drive you back to the airport, but since you only got to visit for an hour, you can spend the night. We have a nice Christian lady here, she takes girls in. Families that are visiting." So I said, "No, I don't really want to spend the night," because I smoked. I thought, "How am I going to stay at this nice Christian home if I smoke?" So these other people from these friends outside, they offered me a place to stay if I wanted to stay. That's a whole other story.

But anyways, in the morning I was able to go visit him and spend the whole visiting hours with him, so it was really great. Then Herb was going to drive me back to the airport. I just saw love everywhere. He said, "I want you to meet this lady, because she is a wonderful lady and next time you come to visit you can stay with her."

I went to go visit this lady, meet her. Shirley Wilson, wonderful woman. Still in touch with her. And guess what? She was smoking. I was like, "Darn it. I could have spent the night here instead of that horrible situation that I was in last night." But it was all great. Just another way God showed me Christians aren't perfect.

Whatever we always think about Christians, we have this stereotype. Then we just started writing, and then eventually I visited a little bit more. After the first visit that we had, Herb had told him, "She is a little bit too worldly for you." Because I had long nails, tight clothes. He said, "She is a little bit too worldly. You are so fresh into the Lord. I don't want her to stumble you." So he's telling him be very cautious.

So I started visiting more, and the more I started visiting, the more I got to know Herb, the more I got to talk. Then Herb, who had been a pastor for many years was burnt by the church. That's why he became this lay pastor. Because of a lot of different hypocrisies and stuff. He never would marry anybody, he had never been married himself. He would never marry anybody because he said marriage is ridiculous because nobody ever keeps their commitment. That was his rule.

So one day he said to us, "I have to tell you something." "Okay?" We are in the visiting room and he said, "The Lord told me I'm supposed to marry you two. Now you know I've never married anybody." He said, "So I know it's of God. I'm supposed to marry you two, and you two are going to be a use to God in so many different ways." It was overwhelming. We both just kind of looked at each other and he said, "You are going to be an example to all those who don't keep their commitments." We are like, "Okay." He actually had the date, August 13th, which is today.

Phil and Sandra Aguilar (center)

SANDRA on the day of the wedding: I was divorced, and he was widowed because he was only married a short time and his wife had died. So the day of the wedding is always exciting, and Herb who is a great man was always teaching us lessons. Phil had all his Christian brothers, and he didn't know which one to pick to be his best man. Herb said there is no choice. You are picking this one person who is like an enemy to him, who hated him. He said, "No, you are going to ask him to be your best man." He's like, "Really?" "Yes."

I had a cousin who lived in northern California, and she was going to be my maid of honor. We were going to get married in a little chapel. "No you are not, you are going to get married in the visiting room, and you are going to be a testimony to everybody there what a real Christian wedding is like." It's going to give us the opportunity to witness Christ to all these inmates and their families. Now there was the Lieutenant in charge of the visiting room who hated Christians. He was always picking on us. Always checking to see if we were holding hands, bugging us all the time. So he said, "I'm not going to give you away. He is going to give you away. He is going to walk you down the aisle. And you are going to ask him to."

He was always giving us lessons of love your enemies. Love your enemies. So my husband asked this man, this prisoner who hated him to be his best man. And the man just teared up, he couldn't believe that he was asking him that. I asked the lieutenant in charge who was just humbled, yes of course he would walk me down the aisle. So it was a big thing, because people didn't get married out in the yard. They always got married in the little chapel. So the day of the wedding everyone is all excited.

I'm waiting to get through the gates and everything, then there is a hold up. No paperwork on my divorce. They can't find the paperwork on my divorce. The wedding can't go on, because they can't find the paperwork. Well, it was I think a weekend day so it ended up where I told Herb, "I guess this just isn't the day." He goes, "Oh no, this is the day. God told me. This is the day you are getting married. August 13th is the day God told me. This is the day you are getting married. The paperwork is going to show up." Well it had got put on another lieutenant's desk. So this other lieutenant was off that day, so this one man went around looking for paperwork and found the paperwork, and the wedding was on. It was amazing. It was just amazing, because it was all for the Lord.

As this lieutenant walked me down the aisle, down the cement yard, everybody was as quiet as could be. There is hundreds of people, inmates, kids, and you couldn't hear a sound. Everybody just stared, and we walked over to where Herb was. It was on. Herb gave the whole message of salvation, the whole message of marriage, commitment and that was all of the Lord. It was a great way to be, a testimony. From the very beginning, we were a testimony. That's how it all happened.

I spent my honeymoon night at my cousin's house. We celebrated, my cousin and her husband. Because obviously after visiting hours, he went back to his cell and I left. I had no idea what was going to happen, but I had peace about it. That was so strange to me. I've never had that much peace. Now I knew I was going to be moving up there also eventually. That was going to cause a big problem with my family. I come from a very loving Italian family, but they'd never, ever wanted me to be with him to begin with. Even more so to marry him. I love my parents. My dad and I were just extremely close. So to break the news to them was going to be really hard, but I had to tell them I was eventually going to move.

ELIZABETH AGUILAR BUCHANAN on seeing Phil in prison: He wrote to us a lot and told us about the Lord. And I wanted to believe him, but I was very hesitant. He invited my best friend and I to his wedding. I was 7 months pregnant with my Ricky, and when I walked into the prison room, I could not believe the change in my brother. It was on the inside and the outside. He had gained weight. He was no longer jaundice. He had this beautiful head of curly hair, and he spoke like someone that I didn't know. It was one of the happiest moments in my life, seeing my brother and seeing the change, the transformation that the Lord did. And my best friend and I said, "Wow, if he could do this for him, he could do it for us," and that night we went to a Bible study with Sandra. Of course, she didn't get to hang around with him - he was in prison. So, we went with her to Bible study, and she led my best friend and I to the Lord who is still my best friend. My brother has made mistakes over the years, but from that

Elizabeth Aguilar, Phil Aguilar, and Clara Loysola at the wedding

day forward, he was a man after God's heart.

PASTOR PHIL on being content in prison: I ended up being on fire for the Lord. I started reading about the Apostle Paul and about praising the Lord in prison. I thought, "I can relate to this guy, he was locked up a lot too." I learned it wasn't my circumstances that I had to look at, but that it was 'greater is He that is in me, than he that is in the world'. So, I was happy to be there. I learned to be content there.

Sandra said, "You don't look like you ever want to get out." I go, "No, I'm just content while I'm here. I've got a captive audience to tell about Jesus. I've got time to study the Word of God" and before you know it, the lieutenants and the other officers there said, "We have never ever met an inmate that has enjoyed his time in prison so much." I got to testify to them and share with them. It's just because I'm resting in the Lord, and I don't want to go out again to come back again. This time, I'm going to get it.

I really am that person that was *sick and tired* of being *sick and tired*. I'm really that person who had a checkup from the neck up. I understand that God can renew my mind. So here I am in there, and just shy of two years, I go before the parole board and they said, "You are an exemplary model inmate here. We believe you are going to make it." Next thing you know, they gave me a release date. My wife is happy, and I'm happy. She's got her son, and he's happy that I'm getting out. God had worked all that out.

My brother Mel, the least likely brother I would have thought of - he picks me up at the prison. Sandra is there, and my stepson, Christopher, is there. The very first night out of prison - I went and spoke at a church. Herb had set me up to go speak at a church and give my testimony.

BILLY AGUILAR on Phil's release: You know right before he went to prison he was really strung out. He was really having a hard time with drugs. He was ripping everybody off, everybody. I really didn't get the whole story why he went down for what he did. I never really asked him, you know? I'm not a very good pen pal or whatever, but I just waited for him to get out. He came out, and he was a whole different guy. I was all excited he was coming out. "Alright, my brother is back out," because I already had the bike, and I was already hanging out at different bars called Little Beaver, Chez Paree, Crystal Pistol; I was a young alcoholic already,

Brothers Mel and Phil Aguilar

you know? When Phil was in prison, I got married before I could buy cigarettes, and I got divorced before I could buy beer. I lived a fast, stupid life, and then he got out, and it just seemed like the whole world changed.

I was just excited that he was free from the system, the bars. Telling you when to get up, telling you when to take a crap, telling you when to eat, you know? Because Phil is a pretty free spirited guy and I was just excited that he was excited about being out. I thought it was going to be a religious thing, I could live with that part of. I'm just happy that he's safe and he's healthy. Because before he went in he wasn't safe and he wasn't healthy.

ELIZABETH AGUILAR BUCHANAN on Sandra: Phil was very popular with women. I was always like, "Wow, what do they see in him?" He just has this charisma that women were always drawn to him. All kinds of different women from all walks of life. We really liked Sandra, very much. I got to know her more after they got married and came back home. She is someone that I look up to very much. I think she is the best wife ever.

PASTOR PHIL on early jobs:
I'm paroled back to Orange County, and I'm on fire for Jesus. I love my wife, I love my kid, and I love my life. My mother- and father-in-law allowed me to move in with them, and they are going, "Are you sure of this jail house religion?" But I knew. I started looking for a job, and I found one at 7-Eleven making nickels and dimes working graveyard shift. I started mowing lawns. I was riding the bus. Got a little hooptie car for $50 that I'm driving now. I started from the bottom, but I worked my way and kept rising up. Got a job for the city of Anaheim, working for the street maintenance department.

Christopher, Phil, and Sandra

JIM BUCHANAN on seeing Phil for the first time out of prison: I'll never forget. It's like it was yesterday. He takes his Bible, which I hadn't seen, slams it on the table and says, "Jimmy, it's all about Jesus," and I didn't say, "Oh, praise God." I said in my heart, "You devil." I said, "I've done a lot of things, but I'm not going to do any BS weirdness concerning the Bible, church, God. You can count me out, oh my God I should have never - ", the first few minutes I thought it was that. He said, "No!", and then he gave me his testimony, and we went to church together me and him.

PASTOR PHIL on finding a church: I knew one Christian before I went into prison, and his name was Greg Lyles. I went searching and found him easily, because his dad had a little M&M market in Anaheim. I always heard he was a Christian, and I was so excited to tell somebody, "I'm a Christian now. I love Jesus." He invited me and my family to Central Baptist Church, now called Victory Baptist Church. I'm going, "Whoa, this is weird. I'm used to prison church. This is weird." Everybody is all dressed up, and preachers got fancy shoes on and stuff. I started going to church there, and it was a little bit shocking because after church one day, they invited me to go to an ice cream social. I'm thinking, "Man, I'm not from this world. I'm a sleazy wannabe thug gangster guy who likes to do drugs." I'm a Christian now and I love reading the Word, but the extracurricular activities are a little bit strange for me.

MEETING SAINT SANDRA AND JESUS

SANDRA on going to church: We start attending any church in the neighborhood that we could go to. What happened was, we would go to church and you put your little visitor tag on. "Oh hey, I'm a visitor," no one came up to us. No one talked to us. Then we go to another church, they come up to talk to us and my husband being very proud of getting saved in prison. "I got saved in prison. Just got out." "Oh you need to go down the block because there is this - "

Then we went to this other church and two people came up to us. "How are you doing?," really nice. And then they literally said to us - my husband is a dark man. They literally said to us, "You know there is interracial church over in such and such an area." Well, we were getting definitely pretty burnt out.

This is not what we had in prison. We had love, no judgment. Don't get me wrong, we were taught very strict things, but our pastor had warned us, "Be careful of churches." Because they are not what we have here. You have to be really careful. So, we started visiting different churches, and it ended up where we didn't go to church because there wasn't a church.

Now he was working for the city, which was amazing. His mom got him a job working for the city as a street sweeper. Now here we are in our little apartment. I'm ready to have our first child together which we conceived in prison. So now you have to remember we didn't even think we would ever leave prison for seven to ten years, so we had built our life around that. So when we got thrown out, it was a blessing and a curse.

Now here we are trying to live in this world with no Christian friends and no Christian family. Nobody knew the Lord that we knew. So we are looking for churches. We had this nice little place, my sister who went to an AA meeting had been invited to a church, a Baptist church to listen to an evangelist. She invited us, so we went. The evangelist, when you go to Baptist churches, you fill out little cards, and they come looking for you. They would come every single Wednesday and knock on the door and try to minister. Try to invite us back to church. My husband would say, "Don't answer the door. Don't answer the door."

Well, I could see he's fading quickly. I wanted to get a hold of somebody to help him and prayed. His dad came to live with us for a while because his dad was a mason, and he was doing some job in the area. He never had a good relationship with his dad because of all his circumstances. He ended up him and his dad got into an argument. He took off, then my husband took off. I knew at that time that something had to change immediately, because I just knew in my spirit that he was going to go out and do no good.

I prayed the whole time he was gone, "Lord whatever you do, don't let him go back into drugs. Don't let him hurt anybody. Just do anything." He ended up coming back, everything was fine, and we had an amazing fire happen in my house. It was horrible.

I was overdue with our first child, my son who was still with us, he had found some matches and was playing with them and set the whole closet on fire. From there, we ended up losing our whole entire house and everything in it. But thank God, not us. They told me I had inhaled so much smoke that they were really worried about the baby, the unborn child. So we ended up moving in with my parents.

Here we are at my parents house, and this church who we wouldn't go and visit after we saw the evangelist there, comes over to my mom's house with tons of stuff. Baby stuff, food, anything you can think off. All kinds of gifts. We were so grateful. We went to church that Sunday, and we ended up telling them how thankful we were.

At the adult Bible study, they had taken up an offering to give us to get into an apartment, first and last. They were just so gracious and wonderful. We had been missing out on this love, because we already felt like the church wasn't going to accept us. Churches were not going to accept us. He was a prisoner. He was dark, whatever. So he went to the pastor there, and he told him how grateful he was, explained his story to him. He said, "I'm not sure why this fire happened, but I know God is trying to get my attention." The pastor said, "Absolutely," and he said, "Son, God has called you to be in the ministry, and you need to go to Bible college. I will pay your way." That's what happened.

Phil and Sandra Aguilar
celebrating her pregnancy

PASTOR PHIL on being called into ministry: I asked for an appointment with the pastor of the church, and I tell him, "I got this yearning inside to study the Bible more." So he suggests, "Maybe God has got a calling on your life." I didn't know what he was talking about. "Maybe you've been called to preach," he told me. I go, "That's a little bit weird. I don't know about that, I just want to study the Bible more." So he recommended that I go to a place called Pacific Coast Baptist Bible College.

It's on the old Cal Poly campus in San Dimas, California, and I go up there and check it out. Everybody is wearing suit and ties, and it's basically an Anglo group. I came back and told the pastor, "That's pretty trippy." I had to pray about it. I went back to work at my wonderful job for the city of Anaheim. One day, my wife gives me a call, and our apartment was on fire. My stepson had lit the place up. I go back to the apartment to see what happened, and they are both okay, but the place is on fire.

I heard the voice of God that day. I believed it was God saying, "I called you to ministry. You need to go to that Bible college and enroll." This was a Baptist Bible college that was a Jerry Falwell

Phil holding Matthew (MJ)

affiliate school. Very conservative, and I'm going, "I've got to wear a suit and tie if I go." So one of my brothers, Mel again, God used my brother Mel there. He had a little raggedy trailer in Perris, California, which he said I could rent for $50 a month. We packed up all of our belongings in this old Suburban we had, because the whole place burnt down. I drove out to that trailer. First day I was there, I went looking for a church and found Temple Baptist Church with Pastor John Lyle.

I came to church that Sunday with my family and said, "I'm here to serve." Pastor Herb had taught me, "When you find a church, tell that pastor you are there to serve." So I went there, and he got me involved teaching junior church. He raised the money for me to go to Baptist Bible College, and he helped me and my family out by getting me a job as a graveyard worker at the Perris airport where they do sky dive jumping. I'm getting helped, and I'm watching God put people in my life now who are helping me along the way in my journey.

SANDRA on moving to Perris: We ended up living in the middle of nowhere in Perris, California. When I tell people I lived in Perris, they go, "You did?" No, Perris, California. Big difference. His mother had a piece of land there with a little trailer. We literally lived there. Matthew our first son was born and then we had my son still, and we lived on this piece of dirt. But it was joyful, because now you are in God's will again. So before you were getting all this stuff and accumulating things, the Lord knew he would never make it, because he was street sweeping up and down the streets where all those bars were in Anaheim. So it was all part of God's plan, and we knew that. So it was exciting, and that's when he went to Bible college. You have to get involved with the Baptist church, and that is where we got involved with Temple Baptist. Which was amazing. We learned so much there about humbleness, that's for sure. They are wonderful, him and his wife are just wonderful people.

PASTOR JOHN LYLE on Phil and Sandra Aguilar: Back in 1979, this young couple, Phil and Sandra Aguilar, came to church. And they were really dedicated to the Lord. I remember they wanted to serve the Lord so we had them work in junior church. They were very faithful to the church. As I recall, everybody received them well. Phil was called to the ministry, full time service here at the church. Wanted to learn soul winning. We had a 12-week program in the fall and a 12-week program in the spring. He went through the 12-

Pastor John Lyle

week training. I trained him as a young future minister. I wanted to do it myself. I trained him, and then he took somebody out for 12 weeks in the spring and trained them. So he became good at leading people to Jesus Christ.

We would knock on the door, and people would come to the door. We would say that we were from Temple Baptist Church, and we'd like to ask you a question if you don't mind. That question was, "If you were to die now, would you go to heaven or hell?" That either closed the door or started a conversation. Many folks come to know Jesus Christ as Lord and Savior. Back then you could do that and got a very favorable response. Very few people would not talk to you. They had some kind of a belief, and they wanted to talk or something.

We would talk to whoever we could. Of course some people weren't home. Some people didn't answer the door. We lead a lot of people to the Lord, and the church was growing through our Evangelism Explosion. We had 11 teams out going two-by-two to the area. The town was running around roughly seven to ten thousand people. We were just blessed to the Lord. It was a great blessing to me to be with Phil and see his eagerness and how quickly he learned and memorized. He just did a good job. The second 12 weeks, the report was excellent. He taught the Evangelism Explosion to his group and took two of the people out and went door to door. So he trained somebody else.

To me the biggest thing was he was really eager to serve the Lord. His whole life was to be a life that pleased the Lord and did what the Lord wanted him to do however that lead. He didn't know, and I didn't then whether he'd be a pastor of a church or what he would do. I don't know if he was surprised, but I didn't know his background too well so when he started Set Free and was working with drug addicts and so on, let's say addicts of all

Phil and Sandra Aguilar

kinds, I thought, "Man, that is absolutely great. Just absolutely great." So it was a wonderful time and a wonderful experience for me to watch him grow and get into serving the Lord.

PASTOR PHIL on working at Anaheim Bible Church: At Bible college, I met Dr. Daniel Davidson who is my psychology teacher, and he offered me a job. Of all places, in Anaheim, near my house, near where my family is from. After Bible college, I go back over there, and now I'm working at Anaheim Baptist Church right down the street from my mom's house. There was a parsonage, and that's where I lived with my family. I worked as an extended daycare worker for about a 150 Christian kids. I remember a school teacher named Holly Palmer coming up to me and going, "Hey, good to have you around. That's a pretty rough job you got." I told her, "One day I'm going to be your boss." She goes, "What?"

God just put a spirit in me, a momentum, a fire in me that He was just going to keep bringing me up through the levels, and I was going to get involved in this ministry stuff. Next thing you know, they made me the youth director, the evangelism leader, and the overseer of married couples. I taught the teens, and I headed up the bus ministry. Next thing you know, I'm the co-pastor of Anaheim Baptist Church with my old psychology professor Dr. Daniel Davidson. It was a great Baptist church, but a little too conservative for me.

ELIZABETH AGUILAR BUCHANAN on Pastor Phil's passion for evangelism: His only business in life it seemed was to make sure everyone came to the Lord, and that's all he did. It was like one by one, all of my brothers came to know the Lord. My dad came to know the Lord. My

61

mom did. Sandra's family, friends. I have so many friends that came to know the Lord through Phil. Everyone of my brothers knows and loves the Lord. A lot of us were, "Yeah, right." So, it took awhile to believe him, that he really did have a relationship with the Lord. It was life changing, and we were happy. Once we really said, "Okay, this really happened to him," we were happy for him.

Aguilar siblings

JIM BUCHANAN on going to the Baptist church: I went to every service, and we were fully plugged in and serving in the church and I started going to Bible college. The doctrine and everything was wonderful, but when we were leading all of our friends to it, all of our friends are prostitutes, drug addicts. They are all these nefarious people, and I'm not talking any more gestalt or metaphorically speaking, any particular conversation. We bring them and they go, "Eww, did you see how she was dressed? She was dressed like a streetwalker." And then our reaction would be, "That's how she pays for her drugs." It was like, "Okay, we need to put down paper." So, we couldn't clean our fish, if you catch the metaphor.

BILLY AGUILAR on going to the Baptist church: My wife said, "Hey, why don't we just go to your brother's church?" And I said, "Well, alright. If you want to, we can. But you know how he is." You couldn't roll that guy two feet he's so square right now. He was really, I'm telling you, he didn't want to make a move unless it was biblical. I wasn't going to put no suit and tie on, and he was going to this Baptist church. He kept saying, "Let's go reach the homeless." He keeps telling me that he's going to try and reach the street people, and I go, "Yeah, sure you are bro. I know that church that you are going to. I was a Boy Scout there, when I was a kid. Those people are nice people, but they are not going to

Billy Aguilar

reach - they just want to reach each other." Finally I guess they told him, "Hey man, if that's what you want to do, why don't you go start your own church?" And, that's what he did.

PASTOR PHIL on going to see Arthur Blessitt: About that time, I hear about this guy on TBN (Trinity Broadcasting Network) named Arthur Blessitt. He carries a cross around, but he's got Levi's and long hair. I'm watching him on Christian TV. I was warned not to watch that, because these people spoke in tongues, and they are a little bit out there. Anybody tells me don't do something, usually it makes me want to do it.

I heard he's going to be speaking at this nightclub called Gazzarri's on the Sunset Strip, and I go up to visit. My brother Bert is there, and he's a big ole Jesus freak. He goes up on stage where Arthur is at. The TBN cameras are rolling, and I'm in the audience trying to be low profile, because I'm not supposed to be hanging out with these charismatics, because I'm a Baptist. My brother is up on stage, meets Arthur, and he tells Arthur, "I'm here with my brother. He's a Baptist pastor, he's right there. Pastor Phil Aguilar." The cameras turn to me.

The deacon board from my church sees me on there, hears I'm running with that crew and next thing you know, they call a meeting together at Anaheim Baptist Church. "You are a little bit too charismatic for our group." So in a nice way, we broke fellowship and here I am thinking, "What am I going to do now?"

SANDRA on starting something new: When we came back to Anaheim, he was working at a Baptist church in Anaheim. The restraints there were where you couldn't invite anybody there unless they were a Christian. You can't invite anybody to church, because when you did they were criticized, picked on. Not in front of them, but behind their back.

So as time went on, he wanted to do a little bit more and there was another pastor there that wanted to do more for the community. He would invite people to church that were his friends that were drug addicts and gang people. They weren't welcome there. So that's where he said, "Okay," and he had a friend there, Doug Dorsey, a wonderful guy. He wasn't a pastor or anything, but he was our friend. He was wonderful to us. He helped so much in

Pastor Phil Aguilar

a lot of was. So he said, "Why don't you just start your own thing?" He's like, "Yeah, why don't we start our own thing?"

He couldn't get rid of the Baptist, so he named it Set Free Baptist Church. Set free from all the traditions and "if the son sets you free you are free indeed". So played a dual role there and became Set Free Baptist Church, but he couldn't lose the tie, and he couldn't lose the vest. He couldn't lose the things that the Baptist had taught him so well, because there was so much good to it. Don't get me wrong, great stuff. It was wonderful that foundation that we had with the Baptist church.

CHAPTER THREE

THE RISE OF SET FREE

With a handful of people, Phil started Set Free Baptist Church in 1982, but eventually changed the name to Set Free Christian Fellowship. Having had a strong Baptist influence, Phil slowly loosened up the style of music, his preaching style, and his own personal look. As the church grew, it moved from location to location and finally settled at 320 North Anaheim Boulevard in Anaheim, California. With a unique music and preaching style combined with an atmosphere of acceptance, the church began to attract people with great needs. In response, the ministry began to operate 24/7 by opening up discipleship homes and other ministries to work with addicts, bikers, gang members, and black sheep.

A relationship with Trinity Broadcasting Network (TBN) opened doors for Set Free to expand its number of discipleship homes as well as produce a weekly television show. This exposure gave Set Free a worldwide platform, and the church continued to grow in Anaheim and start over 100 Set Free churches in the United States and around the globe.

PASTOR PHIL on starting Set Free: In February of 1982, about 10 of us got together at my friend Wayne Palmer's house, and we started Set Free Baptist Church. My in-laws let us meet in their pizza parlor for a little bit, and we got a little office. Then, about 1984, we moved downtown to 320 North Anaheim Boulevard in beautiful Anaheim, California. My hometown, right down the street from City Hall, right down the street from the police station. Police officers all knew me, and here I am now, I'm a new man in Christ, and I'm starting a ministry called Set Free Baptist Church.

We were all Baptists, and I joined the Baptist Bible Fellowship organization - sending in dues. Because I felt like a Baptist, I felt like that was part of my stamp - part of my branding that I was a Baptist. But, as I started doing church services, I'd put a little flyer out and I'd call them "Praise Services". Those words offended some of my Baptist brothers. I had some Baptist preachers going, "You are not wearing a tie anymore. You are letting your hair grow. You've got guitars playing at church. I don't think you are real Baptist." So I asked one of the preachers, "What do you think I am?" He goes, "I think you are more like a Set Free Christian Fellowship." So I go, "Hey, why not?"

Set Free Christian Fellowship meeting in what was previously a bank

SANDRA on the early days of Set Free: There was several people who really liked us and wanted to come join us with Set Free Baptist Church when he told them what he was going to do. One couple Wayne and Holly Palmer who were the wealthier ones of the group that had the bigger house. We started meeting there, and then several other people that came along also who wanted to break away from the tradition. We would meet there every day. Remember, he was not only working at the Baptist church, but they also nobody wanted the little house that was on the property, so they gave it to us. So we had lived in this little house on the property of the Baptist church. So when we left the Baptist church we had to leave that house also.

So now we are living in my mother in law's garage. Not even a remodeled garage, just a garage. Well it was a little bit remodeled, it had a bathtub in there. Which we used to bathe the children and wash my dishes at the same time. Not at the same time, but yeah. It was some really struggling times. Very struggling times. All of my kids in one room. I had just had Trina. She was just born. So it was a lot of sacrificing, but I have to say that I never cared, because I had this peace that this is what God really wants. So I had that joy of, I'm away from that and now we can do what God wants us to do. So that's how we started, in their house. And then it went on that we got another little house that we lived in.

I told my husband, I had just read about Nebuchadnezzar, the King. King Nebuchadnezzar and sometimes you just have to ask for something. I remember telling him, "You just need to ask the mayor," they keep shutting all these places down, because they are going to remodel. They keep blocking them off, and you can't use them. There was this bank that they had taken and boarded up. I said, "You just need to ask him, 'Can we rent it until you knock it down,' or something?" So he did. He went to talk to mayor, and the mayor said, "Yes, I think that's a great idea."

So the first place we had was this bank, and we had it as a church. We always had people that stayed with us, at least one or two people. So it ended up where we had this bank, and it was wonderful. Then before you know it, there was these other houses that were being boarded up. They were getting vandalized. So the mayor said, "Hey, you need a house? You can use the house." I think we paid a dollar rent a month in order to keep it safe, and that's kind of how it just started evolving from there. Yeah, it was amazing.

My husband always felt bad for people. That's the greatest thing about him, which is another reason why I think he gets a bad reputation. Because he cares so much about people that he won't quit on them, never. He just doesn't quit on people. No matter what they do, how bad they are.

So there is guy who used to walk around Anaheim, big old tall guy. He looked like he was from the woods. He had a bag that he carried a sack over his shoulder that was full of shot put balls. That's what he carried in there, he was very strong. My husband kept telling me, "This poor guy. He needs a place to stay. Can he just stay?" So in our little garage in the back of this one house that I lived in, finally I said, "Yes, you can stay there." But he was crazy. He was literally crazy. So at the time, the faith that God gave me to trust was amazing. I was very trusting, because I just felt like God took care of me. God is looking out for me. He is looking out for my kids. I always felt that way. So this guy, he would just do weird things.

Finally, I said I don't think he can stay any longer. I'm afraid now. He's a little weird. He told my husband, "Oh no, I'll cut the bushes. I'll do anything to be able to stay." So he's trimming the bushes in the front, and he has these pliers. Literally, all of a sudden, he starts pulling his teeth out with the pliers. I was like, "Oh my God!" I can't believe it, this person is actually on my front lawn pulling his teeth out. Which ended that one. He moved on. I don't even know where he went. It was just amazing that it took something like that to finally say, "Okay, he better move on."

But anyways, that was just too much to bear. At the same time we had this woman and her two children living with us, right? She had the audacity to actually come out into the living room and say, "Could you maybe keep it down in here? We are trying to sleep." I'm like, "Are you kidding me?"

He would always say, "Sure, okay. We're sorry." That's just the type of person he was. He wanted people to feel welcome, still does. He has never changed on that one. That's for sure.

ALEXA TEJEDA on finding Set Free Church: Back in 1988, my late husband and I lost our business due to the recession back in those days, so we were searching for a church. We were going to Calvary Chapel for many, many years and as you know that is very stoic, very quiet, very traditional. So we were looking for something like that, but my ex-husband met Phil at the city. He used to always advocate or fight about something at the city, and my husband used to do his real estate and try to get things passed through the city. He said, "You know, I met a very interesting pastor today, and I've seen him several times. We got to talk to each other. Why don't you just come and meet him? He says we are welcome in his house." I said, "Sure, why not?" So we had our son, and we took off walking. We get to the house and as soon as we get there I see about 10 guys all tatted up and leather, beards, long hair and just laughing away talking. I'm weak at the knees at this point in time. I didn't know who these people are. I didn't know what to expect.

As we walk up, they started smiling, Pastor Phil said, "Hey, come on down. Your husband told me about you, he said you are a singer. Come on, tell me about it." So, we started talking, and they were just wonderful, wonderful people. Nothing like I would expect. Very warm, very caring and inviting. That's what I loved about the whole thing. So I said, "Sure, we'll show up next Sunday." And as we arrived, I found that there were about maybe 300 people at that time in 1988. It was like a family. I felt very well received

Alexa Tejeda holds her child while sharing her testimony.

even though in the outside everybody looked tough and mean and rough. They just gave you the biggest, warmest bear hugs. These big old guys with just earrings and all kinds of tattoos and bikes and motorcycles. They were just great people.

BILLY AGUILAR on the early days of Set Free: I went there for 10 years straight, and it was a pretty cool thing. I enjoyed being able to ride my bike to church, and then he started loosening up. The tie started coming off. I don't know how many years, maybe 5 or 10 years later Sandra started wearing pants. It was pretty cool. The music was really cool. They played a lot of songs from the Stones and from the Beatles. They used the Word of God into it. It was pretty cool. I enjoyed going to church there as a young Christian.

PASTOR PHIL on loosening up: The Baptist Bible Fellowship - they literally booted me out, because they heard I was going to Hollywood movies. They heard I was dressing in attire that wasn't fit as a Baptist Bible Fellowship preacher. With my hair growing, they just figured I was evangelical or some kind of label they gave me. So, I was happy to be called Set Free Christian Fellowship. Like I said, I let my hair down and started doing some music, got the guitars going, got a little choreography going. I just stopped the ugly

Pastor Phil

contest and started telling ladies, "Hey, put on a little bit of makeup. And the old barn, put a little bit of paint on it. It looks a little bit better."

We were young people, and I read a book by a man named John R. Rice who had eight daughters married to eight preachers. He never believed in any kind of birth control. He believed God would be in charge of that, and I respected him. It all seemed wonderful so I kind of went along with that. Let people know, "Let's not use birth control. Let's just everybody have kids." So by my fifth kid, I started changing my doctrine and teaching a little bit. I said, "God is not smiling now. He's laughing at me."

At that time, it seemed like everybody was pregnant in the church, but we were all young, in their 20s, growing. That's when Set Free started becoming contemporary, and we just went for it. I got back on a Harley, and we just started going forward. Come as you are. I figured Jesus really meant that when he said, "Whosoever come onto me, just like you are." So I started wearing Levi's again. I got rid of the polyester pants. Things started changing at Set Free.

At the same time, I saw how important music affects people's lives. What a tool it is in the hand of God. So I'd been to Christian things where it seemed like, "Why should the devil have all the good music?" I never remember going to a Rolling Stone concert and Mick Jagger going, "Come on you guys, clap your hands. Come on guys, get into it." We just got into it. I went to The Doors loaded out of my mind, but I never heard Jim

Morrison say, "Come on everybody, sing along." We sang along *Break On Through To The Other Side*, because we were into it.

I started hearing pastors say, "Don't listen to my voice. It's the words that count. I'm not here to entertain you." I'm going, "I've got to be entertained, or we might as well put a tape in or turn the radio on." I believe we should be animated.

I believe that Noah when he was building that ark, he got into it. Joshua when he was leading his crew, he got into it. David when he was leading his men and Moses at the parting of the Red Sea, I believe they were fired up. To me, the music out of the songbooks, I love some of them old songs. I still do some of them old songs, but one, two, three, four, boom, boom. I said let's get a little syncopation. I was being taught that any syncopation in music appeals to the flesh. Well part of us, a third of us, since we're spirit, soul, and body. A third of us, flesh likes tasting food and hearing a good beat.

I was thinking what kind of music I like, and I said, "I could take a cool song like *My Girl* by Smokey Robinson and go change it to *My Lord*." Because people know the beat, so immediately when you start playing the music, immediately people go, "I know that song." But, then they are hearing the words, "My Lord". I started seeing, I started fishing, I started doing that music and changing the lyrics to different type of songs, and I saw people getting into it, because they felt comfortable.

Hearing the music, the beats that they liked, everybody loved it. Just changing up a few lyrics, I'd get that song saved. Get it born again. You could take a bar and turn it into a church. You could take a ho house, turn it into a house. Whatever it is, like I said, it might be doing something negative, you can flip the script on it and turn it into something positive.

ALEXA TEJEDA on the music of Set Free: I started noticing that this most amazing band was singing songs of the world, but they changed the lyrics. And it was something that I was not used to. I was used to singing these very straight and narrow songs about God. You don't raise your hands, you don't move around, and these people were going nuts. They were dancing, raising their hands, and praising God. They were singing music that I was familiar with, but with new lyrics and that really attracted me. I have a passion for music. I have always been a vocalist since I was 5 years old. So that was very much something that lured me in. That really opened my heart to this church, and I felt part of the group already as the music was playing. That's what interested me.

When Pastor Phil invited me to come to one of the rehearsals, I did, and I fell in love with the band. They were just amazing. Some of the best musicians around the area, one of them was Kid Ramos, an incredible blues player. Just like that, every single one of them was amazing, so we clicked. I started singing with the church, but it went much further than that. We were serving 24/7. It just served as the platform for me to grow and understand what serving Jesus was. That's when I realized, "Wow, these guys are for real. They are serving God seven days a week."

Alexa Tejeda became a prominent singer at Set Free services.

My ex-husband was still in real estate, so he did real estate and I was taking care of our newborn son. Whenever he was home, I would take off at night and go do Set Free. He came for a while, but he wasn't really into it. So he started doing real estate, and I started coming to church and was very much involved. Eventually, we did a lot of outreaches to other cities. We ended up going to Jerusalem as a group. I used to translate for Pastor Phil for the Spanish community. We just set up shop anywhere. I would go to the beach - Malibu Beach, you name it. Every corner that would receive us at every park. We used to give everything for free, and that's what I love about Set Free. Everything was given out for free and that's the way the Lord wanted it.

PASTOR PHIL on Kid Ramos: At the time, Kid Ramos was playing in bars all over the place - one of the top blues guitar players in the world. He's with the James Harman Band doing it. He was with The Fabulous Thunderbirds. This guy is one of the top guitar players in the world, but he was playing in a bar, and his life just sucked. So, he came to Set Free, and he gave his life to the Lord. At Set Free, I talked to him about getting involved with our band. I can remember all he wanted to do was the blues. For me to talk him into doing a Rolling Stones song cover, it wasn't easy. It took some time, but Kid Ramos actually became the heartbeat and leader of our band.

He helped us win thousands to the Lord. He would get up there and play. He was just a great brother in the Lord. He was an integral part of the ministry there. Him and his beautiful wife, part of their wedding ceremony and part of everything they did. He was just steadfast there all along the journey. He was a major part of reaching out, bringing people to Christ.

He brought dancers who do that west coast type of dancing. Skater friends he had. He drew a lot of people that wanted to come and go, "Kid Ramos is at church now. He's not in the clubs playing anymore. He's playing for the Lord." He was a total volunteer all the time. He'd just come and volunteer, bring his setup, play his best, lead people to the Lord, and just became a great servant of God.

Kid Ramos

PASTOR TIM STOREY on encountering Pastor Phil: The first time encountering Phil Aguilar was from the outside. I saw him speak at an inter-city rally, and I saw the passion. I saw the street swag, and I said, "Wow, that is definitely a guy I would like to get introduced to." It wasn't until later in life that I got to meet Phil Aguilar. I saw him, I liked what he was about, and I just thought, "This is a guy that is definitely kind of beating and walking to his own drum beat." It was a whole different world than I was in. I was in a whole different side of religion and Christianity, so he was a guy to watch. Maybe not to get to know at that point, but it was somebody that I wanted to watch.

I remember watching people roller skate one day in Central Park in New York, and everybody was kind of dancing to their own music because they had on these headsets. Some were probably listening to opera, because they were dancing that way. Some were dancing to rap, because they were listening to that music. Phil Aguilar to me was listening to something else in his head. At that point, I was a well known speaker in the church world, kind of amongst the conservative, powerful guys. And this Phil Aguilar was kind of a guy who was just blowing things up with his way of thinking, the way of doing things. Very radical. I definitely liked him. I didn't know if I understood all of his approach to life, but I liked what I saw in his spirit.

The first time that Phil Aguilar and I had an encounter would be back in the 80's. It was a great thing that happened. There was a football player by the name of Isaiah Robertson. Isaiah played for the Los Angeles Rams. He is a six-time All Pro out of Louisiana. Isaiah had been a friend of mine since I was 15, and I had not seen him for several years. Isaiah said, "Tim, I've got addicted to drugs the last few years, and I'm now in a place called Set Free. And Set Free has taken me in." So now, here was this guy Phil Aguilar that I had heard about, and now he was taking in one of my friends, former six-time All Pro Isaiah Robertson. So Phil and I began to talk about Isaiah, and that was the first time of the encounter. That was probably around the year of 1988.

MICHAEL "TURTLE" TIMANUS on meeting Pastor Phil: When I first met Phil Aguilar, there was a skate park there in Anaheim and him doing such a radical movement there. If you are local from Anaheim and you can ask any kid growing up around that time, you skated at that park. It always had professional skaters there. They were always doing some type of outreach for youth at that park, and he had all the plush ramps back then. Of course, it was free. So of course, every kid in the neighborhood wanted to go over and skate.

One day, when I was down there skating with one of my homeboys who's mom attended the church, Pastor Phil showed up with the Servants for Christ and all the motorcycles and what not, and I actually got a picture on the back of who's now my Uncle Billy, which is a trip how God seems to show you things. I still have that picture at my house, because no one knew down the road that he would end up being my uncle. And he ended up coming out, Pastor Phil came out and shook hands with all the kids. That's when I first met him and was introduced to him and actually shook hands with him. And obviously with the radical movement that Set Free was doing here in Anaheim at that time, everybody in the city knew what he did as far as taking in dope fiends, ex-convicts, drug addicts, homeless people. So we knew what he did and I knew what he did, not knowing at the time that I would end up being one of those people.

Pastor Phil

SANDRA on Pastor Phil's leadership: Phil is a born leader. He was a born leader in the drug world, in the karate world. Any world he is in, he's just a leader. God has given him that personality. I believe people see his sincerity and that he doesn't want anything from them, he just wants to pour into them. He wants to make them the best they can be. I always call him a coach. He's like a coach. You love him, but you hate him, which is exactly how Herb was. You loved him so much, but you hated him, because he was a hard coach too in your Christian walk. And that's what my husband became, just like him. You just want to be around him. His leadership role was natural. So people wanted to follow him. They wanted to do the things that they knew would be great for the Lord.

MATTHEW "MJ" AGUILAR on the atmosphere of acceptance at Set Free: The first thing I would say, maybe it's been said, "It's not just a name, it's a way of life." It really is for me and for many that were around me, you lived it, you breathed it. You almost didn't realize you were apart of it anymore, because it was part of you. It was a family for sure for a lot of people that I grew up with and around. We were always searching for what we know some of us as the Beloved and to be accepted and to feel belonged, almost feel whole. And Set Free for so many people, that was that piece that they were missing obviously we know through Christ Jesus. Still that's what you can see, its what you can feel. So for those times and even for now Set Free was that piece that was missing for a lot of people, where they finally felt, "I'm home." I can breathe, I feel accepted just the way I am even though I've heard that from church and heard that from my mom and heard that at the dinner table. This place actually accepts me how I am and is not trying to reframe me after the first meal. They are good. Obviously, we are all working on things, but the way that Set Free helped people to do that, assisted people in that way, it didn't feel like it until you looked back years later and you are like, "Whoa, who is that weirdo?" You know what I mean? It was just different in that way. So for me, Set Free definitely became a lifestyle and definitely a home for the wanderer for sure.

TRINA AGUILAR TIMANUS on the people of Set Free: I would describe Set Free as a church who deals with people who nobody wants to deal with, that don't fit into any other church. We deal with people when they have nothing. Even the people who had money at one time, when they come to us they don't have nothing. Yeah, we have the poor of the poor that we deal with.

SANDRA on her role at Set Free: Well from the very beginning, my role was kids, no doubt. And nursery, helping with the nursery. But also singing, because my husband and I were the first worship team. He barely played guitar, and I knew some Christian songs. So we would be the music and then eventually others. So that was my role. Nursery, music.

I was a full-time mom. Phil was definitely not a full-time dad. He was a father to everybody, that was his role. He was a young man still at the time, learning. We were always close in distance. We were only a house away or a block away, but he was gone a lot. So he would be doing everything that he does. As you know he does it with a thousand percent. I would say that as much as you try and keep a family situation, dinner and all that, it didn't happen.

Holly Palmer, Margie Kelly, Sandra Aguilar, and Rene Aguilar (Mel Aguilar's ex-wife)

PHILIP "CHILL" AGUILAR on culture of Set Free: It's a wild group of people. It's not your average I guess church-goers as you would say. I believe a lot when I think about it, it was how Jesus was with the disciples. They're foul mouth fishermen, dirty. I pictured them as they were cursing and probably smoking whatever they were doing that day. Smoking the hookah. I don't know but they are a wild bunch and they are radical. They are unchurched and untrained. That's what Set Free was as far back as I can remember as a young kid. It was a bunch of radical people that come from all different walks of life. A lot of times people call it a biker church or a gang church. There was multi-million dollar businessmen there who owned companies, Fortune 500.

So it was a Noah's Ark of a bunch of different type of people, but that's crazy when you throw that mix together. It's almost like a time bomb, a crazy mix of this, that and that. It was definitely a groundbreaking, never was really done like that. You have the Calvary movement, more hippy and nice. Peace and love. Here you had bikers, gang members, beeper people who wore beepers at that time - who worked for Hewlett Packard and work for computer companies. They were all thrown in as a gumbo of different flavors.

To me, that was groundbreaking. Most churches we are either black church, white church, Mexican church, Armenian church, El Salvadorian. So when they did it, it was unheard of kind of. You know what I mean? So Set Free is to me was just a groundbreaking, something that was needed. Thirty-one flavors. It was needed at that time to open up that are people who look different and that love Jesus.

PASTOR PHIL on Lois Trader: One of my first members was this girl named Lois Trader. She came because of an advertisement in the Christian Marketplace magazine. I offered karate lessons from a Christian perspective, whatever that is, but that was my little bait and Lois came in. She was wearing an Isaiah 63 football shirt, and she pulled up in this nice new Jaguar. I go, "This lady is cool." She said, "I'd like to

Lois Trader

help you do a church." She just was attracted to my ministry and myself, so she became a part of our new Set Free Christian Fellowship.

Later on, she became my assistant, and she was fantastic. She was smart. She was able to help me with all the paperwork, and she ended up spending the next 15 years with me. Every step of the way, she was like a mastermind computer. She was a planner, a plotter. Everything I thought of doing, she made happen for me. Whether it's ministering to people, writing letters to the mayor, getting me involved in all these different conferences and stuff that I was doing. She was the backbone and the brains of our operation. She truly was the driving force.

Lois Trader and I were so close, and her kids were raised with my kids. Her husband, we did everything together. Our lives were Set Free, and Set Free started growing at such a rapid rate. There was over 100 Set Free churches, and she dealt with all the pastors. It was her baby. It was like her baby even more than mine in many ways. I loved doing the ministry, preaching, teaching, hitting the streets doing outreaches, takeovers.

TRINA on Pastor Phil's assistant: Lois Trader was my dad's right hand person since I can remember. She was always his secretary. Basically I would say she was the person who ran the show behind the scenes. That was the only person I've ever seen my dad scared of and listen to. I never was close with Lois. I was friends with her daughters, but I never had a relationship with her. She was very much a big part of making Set Free what it was, and she was really smart and did paperwork stuff that nobody knew about. My dad would say 'yes' to anything, so she was the one to make sure to say 'no' to stuff. So they definitely worked as a good team for a lot of years.

BILLY AGUILAR on taking over the motorcycle club: At first, I didn't get involved, because I didn't want to be a poser. You know what I mean? I didn't want to say, "I'm going to do this and I'm going to do that," and really not. They asked me to get into the motorcycle ministry, and I joined the choir. I joined the choir, couldn't sing a lick. I joined the choir, because I wanted to get away from the lifestyle - because

Billy Aguilar

my friends were still dying on these bikes. My friends were Muscularos, my friends were from the neighborhood. My friends were dying from heroin overdoses, and I'm fresh still. I really didn't want to get caught up in this. If I'm going to change my life, I've got to get with the squares and sing the simple songs and join the choir.

And then eventually he asked me, would I take the motorcycle club? We had this guy that was running it for a little bit, for a short time and he had like three Hondas in it. I told him, "Hey bro, I have no problem doing it, but I want to make an MC out of it and no Hondas." I grew up in the lifestyle, and I still live the lifestyle. I park the motorcycle in the living room, the whole thing. I said, "Hey bro, check it out; 900 CC's or larger and American made bikes, period. No girls riding with colors on. No girls riding in the pack. We are an MC. We are a man's club. If you can live with that bro, lets do it." We were the first Christian motorcycle club in southern California with a three piece patch.

The 1% wear them. The top shows who you are. The center is your center patch of course, name of the club. And the bottom is your territory. Well our bottom is "Live or die, the living Christ, die as a gang." I just didn't want to join some cavalry that had a little diamond and pink little bow on it. If we are going to do this, hey let's reach these guys. Let's reach all of them. Let's reach the red and white, the green, the black and the white. Let's reach the dangerous guys, because I believe God saved me to put back where I stole. If that's what I'm going to do, that's what I'm going to do. If I was going to be a baseball player, I have to go Single A first. Sure enough, Phil gave us the green light. He says, "Go for it, if that's what you guys want to do." Thats where Christ's Son's came out of. I'm the president and out of that club came a lot of different clubs, a lot of different clubs.

I was president of the Christ's Son's, and then my brother Bert had a falling out with us and he started a club. He's the founding president of Soldiers for Jesus. And then, I started Servants for Christ with Pastor Phil and got to be a pretty large club, still is a large club. Phil and I had a little falling out, and then I started the Saints Motorcycle Club, the Prophet's Motorcycle Club, the Deacon's Motorcycle Club, and one of my homeboys I just met got out of prison named Big Eddie and he goes, "Hey bro, why don't we do the Christ's Son's over again? Start over fresh from the beginning?" And I got with Pastor Phil and said, "You know what bro? I think God wants to humble me. I just need to start over back to basics. Just back to basics." I still was sober 31 years, 8 months, 6 days, 14 hours, sober. "Sure bro." I told my brother Big Eddie, "Yeah bro, let's do it." "Alright." So that's what we are back to doing, the Christ's Son's, which originated out of Set Free, but we go to all different churches.

I've learned at Set Free, I was trained to serve Jesus at Set Free. I took it seriously. Baptized in the Jordan river, walking the Villa De La Rosa. Been to all the sights in Greece where they wrote the New Testament, not once, not twice, but three times. That was my education, and I really thank God that I had the opportunity to do that. It helped me with my staying married to my wife for 38 years. My wife calls me a Set Free success story.

SANDRA on the incredible growth of Set Free: You know it kind of happens gradually. So it's kind of like if you are working somewhere and all of a sudden you have more production, more production, more production. So you are already in the swing of it, so it just kind of keeps going. I was very much involved with the music and continued involved with the music, so that was a lot of my ministry.

I would be there before, and we would always have the sound check and he would be in the office praying up and dealing with Lois. Because Lois always had some issue that she was dealing with. He used to tell Lois, "Look out the door, the people still there? How many are there today?" He was amazed at how many people were coming. It just got larger and larger and all I thought was how wonderful it is that God is drawing people here, because there is something different about him without a doubt.

Pastor Phil with the Set Free singers at a Los Angeles choir competition

He was a risk taker when it came to how to do church, which is amazing. Because everything that he did as a risk taker that he got put down for by other Christians is all over every church now. So it's kind of funny.

We got so busy that it's never good to get that busy. So we lived right across the street from the church. I homeschooled also. I had started homeschooling, and then it turned into where other ladies wanted to homeschool. So basically we got a Beka curriculum, and we had a real Christian school going on that we didn't charge anybody for of course. But there were volunteers, the moms would volunteer to homeschool with their children there.

We had so much going on that our lives were so busy that we would hardly see each other, "This is great. You are doing this for the Lord. I am doing this for the Lord," music, all the different things, childcare. So we kind of just were in two different directions but in the same spot. So it got overwhelming, the roles became overwhelming.

He couldn't be the husband and dad, because he was a dad to so many other people. I was the mom and the worship singer and the schoolteacher and the Bible study teacher and the mom, but the wife part kind of wasn't there anymore, because there wasn't time for the wife part or the husband part - which isn't good.

PASTOR PHIL on the arrival of Paul and Jan Crouch: Lois' husband, Tim, happened to be a cameraman at Trinity Broadcasting Network, and he mentioned what I was doing to a secretary. Well, she ends up telling the network owners about this Pastor Phil guy who takes people in off the streets. Here I am at my little church on Anaheim Boulevard, and I'm giving out food, bread, counseling addicts in my little warehouse that's got about 50 or 60 members at the time. Who pulls in? Jan and Paul Crouch, the owners of this network that is just mega-rich! They want to come and meet me.

Tim Trader

I can remember Jan Crouch just like it was yesterday with her big eyelashes and colorful hair. She says, "I can't believe that anybody would do what you do, take them in your own house," because she saw that I had a bunch of kids. She goes, "Aren't you worried about what they would do to your kids?" I go, "I'm more worried about what my kids would do to them," was my philosophy because I got some crazy good kids. She was just impressed. The two of them say, "What can we do to help you?"

Pastor Phil giving Jan Crouch a temporary tattoo

I lived like a priest at the time, taking a vow of poverty. I didn't want anybody thinking it was anything for the money. I said, "I will utilize whatever you give me, but I don't want to own anything." She goes, "We want to buy you a house to use." The next thing you know, they buy a house. We call it the House of Paul, named after the Apostle Paul, not Paul Crouch. Paul and Jan have a dedication there, and they showed it on TV.

Back in the 80's, when you see a face like mine, with long hair, ponytail, tattoos, Ray-Ban glasses and wearing all black, that wasn't the normal look of TBN. It was a little bit more country. People from all over suddenly started contacting us, "I've got a son on drugs. Can you help us?"

Then, we got the ranch in Colleyville, Texas, a Set Free ranch, they called it Shiloh Ranch on TV. We had horses and stuff like that, and we eventually opened them up in Chicago, in Arizona, all over the place. All of a sudden, I became a big fish in a small pond.

Pastor Phil with Paul and Jan Crouch at a discipleship home dedication

SANDRA on her experience with Paul and Jan Crouch: When we first watched TBN, we weren't allowed to. That's when we were at the Baptist church. That's one of the reasons they kicked us out of that church. Well they asked us to leave the house that we had and everything because of going to a TBN event with Arthur Blessitt. Which was funny because here we are at this event watching Arthur Blessitt who was preaching at a bar in Hollywood, and then somehow or another they found out that we were there because someone saw it on TBN. Well if you saw it on TBN, then you shouldn't have been there either. You are not supposed to be watching TBN. So it was just one of the reasons for them to get us out of there.

I thought that TBN was a little crazy, tell you the truth. I thought Jan was a little much. She was just too happy and peppy and crazy and so emotional all the time. Of course, Paul, he was just quieter. But after awhile, we volunteered to go on the prayer phones ,and we would take a group and go there and go on the prayer phones. Then, Paul and Jan found out that, because Lois' husband Tim worked there as a cameraman, found out through the secretary that Tim used to share with her, "The church we go to, they take people into their own home." So it ended up where the secretary was telling Jan about it and then Jan was like, "I want to meet these people." "They've already been on the phones here." So it just kind of went from there.

Jan Crouch and Pastor Phil

When Paul and Jan came out to meet and you got to see them in the flesh, they were just wonderful. Warm, sweet, she's just a country girl who over does it, but she was great. They were great. It ended up where they bought another home, so we became more involved with them. I actually would go clean her house, because she didn't really trust a lot of people. So Lois and I and my husband, we'd go up there, and I would actually clean the house. Just amazing people. They are full time ministry people. As you know, they were never home. But yeah, they were wonderful. Jan ended up becoming even closer to us and having dinner with her and things like that, watching movies. That was amazing.

Paul would come also. Jan is a very spunky lady. And as a Christian person you are young, and you get married young, and you are a good person. You are doing all the things that God wants you to do. And being strict, you don't watch certain movies. You don't do certain things. You could tell she wanted to do these things obviously, so there was movies that she's never watched. She'd watch a movie with us, and she would crack up at how funny it would be. That one airplane movie, the name I can't think of it, it's really funny. A spoof kind of airplane movie. Things like that, you just saw her, "Gosh, she's not on camera. She's just a real person." Paul was much more conservative, but he would laugh and enjoy it also. It was great.

TRINA on the discipleship homes: When I was a kid growing up, at one time, I think we had 43 homes with all people that were homeless or people that moved to do ministry and helped out in the ministry. We had lots of really good people that helped us. Elders, deacons, all that stuff.

MAYOR FRED HUNTER on the discipleship homes: Any type of revitalization in downtown Anaheim was just going down the tubes. I had to have my law building down there. I could see what was going on. There were a lot of empty houses, and the city was doing some type of - trying to buy some of these old houses and then do some type of cleaning up downtown. And instead of those houses being empty and abandoned, the city leased them out to Set Free who took care of the houses by the way. Painted them up, cleaned them up, and instead of them being abandoned downtown Anaheim. I was for that, and I endorsed that.

Disney always has annually at the Disneyland Hotel, a beautification awards that they give out, especially to folks, houses, and commercial businesses and others in the downtown area especially. There were several houses I know that Pastor Phil - when I say cleaned out, I mean they scraped and painted and fixed those houses up. A lot of craftsman houses, and once those are fixed up, kind of like my law building, I fixed that house up. It's beautiful, and it's still a house today, because it's on the historical society. So yes, he won an award from Disneyland. A lot of those would have been abandoned and in disrepair, and he had a lot of troops down there fixing them up.

KELLI MORENO on living in the discipleship homes: I was very strung out on drugs, heavily, and I had a friend that told me about this place that I could go get off of drugs. I had no clue what it was whatsoever. So I told my mom about it. She checked out it and said, "Okay, go there on Thursday at whatever time and they'll take you," and I said, "Okay." So I went in the morning, I signed up. I went Thursday for the Thursday service. Left my car parked, and all of the sudden I'm driving in the

Kelli Moreno

backseat of someone's car out to this ranch in Paris. I had no idea where I was going either. I was ready though, because I had been crying out to

TRAINED TO SERVE JESUS

God. So anyways we get there, it was just crazy. It was like this acre of dirt. Two sides, the men's side and the women's side. Trailers, outhouse, water, a shower that was heated with boiling water, but I was instantly delivered overnight. The next morning, I woke up completely free of any desire to do drugs or smoke even which was amazing to me. Because I'm like, "I'm not quitting smoking. I'm going to quit doing drugs, but you aren't taking my cigarettes." But sure enough completely, instantly delivered. It was absolutely amazing.

I spent two weeks at the ranch, and then we moved into the homes in Anaheim. He had about 18 homes at that time, and that was it. I just kind of went with the flow and didn't leave. I loved it. I loved it. I loved where I landed.

We all were assigned a blessing, not a chore, it was a blessing. Mine was to make the oatmeal in the morning. So I woke up and cooked a huge pot of oatmeal for everybody. We did devotions early. We got ready, and then we all met at the building about 8 o'clock in the morning. From there, we would sing songs and do Bible studies and clean and just whatever they had for us that day. Sundays - it was address envelopes, we sent out a monthly newsletter. And then at night we always had something going on. And it always involved food, thank you Pastor Phil for the extra 30 pounds. But everything was just a righteous party for Jesus. I loved it. We had an eclectic group of people so we all meshed. There was about 300 of us when I was living there. And then sometimes we would go to TBN during their marathon. Their prayer week - we would answer the phones there. We did a lot of trips. A lot of concerts which was really awesome.

The thing that I am most grateful for is being trained to serve Jesus. It was honestly the best time of my life. It was very simple. I was 23 when I went there, and I had always worked. I was a very functional drug addict, but when I was at Set Free the one thing I didn't have to do was work as far as provide income and support myself. I was free to minister and go whenever he said we are going. I packed my bags and we were going. It was cool because I knew, "Okay God, what adventure do you have for me today?" But honestly that's it, being trained to serve Jesus and seeing a real Jesus. A Jesus that just loved people for people. I went a lot of places, too. We went to Hawaii a few times. I got to go to Israel. That was just amazing to me. I traveled the whole United States several times. Just the concerts were awesome. Fun. Everything was fun. It was a righteous party. It was always a righteous party, and I really believe that's how God wants us to live. Life is not easy - it's a struggle. But you know what? Everyday wake up and be thankful, be grateful, and be a blessing. I learned all of that from being there.

Set Free dancers with Kelli Moreno (far right)

MJ AGUILAR on his experience at TBN: TBN is a trip. TBN is - okay, let me go back to my first introduction with TBN. I felt like I was walking into Willy Wonka land, because things were made out of things that shouldn't be made out of. I wish it was candy, but it was just the utensils, the painting on the wall. The one in Santa Anna where they first had TBN, their studios, which I think is maybe one of their original studios - you'd walk in, and it was just red carpet, so that was different for me. A good DaVinci Code blood red. And I didn't respect it at the time, but now I kind of have a little appreciation for it. And then you look to the right and it's Jesus, this crazy painting with every child from every country, because you can't miss any races. So they had them all up there so you could make sure to find you or your people.

We would wait in that room, and people would hang out until the studio would open and everyone would flood in. And I say everyone, meaning pretty much my whole house and our ministry at the time, as my dad Pastor Phil started. He would get the third spot or the two minutes where the comedian goes on like the late, late, late show. He slowly worked his way up by putting in work in our city and in the county and the ministry to work his way up. So that way you'd get more people that want to be there, and he was always great at recruiting and had a lot of supporters that really believed in him and what everybody was doing. So we'd flood from the wine room into - after a big prayer that lasted way too long for me - and we would flood into the studio and we would kind of in a movie setting. We would be in there, and we would wait for the show to go on. So it was kind of cool seeing some of the behind the scenes that I never got to see before. The cameraman, how they are rolling around setting things up. And then, I see the stage which again for my age, I'm talking about probably 9 or 10 were some of my first experiences if not a little younger, and I was just like, "Wow, this is a trip. This is crazy."

We would go in, and it was a long time sometimes waiting. And our crowd, we came to see one person and one person only. So I think it was past my bedtime around that time, but again there was Set Free School, so we were good as long as it was for something like this. So we were there a whole group. We'd wait to see my dad at the time, which was pretty awesome. And then you see these people that were interviewing him, which was usually Paul and Jan Crouch who were the founders, leaders of Trinity Broadcasting Network. Because I see my dad and my family with the people that I kind of related to and that were around us for the most part, not that they all dressed the same way or anything but when you saw them you are like, "What planet are these people from?", and more so her than him. And this is from a 10 year old, but maybe someone who is a lot older too from what I heard over the years. It was just different. But this lady and her husband really had a lot of love for Set Free from the beginning. It seemed like they were sold out and really wanted to partner up and do a lot of stuff, and they did.

TBN was cool. There was also other people that would be on that we would kind of get to know or like. Like this group called the Power Team, John Jacobs, and you had all these guys that are all kind of bigger, ex-football players and stuff. They would break handcuffs and break bats and bend stuff for Jesus. At a young age, they would be on the show, and to me, that was pretty rad. Besides Set Free there was nothing on TBN that I was a fan of - yeah, I can't think of anything. But other than that, it was kind of cool.

We'd go and we'd wear our t-shirts that said, "Power Team", but they were made at the swap meet, because we couldn't afford the real Power Team. But I'd always get up - not upset but I'm a young kid, and it was like a Power Ranger for the next generation. As a Christian too, you are almost in your bubble that they want to keep you in. So whether it's music or cartoons, you know how it is. Your parents are trying to keep you from the bad guys. So Power Team was one of the things we liked, so I'm like, "Okay, you are making me like this. I'm down with it. They are cool, but I can't get a real t-shirt?" My dad was like, "No, I know them. I'm on the same stage but that's a $30 t-shirt right there in the name of Jesus."

So we had to go make our own, and they were just like the felt Power Team, just white on black. Now they are kind of cool, they are retro, but at the time I didn't feel so cool. But again, those are some of the things that do stand out that TBN was apart of. I got to be around TBN a whole lot. The people behind the scenes. The ranches they helped us with. Jan Crouch, Paul Crouch, her sons, her son Matt Crouch who I know is a big part of what they do now. He used to play with Geronimo, my older brother, because they are closer to the same age. They would be on the same basketball team, and you'd get to see him - just like anybody else - getting in the flesh because someone fouled you. It was pretty cool.

CHILL on going to TBN studios: I was like 9 or 10 and I just remember - if you watched some old videos, you see me and my brothers. We are in the crowd, and we are just so happy. Because we didn't know about any other secular TV. We couldn't watch anything at that time. So they were like stars to us. Her bright pink hair and Paul and his fake hair wig. So us, we get to go down there and get free snacks and be on the phones. So it was another place for us just to play. And actually, it was bigger than we even knew at the time. You see us in the audience, our hair is all messed up, we didn't care how we looked. We are playing. They had different people on the show, this group called the Power Team that broke stuff like bats and stuff and bent metal. They are power lifter guys so we would love that. They were like our heroes. Like Bible Man, you know what I mean? They have different characters. We were so into church and religion that those were our heroes. Forget watching GI Joe. We loved the Power Team. Paul and Jan were like stars to us, so it was cool. It was fun times, but I don't know too much about them because I was so young. I just saw them help my dad out with homes and stuff, but I never really knew them.

TRINA on her experiences at TBN: There was a couple of years where we were at TBN all the time. I didn't answer phones, but I would go there with them. Answer phones for the prayer line. Set Free would be the ones who were there all throughout the night when nobody else wanted to be there. We were in the crowd quite a few times. Yeah, actually we filmed a video with Vern Jackson. Hebrew was in it. Hebrew was playing my dad as a young kid. We were with Jan that whole day. She is actually really nice. Really, really nice. That was the first time I was ever alone with her. My dad hung out with them a lot.

When we used to go to TBN, it seemed like surreal. It was weird. Your dad is famous on TV - that's how it seemed at the time. But then when all the bad stuff started happening, I was like, "Ugh, I hate living in Anaheim where everybody knows me. I hate it. I want to move really bad." Because everywhere you go, somebody knows you. Then you never know, are they going to say something bad about your dad? Are they going to say something good? So, I'm not the type of person who likes to be put in those positions. But he seemed famous when I was young.

KELLI MORENO on working the phones at TBN: Specifically this one lady called in. Somebody was on air I believe, a kid, a younger kid and he had one earring. So a lady from the Bible belt, Texas, called and she was like, "That boy has an earring."' And I'm like, "Okay," anyways I said, "Well, what's going on with you? Tell me what's going on." So she said she's got some problems so I said, "Well, let me pray for you." So I prayed for her and then after the conversation I said, "Just to give you a little clue on what I look like. I have pink hair, I'm covered in tattoos, I have ten earrings, my tongue is pierced but would you ever know that by the phone conversation?" And she is like, "No." She almost didn't believe me. I'm like, "That's right, that's because Jesus looks at the heart."

Just being able to impact her in that way maybe opened her eyes up a little bit and showed her that people - Jesus didn't condemn people by their appearance or their social status or whoever they were. It was just based on the inward. The inward man and that was one of the most interesting things that happened there to me at TBN.

Pastor Phil standing next to President Ronald Reagan and other members of Set Free

PASTOR PHIL on the expansion of the ministry: There was so much response that Paul and Jan bought another home for us. They didn't stop for another few houses like that. Here I got Paul and Jan Crouch, people are dying to meet them, and they are over there with me, coming over to my house to visit. Well now they invited me to go on TBN to give my testimony. Little did I know, that's a blessing and a curse, but I go on there and I just share my testimony. I was saved in prison. I was a heroin addict. Jesus delivered me, now I'm loving on people.

At the same time I got the mayor of the town, everybody had seen that I'm helping people. They see all these homes, and they see our people every

President Ronald Reagan and Pastor Phil

day in front of the streets, cleaning out the gutters, wiping out graffiti. Doing all these kind of good deeds in the city. So people are noticing all over. The next thing after that, I'm with Paul and Jan on TBN, and they have me as a regular guest going on there. Then, Paul and Jan have a ranch in Colleyville, Texas, and want me to open up a rehab on their big 60-acre property.

By this time, my wife and Lois are taking care of Paul and Jan's Newport Beach homes. They are taking care of their families. We are all the phone people in the 80's that you saw on the phones. Almost all of them were people from my Set Free homes. Addicts, prostitutes, people from every kind of strange lifestyle. So we are counseling America now. People are calling up, and they are getting one of my characters that were mentored in our homes, our discipleship homes we called them. So, God was just using TBN.

We are going from a small little church where every week there is not just 5 people, there is 25 people, 50 people. I got a little office at the church warehouse where I'd peek out the door and go, "Lois, are they coming again this Sunday?" It went from a few hundred, to five hundred, to seven hundred, to a thousand. Week after week, I had letters coming in from TBN from all over the place.

I ended up having 70,000 people in my Rolodex in 1991. In those days, we didn't have the phones and computers. I had eight volunteer secretaries writing letters to everybody who wrote to us. It was in the hood, a warehouse with leaks, no air conditioning, bleachers with two-by-fours. Every service, we brought out folding chairs, and one or two of them would break down in the middle of the service.

This place was a warehouse in a gang neighborhood, not remodeled. This was not a 'how to build a megachurch' strategy, but all of a sudden it was growing.

When Paul and Jan Crouch came to my place into our little warehouse and I started working with them, all I remember, Paul was always business, business. Great guy, kind, nice, but always business. Thinking about his vision of building this and building that. I always remember that very kind, wonderful gentleman. He father-figured me and took me places to the point where they asked me to be one of the five board members of the whole Trinity Broadcasting Network where I'm voting to help approve whether to buy a station or sell a station.

Jan was just loving, soul-winning. God just made a bond between us that happened quick. They would come over to my house, and we'd watch Airplane or other funny things on TV. Jan just loved the heart that I had during those years of taking people in. Just loving people where they are at. She loved being able to get involved. She'd come to our Thanksgiving and help feed people. She'd come to the homes and help talk to the young kids. Jan Crouch, people have said a lot of things about her, but I'll tell you one thing, she cared about souls. Cared about people. She was in a tough spot being in that position, her and her husband, but they treated me like gold. They were great friends to me. They were with me through the good, the bad, and the ugly.

Meeting Benny Hinn and all these other famous preachers was a little bit different, because all their hairdos and the way they dressed took me for a shock. LaVerne Tripp – they are like country people to me. They remind me of country people. Everybody had big fancy hairdos, cowboy boots, Dwight Thompson, all these kind of people, but they all treated me like gold. They were just wonderful to me, and I never had a problem with any of them. They

Benny Hinn taking a ride with Pastor Phil

loved us right where we were at. We were kind of like their little step-children.

TBN and Set Free became friends just like that. We just had a beautiful ministry relationship. Now they gave me a TV show, and I'm reaching millions of people every Friday night. I don't really know what I'm doing. I'm as amazed as anybody else that this is all going on. God has just given me great favor and influence. Now I'm asked to go speak everywhere. I'm going all over the world, all over the nation and speaking at churches. Everything was just going super, wonderful.

MJ on Jan Crouch: I could care less when I was young when she would come over. I'm like, "Hey, what's up? Right on, nice hair. Cool, I'm going to go play with my friends." But it was a big deal of course. When she came, it was like my dad would be telling everyone, "Yo." He's kind of already like, "Hey, be on your best behavior. Be cool." The place was already pretty clean, but she's coming it's kind of like the Pope coming through. It was more her than her husband. She was usually the one that was more around. She would speak at the church a couple of times, which was big to have her come and speak to your congregation and be there. But she would come by once and awhile. She would come to the property and see what's going on. Maybe a new house that they would help rent for our ministry, you kind of cut the ribbon.

I remember being just a kid and being apart of that and being like, "Oh, they are still here. That's cool that they like what our family does, and they support us," even at that young age. And then, even she would just kind of spend some of that extra time - where I felt like even for her, this was a time where she could kind of let her guard down and relax. Because as you know, the bigger you get it's hard to find people and places where you can just be real and honest. That is the thing with our place, there was no reason to front. There was no reason to portray anything and what God made you or what you were or maybe what you always wanted to be but you've always felt you weren't allowed to be or afraid to be.

So even for her, her look is her look, but a lot of her heart was Set Free. It really was. I think if she grew up in another time and place, definitely her. I don't know about the both of them, but she would be out there. And maybe she did, I don't know her whole story either, but she definitely liked to get her hands and feet dirty - which it was pretty cool to see someone like that come off what looked like a throne at TBN. It just looked like that whole thing. So to leave your crown and scepter and come out with us grunge folks and do some work, that was cool to see. It was real cool, because we always went to that side, but you don't see too many people from that side come to our side for whatever reason. So TBN was pretty cool like that I thought. To even allow Set Free to kind of be in their mix, I know it was a big step for them. They seemed like they gave it a good shot.

MAYOR FRED HUNTER on his support for Set Free: I supported Pastor Phil. He and I on a couple of occasions were on TBN, Trinity Broadcasting Network, and we were telling the story of how Fred Hunter, the cop, probably arrested Pastor Phil. Now, Fred Hunter the Mayor is tight with Pastor Phil, because I really had admiration for him for what he was doing. And I know a lot of the old timers downtown did not like seeing a lot of people out of prison and other folks walking around downtown Anaheim by City Hall, because it didn't have the flavor they wanted. But I stood by him, because I knew what he was trying to do.

I call it real Christianity. It's not people just sitting there bored to death. Even today, you go to church, and its rare that somebody is quoting from the Bible. I was raised in the Church of Christ, and it was King James version of the Bible all the way. You go to church now, and you are lucky to hear somebody say, "Jesus Christ." That's what it's all about. Well, their whole sermons and their whole music was all about Jesus. Jesus loves you, and you need Jesus to be saved. And that Savior message brought out a lot of young people, to clean up their lives.

When I was running for Mayor, the Set Free Posse, hundreds of them - they canvassed neighborhoods with brochures that said, "Re-elect Fred Hunter for Mayor". Now a lot of people in politics would say, "Oh my God, Fred, why would you do that?" Because you have these folks out that didn't look like a normal person that would knock on your door and say, "Endorse this guy." But every election Pastor Phil and his posse, they went out all over the city and passed out brochures and knocked on doors for me, and I appreciate them doing that.

God's Casa, one of the many Set Free discipleship homes

JIM BUCHANAN on God's provision: If you can believe, we never, ever, ever passed a plate. We never sold it. Every t-shirt, every burrito, everything we gave, we just gave. And people came and joined us, and the people that come and joined us were those that wanted to truly serve God, because we had no salary. We all got the same salary here, zip. Zip, that is your salary. You are here to serve God, not be paid. So everything we did that way, and God blessed. It was just unbelievable to see the miracles. People would say, "Jimmy, you've helped me so much." I would say, "No, I gave you a light bulb, a table, and a Bible and hours to read. I took care of you, just fed you," and their only duty was to read, to obey, to learn, and to grow. And as they did, God just blessed it. We just watched those transformations over and over again. Jehovah Jireh - He is the provider. He provided everything, before we even asked.

I've been in every branch of our ministry that we've had, but one we had was called 'His Hands'. We gave away food and just clothing and everything. We did it all day. I'd wait about every half hour, and I'd let a new group in so that it would coagulate in the courtyard waiting, and my preacher boys would try out their first sermons. But my point I wanted to make is we had a big place, a line all day long, and I fixed that place. That place was sweet. I had people, three or four people all day long did nothing but sort clothes and find out what was good enough to give in the name of Jesus. The rest we sold to second hand stores, and they sold them in the same neighborhood that we gave.

The point of what I make is, out of all that traffic, I was never able to empty those shelves or those racks. Never, and we had I don't know how many second hand stores were making it a business, and we were giving it away free. We could not run out, because I had another two or three guys, all day, all night. We never advertised. We never spoke from the pulpit. We didn't put out flyers. God directed people to us. They would come in trucks. They would come in cars. There it was, everything we needed. We could not give it away fast enough.

I had pastors call me and say, "I want to start a food ministry. We understand that you are doing all this, please help me." I gave them sincere help. They wanted to start a food ministry, I sent a little flyer and it said, "Go to your cupboard," Lois wrote it, "Find delicious, nutritious food that you like. Go to the street and find a homeless person. Come back to your house and repeat. Congratulations you are now in the food ministry." So this is a sincere pastor with a rather, not a large, but a substantial church in another state. I sent him back that exact pamphlet, and he wrote me back a little later and said, "Brother, why would you do me this way? I came to you in the name of God seeking help and advice in prayer." I wrote him back and said, "I responded to you with good advice prayerfully. This time my dear brother, perhaps you should pray, and then read that carefully and understand that I'm with you and for you."

PASTOR EDDIE BANALES on meeting Pastor Phil: Well, the story is like this. I got saved through Victory Outreach. I went to an Assembly of God church, some of us - not just me, other gang members from different neighborhoods, and our pastor had a heart. We would go to outreach in our backyards. We would take our choirs, and we would take our church team to the parks and to the areas where the gangs would hang out and nobody would come. Okay, as time went on - we still did it. You would find one or two persons here or there and witness to them. But as time went on, I became an associate pastor.

I was an associate pastor in Assembly of God church, and all of a sudden, I heard about this ministry called Set Free. They sing, turned around oldies in a band. They sing rap music that they turn around the music. Harleys and low rider cars and all that. I'm like, "Okay, I want to check this out." So I went and saw them, and this was probably early 1991, down the street here from me. My old neighborhood, my old park. Here, I see these guys on bikes and cars and low riders and their band on the stage. I have done maybe three or four outreaches in that same park with church people and did nobody come. Maybe a few homeless people came for food.

But, when Phil came with his band with the low rider ministry with the Servants for Christ motorcycle and the band, and they start singing 'My Lord' instead of 'My Girl'. the songs that they would sing, I saw a lot of friends that nobody would not come out to that kind of a park, come out. And I thought, "He's reaching people that we're not reaching, and we are supposed to be the church." Again, we wore the choir robes and we just - we had it backwards in my opinion. When I saw what he did that day and the people that came to the altar and actually were relating to people, they were not just dressed in suits and ties and robes and dresses. They were still in biker uniform. They were dressed in comfortable clothes. Their hearts were changed, but they looked the same.

So my neighborhood responded to them, and I just took a liking to him. I met him that day, and I said, "I've never seen anything like this in my life," and I was impressed with that. I felt like at that time I would have been at Tommy Barnett's church in Phoenix so many years watching him do the various ministry he does, but in a different culture setting. I finally felt I met a man that knows how to do cultural setting in the culture that I grew up and how to effectively witness and minister to them. That's how we first met.

Leaders within Set Free Church

PASTOR PHIL on starting Set Free churches: A lot of times people would ask me, "How did you start Set Free? How did God do that?" I just say, "Jesus." I didn't have an agenda. To me, it's a byproduct. When my cup is running over in my life, it's a byproduct that I want to give to others. When I don't have much going on in my life, I want to keep what I have to myself. So Set Free started blowing up. There was no room for people. I even got arrested for a code violation for too many people coming to church.

I can remember this guy named George and his wife, "We want to start a Set Free in Hawaii." Then a guy came to me, "We want to start a Set Free in Gold Coast, Australia." "Hey, we want to start a Set Free in Manila, Philippines." People wanted to start a Set Free in Long Beach, Huntington Beach, Anaheim Hills, Bakersfield. People just started coming. It was just an organic growth. It was a byproduct. I had no plans. I never wanted to be the Pope. Didn't want to have Set Free churches all over, because I had enough trouble keeping an eye on my mess. I'm not a businessman, not a money guy. So I wasn't going to charge everybody. No franchise fees. Basically, like I said, I just started having different people in the congregation going, "I feel like God wants me to start a Set Free in Norwalk."

I'd say, "You've got the Set Free heart. We go where the pizza man don't deliver. We got the gift of inconvenience. Are you ready to be the first one there, the last ones to leave? You got that heart? Boom, I ordain you. Go on out there and do it." I didn't raise an offering for them. I didn't do that. I didn't tell them, "Okay, when you start making money, send back to the mother church." Everybody was independent, autonomous, their own churches, and they went out there and started doing it. They stayed in touch with me as much as they chose to.

TRINA on the freedom to start Set Free churches: I remember we had so many Set Free churches that started. Lots of them. Basically, my dad would let anybody start Set Free that wanted to and help them out. He would get them ordained as ministers. We had a lot at one time. I think we had three hundred and something, quite a lot. Certain stuff he is really controlling on and other stuff we are like, "What are you doing?" Because normally, if Calvary Chapels or bigger churches, when they have a whole bunch, they are still kind of connected. Like ours weren't like that. It was their own thing, they just used the name and catered to the same type of people we did in a different city or different state or whatever. I honestly think because my dad is always the type, out of sight, out of mind person. So if it's not right in front of him, he's not thinking about it, and that's just the way he is with everything.

PASTOR WILLIE DALGITY on affiliating with Set Free: We had started a ministry up at Bryant Street Baptist church here in Yucaipa called Jesus Hands Food and Clothing. We were reaching into the real down and out, the people that with addictions in Yucaipa. We'd been reaching them, and I'd been following Phil on TBN. So we decided to go take our crew down and go and visit on 320 North Anaheim Boulevard.

We went down there, and we had parked four blocks away, filled. It was just incredible. We are going in and

Pastor Willie Dalgity and Pastor Phil

there is just a flow of people of all kinds of backgrounds. We are all walking in towards the warehouse. When I walked in that place, I was sold on that model of ministry. So in '92 Phil had put out a little, "Hey man, if you want to affiliate or join up with Set Free, let me know." So I sent him a letter. He sent one back saying, "Yeah man, come on down and meet." We went down, and we met him and the rest is history.

We began to go down to Hotel Hell. It was down on the freeway down here on Frontier Road. It was just a really beat-down hotel. A lot of dope slinging going on, people living there. We went down and got permission to do outreaches. We'd just go and cook up some hot dogs and some sodas, Phil style. Pretty soon, we saw people peeking out the windows, but they wouldn't come out. So then, we'd go back the next week and somebody would open a door. A couple or three weeks they started coming out. We started reaching them. Ultimately, we began a Saturday evening service at Bryant Street Baptist. It's just a regular kind of a Southern Baptist church. And before long, we were bringing up 60 people on Saturday nights and doing church there. So that's kind of where we began. 1992 is when we affiliated with Pastor Phil. So that was our beginnings.

PASTOR EDDIE BANALES on affiliating with Set Free: Well, I was having a challenge because again the church was kind of boxed in. When a church says they want to reach the community, we pray for the prostitute, but we don't want nothing to do with her. We pray for the gang member or the person that has been in prison, but we don't want nothing to do with them. I'm not understanding, how do you pray for them? Who does deal with them?

So I knew that he was doing the same thing that I was doing. Later that year I left my position and started my own church in October of '91. This year will actually be 25 years for me. But I would not reconnect with Phil until months later when he started a Set Free in Pomona. Another pastor and I wanted to work with him - it didn't work out for that pastor and the next thing I know I have 20 or 30 people coming to my church saying, "Phil sent us here." So I wanted to ask him, "Hey, what are these people dodging?" "They have to go somewhere."

And he at that point was making a transition. He was too big. He was going through his personal challenges, the buildings on Anaheim Boulevard, and all of that stuff. He was going through changes, so he started launching at that time. I wasn't really aware of the details until later that I would be the one in charge of everything, but that would be later to come. So he said, "Send them to me." So then he asked me, "Why don't you become a Set Free?" And I thought, "Okay." So I incorporated what I did have into Set Free Pomona at that time. And it started, and when he sent me those people, I went to them and he ordained me, licensed me and I became a Set Free. I think it was in January of '92. And so that was the beginning of journey.

Remember, he had a lot of pastors at that time. He almost had 60 or 70 if not more at that time that he was launching out. I'm talking about all over the place. People had a vision, they had a goal. Now, truthfully and you want me to be truthful, most of them didn't know what the heck they were doing. But they had the zeal. They wanted to do a Set Free Posse which was a rap group at the time. They wanted to organize a rock and roll band that sang Christian music at the time, which is still popular to this day, but church is more than that. The administration part and all that stuff. So that's kind of how we began.

PASTOR WILLIE DALGITY on the Set Free style of ministry: The Set Free way, at least from a Biblical perspective is Matthew 25 - it's where Christ said, "When you've done unto the least of these, you've done it unto me." And that's what we do. The disenfranchised, the people that are on the fringes of our culture and society. We really take it to heart and I know Phil, this is where it all came from. You just open your doors. You meet them right where they are at, and you just love them. I believe that the Set Free way involves deeds of mercy. Giving people what they have the right to expect nothing good. Giving them everything good. That's really what mercy is. That's really to key Set Free. It opens the shut doors of people's hearts where you can give them the gospel.

We do it in several different ways. We have our outreaches where we go out on the street. We do outreaches. And outreach for us is where we go set up a place in a parking lot or a park. It doesn't matter where and we cook up some hot dogs, some sodas, and we play some loud music and some hip-hop or something. We flyer the place, and they come. We give them Jesus, man. We give them the gospel.

This is the cool thing about Set Free everywhere, we say, "Hey, you may have given your heart to Christ but if you need a place to go now, you can come." So we'll bring people home. That's when they go to our ranches. And we have a ranch out in Lake Elsinore right now, about 62 guys on the men's part and 27 women on the other part. So that's where a 60 day commitment, get hooked up with the Lord and discipleship begins. Just trying to teach them to be followers of Christ.

After they are done with that, if they would like they can come into one of our residential discipleship homes in Yucaipa, San Bernardino, Redlands, wherever we have our Set Frees in the Inland Empire. They just continue in that. They continue to learn Jesus, and then they start taking steps in employment, taking care of their old warrants, getting their driver's license back, turning themselves in. All that kind of stuff. Then they are able to continue in their lives in that way.

THE RISE OF SET FREE

PASTOR PHIL on the type of person who started a Set Free Church: I'd say probably 125, 130 churches at its height. There were that many churches really rocking and rolling – Lake Havasu, Arizona, Oklahoma, Chicago, Florida, just all over the place. Lois kept more in touch with them more than I did. I was busy taking care of my own stuff at home.

One of the things that I've learned in ministry, and I'm still learning all the time, I see people who go to a three-year, four-year seminary Bible college.

Sandra and Phil Aguilar

Then, so often times, they pray about where they're going to go do ministry. Then, they pray by the paycheck they are going to receive. Whether it's in Hawaii or some desert place. So, to me, when people are called by God, nobody can really say yes or no if they are called to God. It's a personal thing. Everybody that wanted to become a Set Free, they were people that had spent time with me.

They came to the church, and they saw the vision. They had been walking with the Lord for some season of time. They've been through many things in their life that they believe they could do it. It's always a testing ground. I remember Jesus disciples. They walked with him for a few years, hung out with him day and night. They are still cutting people, and they are still cursing. You just never know who is going to be the one to really succeed, and I don't think there are enough things that you can put somebody through to see if they are going to make it in the long run.

Nobody thought I would still be married. Nobody thought I would still be doing ministry. A lot of people counted me out many, many times. So there are so many people who started with a Set Free, now maybe they are called Free Indeed or Freedom Bible Church or New Wine or something else. But it's cool, because they are still doing ministry.

PASTOR WILLIE DALGITY on Pastor Phil's leadership style: This is Phil. When we hooked up, I thought I'd get some mentoring from him. How are we going to do this? And he gives me that little pamphlet, "How to start your own ministry". You've heard about it, so he gave that to me. He goes, "I'm not joking you Pastor Willie, just do it like this." We'd been doing it that way, but he just meant, if you come to Phil and say, "Can I do this? Can I do that?" He goes, "Do it." That's his leadership style. He just says, "Do it, but don't expect me to sitting there championing your cause. Just get it done."

There is a pastor up here in the Pass area who was down there in the early years too, but he kept coming down to Phil's wanting him to do something similar out here in the Pass. He kept showing up here at the outreaches with Phil, and he told Phil, "I want to do something like this." And he said one Saturday when he went down there, and Phil said, "What are you doing here? What are you doing here?" He said, "Well we came down to do an outreach," and he said, "I thought you wanted to start Set Free? Don't come down here anymore, get out there and do it."

This pastor, he did. And he's had a church for years out here in the Pass area. It's not a Set Free per say with the name, but it's got the same style. So that's kind of Phil. He just put it right on you and say, "Do it man, don't just be talking about it. Be about it." That's Phil.

Pastor Phil and Sandra Aguilar

PASTOR PHIL on money: One of the things that I can remember when I first got involved in Christianity, I went to a church after I got out of prison, and I saw this thing called an offering. These tithes and offerings. I remember seeing Dr. Bob Well pulling up in a big white Lincoln Continental. Fancy shoes, fancy outfit. I started learning a little bit about giving. I would go to church literally with a $5 bill in one pocket and a $1 bill in the other pocket. If I liked the message, he's getting the $5. If I didn't, he's getting the dollar bill. It depends how I feel about it after the service when it's time to give the offering. Then, I started learning about giving a little bit more.

I realized you get blessed from giving - that it's the right thing to do. I became a tither, a giver. Ten percent of my earnings. Now when I started Set Free Church, I'd seen so many people upset with preachers asking for money that I legally did a thing called a vow of poverty - where I did the paperwork so I was treated just like a priest. I could not own any personal belongings - houses, homes, cars, things, bank accounts. I took that vow of poverty.

I'm not saying it was the smartest thing now in retrospect, but I did it. I never one time - in all the years of Set Free - passed an offering plate. I didn't talk about money, because I didn't want people to think I was in it for the money. But, people always said, "Let me chip in this. Let me chip in that." They'd help out.

My assistant, Wayne Palmer, was our bookkeeper, and he took care of all the banking. When I started going on TBN, little did I know grandmas from all over the country would send in checks, $25 check here, $25 check there. I would have some family go, "I want to give you this car." Somebody, "I'd like to give you this bike." So people started donating stuff. Paul and Jan donated homes. I said, "I can't own them Paul and Jan, but we'll utilize them."

I never, ever all through the years owned a home, never owned a car, never owned a motorcycle. It all belonged to the ministry, and the ministry people utilized it. Living in the homes, I always had 20, 30, 40 people living in my own home - lived right across the street from the megachurch.

When we'd go on a bus to do outreaches, we didn't have credit cards. We didn't have the way you do things nowadays, so it was cash. We'd stop at a market to get groceries. Go to Sizzler to get food and do stuff like that. Everything that did come in was totally utilized of the ministry, but I've always had people, "You are rich." I go, "Well my dad is rich. He owns cattle on thousand hills." But when it comes to money, I've always lived real simple. Always ate with everybody. Always hung out with everybody. Never stayed in hotels - we stayed in church pews everywhere we traveled.

I think people have always thought – still think – I'm rich, and it could be the crew I've run with. I work with addicts every day who will spend thousands of dollars a month on drugs. But I'm spending $500 a month on car payments, so I'm a big fish in a little pond. I'm dealing with people that come straight off the streets. They are broke, and they haven't got anything. They are trying to get EBT cards and Obama phones and all that stuff.

In the circle that I run in, I'm kind of a big thing. To them, I've got money, but I rent a house and pay payments on a car, and I make bike payments. In the world that I come from, there is just a lot of people that are dirt poor. I work with the poor. I'm sure Mother Theresa looked like she was rolling big time amongst the people she worked with.

SANDRA on their family's financial position: Poor most of the time. We always, from the time we gave our life to the Lord and started doing ministry, we always were very basic. We didn't have much. Used everything. Used cars. Never bought anything brand new. We were always in that situation and any monies that we did have went to the church. Back into the church, back into the people, back into our homes. That was the biggest thing where the money went. I can't think of anything that we bought new, honestly at that time. Then as time went on, the banking became where Wayne Palmer and Lois and my husband didn't have his name on any of the banking stuff, because he's not good with books at all or money in the sense of checks and all that. He had no knowledge. So it ended up where the bills were being paid.

Wayne would be the person who paid all the bills, electric bills for all the houses and gas bills and the food. Then, my husband had petty cash. So the petty cash, he had it in a drawer in his desk, and everybody knew it was there. So the kids would, "Can we get some money to go across the street to Savalas?" So that was like a treat. Of course I was able to buy them clothes and things like that. I didn't get a paycheck. He didn't get a paycheck. No one got paychecks. He gave love gifts to people. My husband would give love gifts. He would tell Wayne who he wanted to give a love gift to for their ministry work that they did, and that was about it.

I've heard we had money in the Swiss banks, and if I wasn't afraid to fly, I would fly there and find it. It's so ridiculous. I don't understand - when I see somebody has a nice car, I really don't think they are rich, I just think that they have a loan. I don't really understand all that. Then, I think what happens is gifts were given to my husband. Like I said, I don't think he ever bought a motorcycle, they were given to him. We didn't have new cars. I don't know why they would think that. It's not like we wore gold jewelry all the time. Come on, we did not look like Paul and Jan or anybody else on TBN. We didn't look like any of the people that go to most churches. But yeah, we had that reputation and still do, but it's ridiculous.

It's hard to say. You can look at my bank account. I'll show anybody my bank accounts. I always think it's funny, I don't think you or anybody can really comprehend how generous he is with his money. Its very hard. We argue about it a lot.

It just doesn't make any sense to me. To this day, there is a man who he has known for years. This man comes about once a month and my husband gives him money. He's just an old friend who is a veteran. There is a biker guy who was the president of a real outlaw biker club. They threw him to the wind when he got older. We call him Mr. Walmart, because I go there at least twice a month to send him money. Walmart to Walmart. There is so many people like that where I think, "Wait a minute, we need this for something else." But it's amazing, because God always just ends up blessing us. We've never been out on the street, that's for sure. That why I said people don't know how generous this man is. He's so generous. It's very sad.

PASTOR PHIL on fitness and dancing: One of the things that I realized in my Baptist circles, and I'm not saying all Baptist circles, was you couldn't dance, drink, chew, or go out with girls that do. Basically, the only thing that we were allowed to do was overeat, and we called it having "fellowship". It didn't seem like there was anything else to do. When I started Set Free Baptist Church and we became Set Free Christian Fellowship, I had a lot of young people, so they wanted to play sports.

Set Free Health Club

I got involved in the basketball leagues, the football leagues, handball leagues. You name it, I got involved in it by using it as a tool for ministry. We would challenge gangs and other teams by saying, "If you win, we'll give you a hundred dollars so you can buy a keg of beer, but if you lose, you've got to come to church." We won all the time. We were winners all the time.

I figured, let's not have an ugly contest for the ladies. Let's get into the gyms. Let's get exercising, because we do have a body that is our temple to take care of. So we started fitness class. We started a little bit of Zumba in the 80's - Jane Fonda type of things.

All of a sudden we started caring about our whole body, our temple so we'd be healthier and stronger. It was attractive to a lot of people coming to church, not just wearing the same things and eating, but having entertainment, games, concerts. We started Christian punk rock bands, Christian hip-hop, dance crews, all these kind of things.

I asked myself, why should the devil have all the good music, and why can't we dance before the Lord? I know that King David got in trouble for dancing, his wife got upset. I'm not sure what kind of dance he was doing. Square dancing, all kinds of fun dancing we can do. I'm not talking about the bump and grind. I'm just talking about having a good time, moving our bodies to mu-

Pastor Phil coaching a player

sic. I just believe it's part of what God's people did when they got set free from captivity to Pharaoh – they danced. They were rocking and rolling, and it wasn't just the Christian little kick it up vibe. They got loose.

SANDRA on the many ministry trips: The first trip we took, our young-est son was only 6 months old, and we went to Israel for the first time. I hate to fly. At that time, it was very different. We flew Jordanian, and it was a whole other experience. But that was our first trip to Israel, and it was wonderful. As a mother thinking about your 6 month old child and your other little kids, even though they are with good people, Doug Dors-ey and his wife, it was still very hard. There was no cell phones in those days. It was very hard to be away from my kids.

My husband told everybody on the plane ride, "Don't look at any pic-tures. Forget you have children and enjoy what God is going to show us." So that was my first trip. Then I went to Israel two more times after that. Then, you couldn't get me on a plane anymore. It was too long of a flight.

Then, we had motorcycles. We had trikes because I never wanted to be on a motorcycle. Like I said, I wasn't a thrill seeker. On the three-wheeler, that was fine, because you are almost like you are in a little car. But then he advanced to a real motorcycle, because someone had gotten him one. So now we are on a real motorcycle, but it's got a great big backseat. So that was pretty good still, right? We would go all over the place. We would take trips to San Francisco on the bike. Gosh, Palm Springs. All these different places. My kids were a little bit older now.

You got to remember, one part of the Baptist thing that my husband never changed was, women don't wear pants. Because once women wear pants, they start acting like a man. That was one of the Baptist things he stuck to real hard. So I never wore pants. I had a skirt all the time. So now I'd have this long Levis skirt, and I'd get on the bike. Everybody would follow in suit that was really close to me. They would wear dresses, too, but not when they got on the bike. They would wear their jeans when they got on the bike. But most of the time they would always wear a dress or a skirt. That was just what you did.

We went on lots of trips - crazy trips like you can't even believe the things that we did. All of this time, I would always say, "Lord, I wasn't an adventurous person. I didn't like motorcycles. I hate to fly." God was always showing me that I need to get past these fears. I need to grow. I need to become stronger in areas that prepare me for what I really had to be strong for.

KELLI MORENO on her role as a Set Free dancer: We had the rock band, which was awesome, and then we had a reggae band, which I was pretty involved with, and then they had the Set Free Posse, which was rap music. So, I was definitely punk rock. For me, the rap music definitely was not my forte so me and another girl started talking and we said, "Well, why don't we start our own dance crew?" So we did, we started a dance group called the Hard Core Crew, and we were able to do mu-

Jennifer Yace Mendoza & Kelli Moreno

sic - more of the rock music, like Rage Against the Machine and Metallica. Fun stuff that was just a little more our level - so not just reaching out to the - because the kids loved the rap music. It definitely drew attention, big crowds. But when the rock came on, we were able to be a little more involved. I'm not a good singer so that was one way I could contribute.

We choreographed, and they did the music. I was never a professional dancer or anything, but I loved to dance growing up. Which was interesting because I grew up in a church, a Brethren church, and they are 100% against dancing. So for me, it was very difficult, because I grew up in Christian schools and a church that totally taught against dancing. But everything in my body wanted to dance. I just loved to get out there and express myself. When I got to Set Free, it was just like, "Wow, this is it! These are my people. These people love Jesus, and they are out there." It just makes me think of David in the Bible, when David was dancing, rejoicing down the streets with the Lord. I'm like, "Gosh, this is it. We are doing it, and we are doing it for Jesus." It was just awesome.

Of course, Pastor Phil who has a gazillion ideas said, "Oh, let's make a

Donna Herman Horner, Kim Milwee, and Kelli Moreno

band." So he formed a band with Geronimo and a few of the other rockers, and they did a little heavier rock music, and then we started performing doing that as part of the concerts. We would go through several stages of music when we were doing the outreaches. So we'd have the old school rock band, they'd do oldies. We'd have the rap group. We'd have reggae, and then we got up and were able to do a little more hardcore music. Just a little more aggressive style dancing. It was fun, flinging the hair and that kind of stuff.

Everywhere we went we drew tons of people. One of the things that we did is we would go into the public schools, and we weren't allowed to talk about Jesus there but we would just go perform and give a positive message about staying off drugs and that kind of thing. And then, we would invite to them the concert at night. So that's how we would get them to come. That's when people would just give their lives to Jesus. Just tons of people. So one of the coolest things Pastor Phil did was, he would do a dance contest towards the end of the concert. And I'm not kidding, that would draw everybody tight to the stage. Because everyone's kids would be up there and everything.

We had this big dance off. He would award them $20 or something, but then he'd give them the invitation to Christ, and that's where you could just see it. It was just so amazing. The interaction with the people. And I think people seen a real Jesus. The thing that was awesome that Pastor Phil did is, he took music and stuff that people were attracted to. He changed it so that the common person would want to come and hear and see what was going on. It was real creative. It wasn't like, "Oh, you have to adjust to what we are doing." He adjusted to what the world was presenting, gave it a little twitch for Jesus, and that's what drove the people to us. Just the love and I think people seeing that you could just be you and Jesus accepts you that way.

I think Pastor Phil, that's what he really saw. And that's what I love about Pastor Phil too, because when you talk to him one on one, you can tell he doesn't care about all the other stupid stuff. He is looking at you through the eyes of Jesus, and he's teaching people how to serve Jesus. And he's not just doing it himself, but training up other people so that they can go out, start the new Set Frees. Like now, I'm the Sunday School teacher at my church, because he gave me a chance and he showed me the way. So, I really appreciate it.

He's like a dad to me. The closest thing I've ever had to a father, and he didn't let me get away with anything. Like one time I was throwing a fit, and he said, "Get your butt in the van right now and knock it off," I said, "Okay," and that was it. I'm like, "Yes, sir," and I never had that in my life. When I did, I knew that it was just out of the love of his heart and my best intentions. I was so thankful for someone just to put me on the right path I guess. Sorry. I didn't mean to get emotional.

PASTOR PHIL on loving Lonnie Frisbee: Throughout the years of Set Free, I got to meet a lot of trippy people, and Lonnie Frisbee was one of them, a well-known character especially in southern California. He's this crazy hippie preacher. He hooked up with Chuck Smith, and the two of them together started this movement together called The Jesus People Movement in the 70's. Then I heard this Lonnie went with John Wimber and started the Vineyard movement. When he spoke people fell over, all these crazy things. So I still got a lot of Baptist in me, and I think this sounded a bit crazy. I don't know, I think those people at Calvary

Pastor Phil and Lonnie Frisbee

Chapel, I hear they cross their legs and get in yoga positions and smoke a lot of pot, take acid.

I had my own little view of him, but one day he shows up in my church in downtown Anaheim with a whole crew, maybe about 10, 12 people with him. They looked like a bunch of ragamuffins. They looked like a bunch of ragtag disciples of God who looked like they had their butt beat in life. Lonnie came in, and I associated him as a real famous evangelist for Calvary Chapel. But, he was carrying picture albums. His crew started "Hey, Lonnie Frisbee is here to see you." At this time, I'm rocking and rolling. I got thousands of people coming to church. I'm on TV, so I got a lot of people who know me.

I was a little bit of a big deal, and I had my two minutes in the spotlight, so who is this guy? They go, "Hey, he'd like to talk with you." I said, "After church," because I stayed and talked to hundreds of people after church, so they hung around and waited. We sat down, and I could tell that the spirit of bitterness was all over this guy, and his friends were just like helping a crippled person. Kind of like in the Bible where they let that crippled person from the roof in to get healed.

I talk to people every single day, every single night, and it's just what I think is common ordinary talk, a lot of people think it's enlightening. It can be just a word, it can be a sentence, just a conversation, but you get people off their seat or get them in a conversation with somebody else. Good, bad, or ugly conversation, but it's a spark like a fire starter.

He starts showing me pictures, saying I did this and I did that. But, I could tell he was a little pissed off about people in his life. So, "I'd like to come here and help out at Set Free." I go, "First off, my advice to you is this. You need to just chill and for the first year that you are here, you need to just kick back and receive and receive."

That was a little difficult, because he'd been a rock star for Jesus for a long time. Now, he's got somebody who's telling him to mellow out. At that time, I had preachers from everywhere in the world want to come and speak at my church, wanted to come on TBN and my program. I just wasn't into the superstar thing. I didn't want to have The Beatles this week and have to have The Rolling Stones next week and somebody else next one. I kept it simple.

Lonnie wanted me to see if I would get in the middle of trying to help him restore his relationship with Pastor Chuck Smith, the founder and leader of Calvary Chapel, because they had a falling away. He also asked me if I could help restore a relationship with John Wimber, the senior pastor of all the Vineyards worldwide. So I started speaking to him and told him we can't come being bitter.

Whatever the thing is, let's see if we can do it. I took him to Chuck, and Chuck wouldn't come and see him. Lonnie wanted to be like a kid whose dad would pat him on the head or give him a hug, "Yes son, go do it." But I guess some allegations had come out, I wasn't aware of them all, about Lonnie having some homosexual affairs. I don't know any of that to be true if it did happen. I wasn't there to judge him. But Chuck and John had pulled the blessing of their ministries off of him, so he wasn't allowed to go to South Africa, to other countries to do work in an orphanage. He wasn't allowed to do that, because he didn't have their blessing. I didn't quite understand that, because I'm not part of those types of denominations. But I just said, "Chuck isn't going to give it to you. It just doesn't look like that stuff is going to happen."

Lonnie Frisbee (seated)

Lonnie started getting sick - realizing this AIDS virus had hit him. We gave him a place to live. Started loving on him. All of his family, his blood family started coming to church. So one day I'm sure it was within a year there when he first started coming to church, I let him get up and speak wearing a priest collar. He's just a trippy guy, but the guy had been around. He used to say things like this, "I've been with all the big bozos, and Set Free is the new Jesus People Movement going on in the world today."

There were hundreds from Calvary Chapel Costa Mesa where the Jesus People Movement started in a tent they tell me. They said, "This old warehouse, this old building. The same spirit that was there is here in this building." It was that kind of thing where I would get up and speak, and it didn't matter what I spoke about, hundreds would get saved. It was a real revival. It was the real move of God. Lonnie was there to say, "I'm part of this now. Set Free is where it's at now." Lonnie said for 15 years, he preached to his family, and none of them had ever gotten saved. But at Set Free, every one of his family members gave their life to Christ. So here's Lonnie, he's getting sick. I go, "You know what, you haven't got that much time left. I'm going to license you up, ordain you and help you with some finances." And we sent him out to South Africa and other places to go minister.

He got to go out strong, and he went out preaching and teaching on fire. And all of his motley crew of wonderful brothers and sisters stayed there with him until he got on his deathbed. He went to one of their homes over there, Balboa, Newport Beach area. I went to visit him for one of the last times. But he was there in his bed plotting, planning this funeral. To bring John Wimber. To bring Charles, this guy Ortiz. To bring this other famous preacher, Chuck Smith.

Bring them and all of us together at the Crystal Cathedral of all places. He was a Samson in his last days and wanted to bring the house down for Jesus. There was still infighting going on even at that funeral service over there, but I got to speak at Lonnie's memorial - trying to get everybody to love each other. That's how Lonnie went down just wanting to get people all loving on each other.

CHAPTER FOUR

GROWING UP AT SET FREE

MJ, Chill, and Trina share what it was like growing up at Set Free and living with recovering addicts, prostitutes, and gang members in their homes. They share about Set Free school, numerous ministry trips, their unique roles in the ministry, and the challenging experiences. They also open up about their relationships with their Mom (Sandra) and Dad (Phil), how it differed, and how that has shaped the course of their lives.

CHILL on the uniqueness of his childhood: As far as my life being different then other kids, I didn't really know any different. Everybody I was around went to church or lived in the programs. I grew up with all the kids that their parents were addicts. So all I knew was dysfunction. That was normalcy to me. That's all I knew. The drug addict mom with the kids, those are my friends. I didn't know that you go to other schools and get to play football and baseball. I didn't know that. Everything that we were taught was ministry, Jesus, helping people. That was our normalcy. So I didn't know anything else. When we would go out and kids would be staying the night at their friend's houses, maybe doing different activities outside of the church, that was odd to us. We were like, "What? You don't go to church five nights a week? You are not going to come to our church?" We were just trained that way. Our normalcy was different, so we didn't know any other. So to us, it was just normal. This is who we are.

MJ on the differences between him and other kids: Everything was different. Until later in life, I didn't realize how different it was. As you grow up and you have your own kids or you just kind of see life from a different place, I didn't realize. I tell people all the time, "I'm still looking for someone who had the same childhood I did, I haven't found them. Not one person. Unless they were related to me and they grew up in the same house." Because it was so unique. So different. So cool. So crazy. It was a lot of fun, but it was so different because of what we would do or what we were allowed to do or what we weren't allowed to do.

We can just start with school. If you get to know my dad for awhile, he can care less about math and science and more about Matthew and John, you know what I mean? Which happen to be my names, you know? It's the good news, it's the gospel. It's soul winning, it's outreach, it's love, it's people, it's forgiveness. And then you know how you have the test and some of us who have kids know now, you get the math and you do all these things and you are like, "Oh cool, my boy is doing good here and doing good there," and then you get to more of the attitude and more of the self-respect and the respect for teachers and class listening. He was always more into that part of my report card. Is that outstanding? That way you look out for someone. Your teamwork. The way you respect your teacher and family. I feel like that's kind of how it worked

Geronimo, MJ (back) and
Trina, Roc, Chill (front)

from that time. We are talking kindergarten young age, where he is like, "Yeah, that's okay, but how are you treating people?" That's how it was at a young age in my house in our world.

After awhile, we had a school which was the Set Free school. It's only funny if you were there, because we do school for a certain amount of time, but then really it would be like our extracurricular. Phys-ed was walking to hand out tracts like, "Hey, Jesus loves you," "The big question." These famous tracts, "It's hell without Jesus." Some that at the age you don't really know what you are always handing out. I wouldn't even read everything sometimes, but that's what we did. Again, that was part of our world. So that was already different, because most kids aren't doing that. They are just going to sit out at lunch and eat their nachos. And for me, I'm going down to City Hall in Anaheim and handing out flyers of how cool God is and come to our church. So there was that whole thing.

Everything was there. Everything was at the school and at the church in the ministry. You didn't have to go anywhere. It was Truman Show. It was its own island. This part of Anaheim for a certain amount of years was - I didn't even think about anything else. Really, a lot of my friends loved that. So the ones that did go to normal school or did have what maybe was a normal setting or life or home would all love to come and hang out with me at my house and my family. They loved it. They absolutely loved it. They'd all come, and they wouldn't want to leave.

My dad was like that, he'd rather have our crew - even though we had a million people living with us, he wanted a million and one. So he had no problem with kids, friends of mine coming over and staying. He was always pretty cool with that. He'd rather have them on our property where he knew it was in his mind the safest, funnest, most Jesus possible than me going somewhere else and not knowing how they ran their house or what they believed. I might be brainwashed at 10 years old during a sleepover or something for whatever reason. In his mind, that's how it worked. But he is a controlling guy, and it started at that age too where he is like, "No, we can be here and we can have fun here too though." So that was a pretty cool part as my youth growing up, having fun, hanging out and doing music, which was a big part at a younger age. It all happened right there during those times. So it was, man so different. So fun. It was awesome. It really was.

A lot of times I wish that there was something like that still for my children to create that. A lot of places have that community and a lot of churches do a good job at it, but not like this. This was from the corner liquor store - even though they sold more than liquor and hopefully not to any people from our ministry were purchasing that - but from the liquor store to the pizza shop to the church to the many houses that lived in that area to the taco shop. That was it. We would just cross one street from the other, and you would see and you knew and you know. I couldn't even do any good sneaking out because I'd run into someone who was an assistant pastor not even a block away on my bike. He would rat on me and tell my dad, "You know you're not supposed to be out or on this side of the street or with these guys." So, for that part, it kind of sucked, because everyone knew me and knew us in the area. But other than that, it was pretty rad.

Phil Aguilar (right) and teachers at a Set Free School graduation

TRINA on Set Free school: Well, we never went to a real school. We basically had our own little world. I know they say he is like a cult leader, that it was like a cult actually. But to us growing up, it didn't seem like that. It was just normal. We had a Set Free school, so that's where we went. It was basically a whole bunch of people from our church that taught different grades. We had real curriculum and stuff, but those were the only people we ever saw. We never saw anybody outside of our church unless we went to an outreach or something. I liked the way we grew up. I thought it was fun. We always lived like 40 people in our house. I don't remember ever living alone until I was - I think 17 is the first time I had my own room. But we still had people in our house, but I had my own room at that time. We always had tons of people around. It was just normal. Everybody was aunt something, uncle something. It just seemed normal. I didn't think anything different until I got older. And then I realized that it was just a world that my dad created for our church and everybody involved.

CHILL on his role at Set Free: I remember being younger, but nine is about the crucial age where I started. Thousands were getting saved, and I didn't even really know what was going on to be honest. I'm nine. I knew that God had put something in me, and everybody would say, "Oh man, you..." I would tell people about Jesus as a young kid, "Hey you are going to hell if you don't..." I was just watching what my dad did or that guy did. So I liked that. I was attracted to that, because that is what I respected. I liked seeing people fired up for the Lord. But I didn't really know what it was, I was just in it. So as it went on, me and my brother MJ, Matthew, we started rapping at about nine or ten. My dad always pushed us to get on stage and do music or whatever our gift was. He always was definitely an encourager in that area, "Hey, get out there!" Music pretty much saved our life. If it wasn't for music and God using that, we probably would have got in a lot more trouble than we did. So music at a young age, that was what we did in the church. It was fun, it kept us out of trouble. It gave us activity, writing songs. I think that helped me for where I'm at now. Doing music all over the world with worship. It came out of there, it was birthed there.

My dad when we are at the Dream Center, I was 15. I never sang, and I just wanted to be cool with all the homeboys on the corner. My dad would be like, "Son, get up here. Get up here." I'm like, "What? Get up here? I'm gangster, we are gang-banging right now." I wanted to be cool and be part of the culture and I have to get up there and sing, "Oh Happy Day." I was like, "Oh, happy day -," and everybody is like, "This kid sucks." Kind of over time grew and it was just something - it was like God birthed something in me as a young child.

GROWING UP AT SET FREE

When I was 12 years old I had problems, I would lose my voice all the time and I couldn't talk. Real raspy voice and I just sounded really bad the way I would talk. It's a crazy story. My Mom took me to a doctor or specialist, they put tubes down my nose and down my throat. They told me at 12 years old, the doctor said I had polyps on my throat, and he said, "You'll never sing, and by the time you are 17, you'll never be able to sing, rap." So I know that God birthed something there, because if I would have had the surgery, I may not even be able to speak again they said. Back then it was in '89, '90, it was different how they did surgery. That was a miracle right there. As I think back, God was working something out then for the future. It was definitely something that the church and the music, it was a huge part of my life.

The Set Free bus provided the backdrop for an outreach.

MJ on his role at Set Free: On some of the roles that I played with Set Free and throughout the years - it started out as, I'm a son. I'm tagging along. I'm just trying to get a good seat of the show, not realizing that my dad is the ringmaster and my brothers are the main act and my mom is the host of this. So I'm just like a kid who's dad is kind of running the circus and I'm the guy with the maintenance man, you know? Trying to get some peanuts and get a good seat. That's how it started as a youth.

I guess around 9 years old, I believe it was, my older brother (Geronimo) who wasn't around for any of my life to that point, there is that whole history there, came back into our lives. It wasn't long before he moved back into our home, which was our ministry home at the same time. So he moved back in, so he was about I think 17, 18, a good few years older than me, so he was already out there living the life.

He was a DJ at nightclubs and I'm just old enough to kind of get into music. So he turned me onto music, to hip-hop, to funk and to rap, a lot of good stuff. And then he started doing music, like a hip-hop as part of the church which was a big thing for years to come. So apart of it was for the first time, I had a big brother, you know? I was always the big brother, now I had a big brother, a lot older. Someone to look up to. I thought he was fresh and cool and dope and all that stuff during that '86 or '87 or whatever it was.

I got into music real quick and enjoyed rapping and DJing. So I just right then and there, I was like, "I want to do that." We had opportunities with our ministry where you could rap. And I knew people, so I kind of got in. At least, I'm still just the kid, just kind of tagging along. But my foot was in the door, and I was there and I was hanging out and I was the hype man. I was happy to be the hype man in the background. I didn't care. Just to be somewhere on stage. Just to be around people. Just to witness what was going on with this music that was playing a big part in culture just in general. But the fact that we were able to do it in and around a church and a ministry and use it to kind of transform or invite people to Christ, it's pretty rad. I'm figuring that out all at a young age.

Sandra, Phil, Roc (front) and Chill, MJ, Trina (back)

So I started out doing that, and I really did the music part of it just until maybe a few years ago, I stopped doing it actively. So I had a good run. I did it for a long time. So I was always apart of that. That was kind of my role all the time. I moved from the background to the front and center over the time. Whether my older brother was still doing it, then I did it with my younger brother (Chill). We were partners for a long time doing the rap thing. We were kind of like the B-team and the older brother was the A-team. We kind of got a little shine, but then we had to start our own little subgroup on the Set Free label, because we weren't getting enough time.

So that was okay, because there was always a whole bunch of people who felt the same way. So we had crew of a few that we called the Peace Posse. There was a Set Free Posse, and we were the Peace Posse and that was around 11, 12, 13, that age. Everyone lived with us, so we had plenty of time to write and rap. And because we only needed so much math and science in my dad's eyes, we can go and write rhymes and hang out and be kids in a lot of ways. So I kind of ran with that forever, and that was a big part.

TRINA on her role at Set Free: Well, when I was younger, nothing really. Because I didn't sing or dance or nothing like that. Basically everything was some kind of performance, because that's what Set Free was known for. So I didn't have any of those talents. I was just like the background. I did other stuff. I always helped in the nursery and stuff like that.

As I became a teenager, my dad kind of forced me to perform with the Posse, which I hated that. I was always a person who hung out with the people that we had in our homes. I kind of took on more of that. I was one of them instead of one of the kids more than my brothers. They were the performers that went everywhere.

I just don't like people staring at me. I just don't like to perform. It's not one of my gifts that I got. I don't dance. I don't sing. If I could sing, I probably would be singing, but I can't sing. I just don't like to be the center of attention anywhere. If you don't really have one of those - not that you get forgotten about, but you kind of just have to figure out what to do. So that's how I ended up getting into the trouble I got into.

MJ on his look and style: My look back then, back in '80's, '90's - I probably around 9 years old when I started growing my hair long, and I don't think it was my choice. I'm pretty sure it was my dad's choice. This might say a lot. I'll talk to my therapist about this one. I never really thought about it. My grandmother would make my dad cut his hair, because she didn't want the dirty hippie. And she was living in an area, she was Mexican, a lot of white. She was trying to blend and fit in, not cause any problems, and then you have my dad who likes to cause issues and stir it up.

He did that I'm sure at a young age, so he wanted it long. He couldn't at the time. Later on of course, he did a lot of things that his mom wouldn't let him do. But I think through us, he was like, "I'm going to have my kids grow their hair long."

Pastor Phil and his Mom, Celia

So at first it sucked, and I'm playing sports, but after awhile it became a big part of my image to have long hair. Like it got long, it got real long. I think I cut it at 19 or 18 years old, so I had it for a long time. Nine or ten years, and it was down to my butt. That was a big part of MJ. A huge part. For a while it was like, "Ah, you look like a girl," and then it was like, "Oh, he's getting girls." Oh yeah. I wasn't mad at that. But when I was a kid, I still had kind of a baby face, and I wasn't a fan of that. But then, later on, it was alright. The girls would be braiding my hair. I was like, "I can dig this." So I mean that's cool. But it was a huge part of my look.

It could have be a '90's thing too, but a Set Free thing because my dad had long hair, pretty long. All my brothers had long hair, and you would look in and around the Set Free and you'd see a lot of ponytails which I knew were a Steven Seagal '90's thing, but there's a lot of people that got it from a certain time. But I was a little proud, mine was the longest at the time, and it was kind of cool. It kind of even went into our look for music. Because you would see me - even today, I'm always usually wearing a baseball cap, so you wouldn't know that I kind of had a ponytail until I turned around and that was its own look, which was kind of cool with music because it was different. Especially in the hip-hop world. I had long hair usually it was rock and roll or heavy metal or something like that. So for me over the years when I had it, it kind of set us apart in our own way too. In a lot of ways, I still dress the same way I do probably since when I was in high school. A lot of the same kind of neighborhood clothing that we all purchased from the swap meet. So not much has changed.

CHILL on ministry trips: We had amazing times. I think about my life and I tell people about the places I've been, and they don't believe it. Because most people live a pretty sheltered boring life and that's cool. I like boring now in my life, but at the time my dad took us everywhere - but we really weren't with my dad. He would go, and he's the preacher and he'd go preach, we'd just kind of be where the luggage is. We traveled with him all over. Been to almost every state. A lot of countries. To see Israel where Jesus walked. There was some breathtaking moments. We performed for the troops in Kosovo in Bosnia and Iraq. So we got to go all over, but the thing about it during those times, I don't even think I got to enjoy it like I would want to.

As a kid, my mother didn't go on a lot of those trips, and at 12 or 13 my dad said, "Get on the bus, we are going." You need your mom, you know what I mean? And my mom didn't go too much stuff, because we had my little brother at home, and she had to take care of the church. My mom would go and the stuff I'd seen was rough. As a 13, 14 year old, it's very hard to take in some of that stuff that you saw. Guys that were married with other women. Their wives aren't there. Just some foul stuff. There was some good to it, but again there was some bad. So I would end up faking sick and say I was sick during the old Set Free days and say I didn't want to go, because I didn't want to see what I was seeing with my brother. More on my brother Geronimo, I focused on him. I don't know. That's weird. It was just that I saw him more than I saw anybody else. Does that make sense? I don't want to be around it. But there was some great, great times for sure.

MJ on the challenges: As you get a little older, you have a little more now that you look back and go, "Okay, maybe that wasn't the best thing or the right thing or normal," whatever that is. Obviously, when we were younger, some of the places we lived was pretty rough being just poor. With my parent's story and him coming out of prison and making a job, anyone who has been around ministry knows there's no money in that. So it was pretty rough. So he's working at 7-Eleven - he pretty much would just bring back whatever is on the little toy rack. So I got good at the paddle ball and tic tac toe, but that was about it. So it was tough, because other kids had things that you didn't have.

I did get used to going to what was a local place called the CHOC Thrift Store. And all I knew was second hand toys, but at the time you are grateful. You don't still kind of know a lot, so I liked it. I wore the second hand jacket and played with the second hand toy and did the whole thing. We lived in my grandmother's garage. Shared beds, sheets, no sheets, sheets were our towel, our curtain and our blankie. It was just a difficult time. Its what it was. Certain shoes, everyone had Jordans and I had some Payless XJ900s. For a while, your parents can get you where you don't know any better, but after awhile when you get to a certain age you go, "How come mine are the only ones with the guy is turned upside down?"

You look at it now, it's small in comparison for what they did. But there was challenge, and it was because you are just a kid, you don't know any better. You want to go there, eat there, play there. I'd have to find someone. I guess I was blessed to have some cool people in the church and around. Even towards the beginning, some people were rich to me, because they had a swimming pool and diving board. Man, thats another level. I think I used to tell one of my friends, "You're rich." We didn't know what that is, but in my eyes he had Super Mario Brothers. I didn't have Super Mario Brothers. I used to go to his house to play it. Then when I did get it, I had to share it between a few brothers and full house of people. So again, you got to kind of wait your turn.

But other challenges probably later on that I was maybe a little more aware of was probably quality time with family. There was no such thing. I can't remember. I honestly can't remember one meal that was just our family, not one. It was so many people. It would be at our house in the backyard, and it would just be five rows of picnic benches and tables of people that lived in our home so there would be 30 to 60 plus people. Just kind of a big Last Supper kind of a setting.

You used to have to kind of have your own, in our ministry homes at least, have your own cup. So I'd have to bring my cup out there just like everybody else to get some Kool-Aid, and that was just a part of what we did. You ate with everybody. It wasn't my mom so much just sitting around. She did her best and tried, but you can only try so long. When you have so many people there, you are not really going to have this love home cooked meal. Everything was for the masses. Everything was for the 500. Everything was for the group. So again, you get used to it, but there was a lot of times where you wish it was just different. If I would go to someone else's house, I would be there as maybe a guest, and it would just be them and their family. Again you would be like, "How come no one is knocking at your door? Forget knocking, how come they are not just walking through your backgate and walking through your door and sitting down and eating with you and asking your dad questions and your mom leaving to help somebody because they are in pain or they are hurt or they are going through it? What's going on here?"

It was weird, like they were weird. Not me, those were the weird people, because that didn't happen. And in my house, that's what it was. I mean the front door, I don't even think we used front doors. They were locked, and everybody would go around the side. Maybe you needed help to go to the ranch to detox. You got an addiction? Maybe you want to know about the ministry? Maybe you need someone to help you clean out your garage? Maybe your friend needs someone to write him in jail or visit him in prison? That was my dinner conversation. You know, people didn't talk about that stuff. People still don't as adults. We all talk about everything else but real life sometimes. So with me, that's all there was. That's all I was sitting around. That's all that was gathered around me, so again just the time with the family was pretty tough. It really was. Obviously, later on is when I really kind of figured it out. It's like, "Wow, I never had that one on one time."

It wasn't like me and my mom that I can remember doing homework. Not that I like homework, but I like my mom, and there wasn't that time. There wasn't just me and my brother playing a game. There wasn't me and my dad playing catch. He's not a big sports guy, but still that doesn't matter, it's my father. I only have one of you, let's do something like that. But it wouldn't even be possible. If he threw one pass, it would be intercepted by a need of someone else. And that's pretty much in a way my life - not my life, but a big part of my life during that time was that.

I believe in his heart he wanted to do those things with me, and I definitely did with him, but every time it would get intercepted to use my football reference, and it probably happened in that way too, many times. Where he would throw it, "Oh hold on," but he never came back. But, this need was greater because, "Their life is on the line and this is just me and my son playing catch," which we know later on can lead to some other things, and obviously things that I still hold onto in ways and always trying to work through.

But a lot of things were interrupted and intercepted at that time. And because of ministry and because of the calling and because of even me at a young age, I'm like, "Oh, these people are in pain. Their need is greater than my need. They are going through stuff, I see them hurting and crying and homeless and my dad and my mom or my family is helping them. I can't cry about it. I'm not going to go tell him anything. I'm not going to tell my mom something. I'm not going to whine. I'm just going to go play catch with somebody else."

There was 30 different other guys that lived in my house, and I'd go play catch with that guy who just maybe came in last week with his baggage, and he taught me how to throw a spiral. That's who I was raised by in a lot of ways, was a lot of those people. So times like that were pretty difficult. More later in the years were pretty tough of just sharing. I learned how to share at a young age, and I wasn't sharing my truck or my Hot Wheels, it was sharing my parents. It was sharing my house, it was sharing my family, it was sharing my time. I became a pretty good sharer.

CHILL on growing up in a home full of people: There is exciting parts about living with a bunch of people and then there is unexciting parts. One of the not-so-fun parts was waking up, and you got a guy hanging out the window on the second story. One of the guys that lived in our room, me and my brothers, he's like, "Pretty bird, pretty bird, cuckoo, cuckoo." He's about to jump out the window. He's like, "Dude, they are after us." We are like, "What?" We are 11, 12 years old. Basically he was on drugs, on meth. Or a guy you wake up, he's nodded out from shooting heroin, and he lives in the bed next to you. But this was normal for us. That was not really the exciting parts, that was scary, but you didn't say nothing because you are now in a culture. You are around all these gangsters and thugs. They taught us to be tough. You can let nobody push you around. So we didn't want to go cry to our dad. We knew we were in the ministry, and we were helping these type of people. That was the not exciting part. Or waiting an hour to get in the shower, a bunch of men are before you. That was not the fun part.

But the fun part, exciting was we had free reign to do whatever we want. My dad let us run wild. He let us do cigarette checks. You weren't allowed to smoke back then in the program. So we'd go in the guy's stuff and say, "Hey man, you can't be smoking." We'd break all their cigarettes and throw them. They would be so pissed, because their parents once a week can bring them. It was kind of like jail a little bit. We were like the wardens, but we were eight or nine. I still have people mad at me to this day. They are in their late 60's and they go, "Dude, remember when you were nine you used to do that. I'm still pissed at you." So those were the fun parts.

Playing with my cousins, the community. We had basketball courts. My dad always made it fun. There were pools. It was definitely as a kid running the buildings and the halls. Kind of doing whatever we wanted, because we were the pastors kids.

TRINA on getting into some trouble: We moved to Los Angeles, and that's when I got mixed up in the wrong crowd. Even though it was our own world, and we weren't allowed to go outside of it. I found people inside of our world that I could connect with. I was always overweight, and that was always a thing. Growing up - I know it sounds funny but the people in the home's, me and my brother we weren't allowed to eat certain food at all. We'd get in trouble if we ate. So we are the big ones of course, and now we are still big. We had to sneak food so it was hilarious. I know it sounds funny, but it's true. So I always had a weight issue, so when we moved to Los Angeles somebody told me about speed, and you could lose weight. So that's why I originally started doing it. Then I think now that I'm older and I look at things, I think maybe I did it more because I felt no place and that's who my dad helped out all the time, people in need. Maybe I was seeking the attention. I didn't know. But then it became a problem, and then it was just a problem I'd say from 15 to 2001 is when I got sent to the ranch, so 2001.

When I was 18, on my 18th birthday, I moved out the next day and was staying with people who I was using drugs with that I found. We already moved back to Anaheim at the time, but I was still sneaking out and going to Los Angeles where my friends were. So I moved out. I was only gone for a few months, and then I decided to come back and when I came back I said I was going to stop doing everything. But I didn't. I kept doing it. I think my dad was in denial at the time that I had a problem. So it took him awhile to finally admit it.

Then, what was really weird, they call me in to our living room one day, and it was all my brothers and my parents and Matthew had little Matthew at the time. So, we were all helping raise him or whatever. They had a meeting to tell me that Matthew didn't feel comfortable having me around his kid. And I was like, "That's pretty ironic because we were raised around drug addicts." So Matthew is the favorite for sure. My dad was like, "You got to get out or you got to go to the ranch."

Trina and Pastor Phil

TRAINED TO SERVE JESUS

There are ranches all over, but the one that I was supposed to go to was in Del Sur. It's basically like a dirt lot. This one was the old Chargers training camp. So it had some kind of old dorm thing on there. But basically all you do is read the Bible, sweep dirt, rake dirt, and read the Bible. It's all Jesus, Jesus, Jesus.

So anyways in my mind I decided I wasn't going to go, but I didn't tell him that. I just said, "Okay, I'll think about it." They used to come down to church on Saturday nights, and people would go back up with them. So I was supposed to go on a Saturday night, and I used to go to church early because I was always in trouble. So he would make us go early with him, me and Hebrew. So, I told him, "Oh, can I go later with mom? I'm going to pack my stuff. I'm going to go to the ranch." So I called my friend, and he was going to pick me up there, because I wasn't going to go. So I was like getting high, before I went to church because of whatever. Then I don't know, when I got to church, my friend came to pick me up, and then God just changed my mind. I don't really know. I told him, "No, I'm not going to go. I'm going to go to the ranch." The best thing I ever did.

At first, I was nervous of course. And then at the time, there was only a men's ranch, and there was only one other girl there. Then the guy who was in charge, the first thing he said in front of everybody was, "Just because you are Pastor Phil's kid, you aren't getting any special treatment." I was like, "What? I didn't even ask." I wasn't even going to tell nobody I was his kid. So that made it awkward, but as the days went by, it was seriously one of the best decisions that I ever made. Because you grow up in church and people think you are a Christian just because you grow up in church. But that was like the first time I truly surrendered and gave my life to the Lord and changed my life forever.

I was only there for like 60 days. We would wake up in the morning, have devotions, which is Bible study. Eat breakfast. Then we would go out and seriously rake dirt. That's what it was. It was just a whole bunch of dirt. I don't know why we were raking, but we were. And then we would do chores, like all the others chores, the house stuff. And then we would go have lunch, then more Bible study. Then study time. Then more Bible study. We would go off the mountain a couple times a week for Bible studies. Or on the weekends we would have to go do car washes. That's what we did everyday. Seriously, everyday. When I came back from the ranches, that is when I really got involved with helping out because we had ministry homes at the time. So that's when I really started helping out and became kind of like an overseer under my dad working.

CHILL on the difference in his relationship with Mom and Dad: My mom was the safe place. Mom was always one you could run to and cry, "Dad doesn't understand me," or "Dad yelled at me." My dad, great provider, but terrible hugger. He's the worst hugger, until this day, he is just learning to hug. But my dad has something about him. He was special. We wanted to please him and you couldn't make no mistakes. We'd get on stage or rap, it was never good enough. We go off the stage and he'd be like, "You could have done better." They clap for anybody. Seven thousand people, and you think you did a good job. They are clapping.

He was always pushing you to his way of being better. So mom was always the caretaker - always the one you cry to when you are sick. My dad didn't believe, "You're sick? Go to your room and pray." We are like, "What?" I got to go to the doctors. "Lay hands on yourself." He didn't know how to handle it. It wasn't in him. That switch never turned on until later on in life about compassion for certain needs of his kids.

MJ on his relationship with his parents: With my parents and how I was impacted as far as my relationship with them and how they were or were not with me or my siblings - you know, I feel like a lot of it - I don't even want to say, maybe forgave. I tried to get over it, because I felt like - what's it going to do to just dwell on it? I really did. There was never really a long period of time that I can remember where I didn't have a relationship with either of my parents. Never. I mean there have been some moments for sure, but nothing.

The better my relationship got with Christ, the more I understood. It helped me to understand where my dad especially was coming from. And that he didn't know any better almost. At least that's how I look at it, maybe still do. That could just be me as a son or wanting something else. It works for me, and it has. I'll probably continue to use that method, but I felt like he was doing it for the right reasons.

It came from a good place. It wasn't just because his dad abandoned him at a young age. In a lot of ways at a young age, my dad abandoned me for the ministry. I believe that. That's really the only way you can put it. He chose that over us. But over the years, I've begun to accept that. I've said, "Well, if he's going to choose us over something, I guess the ministry is not so bad." And even later in years, I kind of came to grips with that. That he's always going to choose the ministry over us. To this day, when he is hanging out with somebody - me and my siblings even to this day sometimes still joke, but it comes from probably a place where there is definitely some tears behind the clown kind of thing.

That's who he gravitates towards. That's what gives him the most joy on this earth, is people that are addicted, are afflicted and broken and hurt. Although I've got plenty of issues, I'm not hurt enough or afflicted enough or bad enough that he's like, "Oh, he's good." You know what I mean? And my siblings again we've joked over the time and serious as well, that we have to do some more stuff for him to hang out with us or talk to us and do that. Which obviously that's more of a joke, but there is some truth to it too, because that's his heart. Always just runs to that need and those in need.

TRINA on the difference between the relationship with her Dad and Mom: We had so many people around. After church if you wanted to talk to him, it would be a three-hour line, and I wasn't going to wait in line to talk to him, so I would just go do something else. So even though he was around, we weren't really with him that much if that makes any sense. I don't know if it makes sense to you. And then my mom, me and Hebrew were with her a lot, because we were the younger ones who weren't really apart of the other stuff. She was like a real big enabler probably, because she felt bad for us at times. So we were always closer to her for sure.

Me and my dad bumped heads all growing up. I just didn't like the way he did certain things. Not anymore, but at that time, I was real mouthy and opinionated. Just a kid thinking you know it all. When you are younger, you don't see it from an adult perspective. So I just was looking at how it affected my life at the time, and I didn't like it. So everything - we lived around all these people, but when I wanted to be like them, it was like a no-no. "No, that is not the life you are going to live," so it was always constant. I think honestly now that I'm older, I just felt left out. So I was just being a brat just to be a brat. I don't know.

My mom didn't want me to go to the ranch, my dad is the one that said, "Get out or go to the ranch", and my mom fought that. When she came to visit me she was crying, she was like, "This is where you sleep? I can't believe it." I actually really loved it up there, I did. I don't complain about that.

CHAPTER FIVE

PRESSURE MOUNTS

After 14 years apart, Phil and Geronimo reunite, and Geronimo soon plays a significant role in the ministry as a singer and dancer. He begins to date and eventually marries Stacee Davis, and they have two children. Meanwhile, her parents, Dave and Toby Davis, become displeased with their lack of access to Stacee and their two grandchildren. The Davis' were concerned about Geronimo's control over their daughter, Phil's leadership style, and a cultish atmosphere at Set Free Church. With these allegations, they enrolled Pastor Oden Fong, director of the Calvary Chapel Association, in Costa Mesa, California, to address the situation.

Disgruntled members of Set Free reached out for help from cult experts Bill and Jackie Alnor as well as Ron Enroth, and these allegations against Set Free and Pastor Phil Aguilar spread to churches throughout the United States. Attempts at reconciliation between Pastor Chuck Smith, Pastor Oden Fong, and Pastor Phil Aguilar included multiple letters and a meeting initiated by Paul Crouch, founder of TBN, but the rift was never settled.

Meanwhile, the city of Anaheim, California, and its new mayor, Tom Daley, were not interested in helping Set Free continue its ministry. In fact, Set Free was restricted from meeting in both of its facilities due to code violations, and the church was forced to move outside the city. After investing significant time and money in a new building in Fullerton, California, only one service was ever held in the facility, because the city shut it down for code violations.

With rumors spreading about Set Free as a cult and Pastor Phil's personal behavior, Set Free Anaheim held its final service on Easter Sunday 1993 at Glover Stadium in Anaheim, and the congregation was informed that Pastor Phil was leaving.

PASTOR PHIL on reuniting with Geronimo: While Set Free was blowing up and we're on TBN, my son returns after 14 years of me not seeing him. I heard he was going through some tough times. I heard his mother was murdered, heard all this bad news. So I was praying for him, that God would just touch his heart wherever he was. I didn't really want to see him, because I had the fear of rejection. I was worried he was going to say to me, "Where were you at? This happened to my mom." I had a lot of shame and guilt about all that, still do to this day. But when he came back, it didn't take long for us to bond together - his brothers and his sister. We became a family.

The Aguilars - Trina, MJ, Phil, Roc, Sandra, Chill, Geronimo

SANDRA on Geronimo: Geronimo was a very confused boy. He was living with his grandparents after his mother was murdered and never had any knowledge of him living with his grandparents until we ran into a lawyer one time when we were at a courthouse. We were there for somebody else, and he ran into the lawyer. The lawyer had told him what happened - that Geronimo's mom had been killed and that he lives with the grandparents now. So he was about 14 at the time I think when we found out. So of course didn't want to rock his world like, "Hey, I'm your dad who deserted you."

So little by little, Lois who would snoop around and all these things. She found out where he would playing basketball - so she would kind of sneak around and watch him play. Eventually got to say, "Here I am." He was with this girl who he had been with for awhile, and they were a little bit into drugs and different things like that. So eventually, he ended up actually coming to the church one day and talked to his dad and gave his life to the Lord and wanted to change. But he didn't want to hurt his grandparents, so he kind of didn't move in right away.

PASTOR PHIL on Geronimo's role at Set Free: I saw that he had talents. He was a DJ, he was off of drugs now. He's doing well. Good looking young kid, a rapper, did hip-hop. I said, "Hey, let's turn this rap hip-hop music into something." This was during the Hammer Time when MC Hammer was doing the rap. My son's a young teenager, and he starts learning about God and doing hip-hop with Christian lyrics. All these young people are wanting to be part of it. Before you know it, him and his younger brother MJ and Chill and Hebrew, they are all starting to rap and dance. Together we started a dance crew, we got a hundred some kids that all want a part of that. Everybody wants to be a rapper.

We are rapping about "give God the glory, no drugs, no booze, no sex". We paid respect to God, "I'm down with G.O.D. Ya, you know me." Kids loved it. The older people loved it too, the beat. Now it's about God. Rap was real popular then. It wasn't all gangster. It was a real positive thing, and we have kids joining but the churches were still leery, "rap was the devil's music", and all that, but I had my son Geronimo back with me. Now we are a part of a family, and everything is going good. But my son is tall, dark and handsome, and I said, "You've got to watch out here, because these girls are looking at you. You are the performer. You are the pastor's son. You are kind of a wanted product here. Somebody is going to want to scoop you up, and the enemy is going to want to pull you down."

Then, this man comes in with his wife, Dave and Toby Davis, and they told me they were professors at Jerry Falwell's school - Liberty University. They are coming out here and asked if I could help them out with their teenage daughter, Stacee, because God has always seemed to be able to have me have an insight to young people. I said, "What's her problem?" "She's hurting. She's got some real troubled issues as a teenager. A little suicidal." I said, "Alright." She gets real involved, and the next thing you know, she and my son kind of hit it off like that.

Maybe six months later, my son is talking about, "Hey, I'd like to maybe marry her." She was about 17 and a half at the time. I said, "You've got to get the dad's permission." So, the parents were really happy, because she's going to marry the pastor's son. He was real involved with me, and everything was just great. We set up the wedding, do the wedding, and they go to Hawaii for their honeymoon. They come back, and everything's going good.

Geronimo and Stacee
speaking at Set Free

SANDRA on how things changed when Geronimo arrived: I think the turning point was when Geronimo came from the very beginning. Because the turning point when Geronimo came, it was a turning point in my husband's life also. A lot of things changed. He wanted to impress Geronimo all the time with anything. With material things, with love, with people. For all the years that he had lost with him, for the things he had gone through. He didn't go

Geronimo (seated in sidecar) with Phil and members of Servants for Christ

about it right as far as I was concerned, and I'm sure other people also. He kind of put him on a pedestal. He kind of pumped him up a lot.

Don't get me wrong. Geronimo had great talents. There is no doubt about that. He was as charismatic as his dad. There is no doubt about that and just as handsome as his dad. They have that charisma about them. So Stacee was this sweet little girl who was in a Bible study class and one day when I saw her, it was the cutest thing. Her mom was putting her little sweater on her. I just said to the mom, "Okay, this is the girl I want to marry my son Geronimo." It kind of went from there, and they got introduced. It was kind of like this is the right thing to do, marry this sweet young girl. That's kind of really how it was.

Phil thought she was wonderful. She wasn't even 18 yet though, so we met the family. The family was very loving, and they were very nice. She had two sisters. And the reason they started coming to Set Free was to begin with was because of Stacee. Stacee had depression problems. So they were concerned about her. Beautiful girl - I don't know what her depression problems were. She was the youngest of the girl. So they started coming because of her, which changed her. She's such a sweet girl.

So it ended up where the family loved it, because she was happy now and things were going good. Well then, it got to be where the part comes in where, "You need to be at this. You need to be at that. You are expected to be here. No, you can't go here because you have to be here ," and she was just engaged at the time to Geronimo. Parents didn't like that. They were losing control of their daughter is what it was. First, they give her to you to help her. Then, they want to make the rules of how you are going to help her - which is basically what happened. So they didn't like it. She became more distant. She wanted to be more with us.

PRESSURE MOUNTS

The wedding was moved up. And it was a very sad thing for Stacee, because the day of her wedding as she's getting dressed, her sisters and her mother were in mourning. It was very sad for Stacee what they did to her. Especially knowing her past depression moods and things that she had gone through. So the poor little girl, she comes, and she's in tears about how the morning went. So we are all trying to cheer her up, her little bridesmaids were all getting her going. So here we are, the ceremony is going to start and looking at that family it was very sad. I felt really bad for her. So they had already had a problem before she was married to him. It just got worse. Then it got to the point where Stacee had to make a choice. Am I going to stay with my husband and serve the Lord or am I going to serve my parents? I know that choice. It's a hard choice.

Family - I missed many family things. My family, my father told me if my husband stayed out of prison for a whole year, he'd even go back to church because my dad hadn't been to church in years. He got disturbed by the Catholic church. So after a year, he had to come to church, because he said he would. So it was like my relationship with my parents was great, but I had to miss out on a lot of things, too. It was just part of ministry. Now, Stacee was in full time ministry. They couldn't accept that. They felt like we were trying to keep her from her family.

Pastor Phil, Sandra, Geronimo, and Stacee

PASTOR PHIL on Stacee's parents, Dave and Toby Davis, turning to Pastor Oden Fong: The church is blowing up. I'm on the board of TBN. We are doing outreaches all over the place. We are traveling on our buses, touring around doing hip-hop concerts. Our band is rocking. Everything is just going good, but one day Geronimo's in-laws were a little upset, because his wife wouldn't go with them to some family thing they were doing. They have a very close family, Geronimo's in-laws.

They started feeling like Geronimo was trying to control their daughter. Now there is a little butting heads going on, and I'm just doing ministry. I tried to stay out of it, but I'm the ringleader, I'm the pastor, I'm the dad. They think I should be telling the son this or that. There started to be a rift, and Geronimo's father in law was upset about it. I didn't know how upset about it at that time, but he goes to talk to a pastor who was the overseer of all the Calvary Chapels worldwide, Pastor Oden Fong. Little did I know that this was going on - that they were upset with me. He's got half a dozen people from Set Free that don't like what I'm selling, and they get over there with him. I've got a little hate crew going on, and I don't even know it until 1990, about December.

I get a letter in the mail from Pastor Oden Fong telling me, "Maybe you heard some rumors about what's going on in your church?" Pastor Oden writes, "If they are not true, then you truly have a conspiracy planned against you and many people are lying, trying to destroy your reputation. If they are true, then you are heading down the same pathway of Jim Jones, The Children of God, Tony and Susan Alamo Foundation and other shepherding

Pastor Oden Fong (right) being interviewed by Hal Eisner, Channel 13

cults built around a super egotistical dictator and not the Lord Jesus Christ."

I get this letter and I'm going, "Who is Pastor Oden Fong? Overseer of all this stuff?" The letter says, if this isn't true, give me a call. The very first thing I did is called him right up and I go, "This isn't true, what's going on? Let's meet together."

Before I can even meet with him, this letter went to his secretary, Tracy, who passed it to all the Calvary Chapels, and of course, they passed it to their best friends. Before you know it, there are pastors worldwide going, "Hey what's going on over there? I heard there are these allegations against you."

I'm trying to meet with Pastor Oden, and I'm trying to work out something. "What seems to be the problem?" I realized the in-laws are upset with me now. They are upset with Geronimo. Stacee is saying, "My parents are just control freaks." She's telling me this at the time. I don't really know what's going on, but now the ministry is jumping.

CALVARY CHAPEL OUTREACH FELLOWSHIPS

3800 Fairview Road, Santa Ana, CA. 92704

Pastor Phil Aguilar   Dec. 19, 1990
Set Free Christian Fellowship
320 N. Anaheim Blvd.
Anaheim, CA. 92805

Pastor Phil,

I am certain that by now rumors are flying everywhere that there is a united front led by Calvary Chapel coming against you and Set Free. This is not true. It is true that some very serious complaints have reached us and that we are concerned not only for the sake of the Body Of Christ, but also for your sake if these allegations are true.

If they are **not** true, then you truly have a conspiracy planned against you and many people are lying, trying to destroy your reputation. If they **are** true, then you are heading down the same pathway of Jim Jones, the Children Of God, Tony and Susan Alamo Foundation, and other shepherding cults built around a super-egotistical dictator and not the Lord Jesus Christ.

Everyone of these fellowships started right and ended up wrong...isolating themselves from the rest of Body Of Christ and thinking that they were the only ones doing the real work of God. Each of these leaders gained large followings but in the end were cast down by God. These were men of self-deceit. They had become gods to themselves yet did not realize it. I spoke with one of our associate pastors who left the Baptist Church with you to start Set Free. He said that you discipled him in Christ and that you were the most humble, loving brother that he had ever met. He said that you were the kind of man who would lay his life down for others.

It sounds like we are describing two totally different people here. My question is: What is the truth about you? I'd would like to talk to you and find out for myself. Would you be willing to meet with me? I'll meet you anytime, anyplace, anywhere. You name it. It might serve to clear everything up.

My bottom line is that I believe in Set Free. We need a Set Free ministry. We need a ministry that is reaching the street level people (something that much of the church is failing in). If Set Free is truly setting people free I would personally back you 100% and support and defend you myself. If Set Free is freeing captives from drugs and alcohol and but bringing them into another bondage, then the whole Church of Jesus Christ has a problem.

I have enclosed a list of the complaints and testimonies that have been directed at you so that you will know what is being said about you. Please let me know what you decide.

In Christ,

Oden/CCOF

133

SANDRA on Stacee's parents: I don't take any blame off of Geronimo, but I put a lot of blame on her parents. Parents started the problem with that little couple, because they would harass her about it all the time. Like, "You are in a cult, you need to get out of there." So her and Geronimo would have fights, strife all the time because of that. Now here they had two beautiful children together, and the parents wouldn't come to church. They wouldn't come over to visit, but for her to go visit them Geronimo would say, "No, they need to come visit you. Why should you go there?"

It just got worse and worse and worse, and Stacee and I somehow or another, we were going to meet up with them and just try to make amends. We were going to meet at Knott's Berry Farm Chicken House. We were just going to try and make amends, get it where they could understand. Because poor Stacee, she was so frustrated. She's trying to please her husband, please God, please her parents. So we went there with the two babies so they could visit the boy and girl. The sisters were

Dave Davis, Stacee Aguilar, and Tobyann Davis interviewed on OCN

there, the brother-in-law was, there because the other one wasn't married yet because of the mother and father. What a setup. The whole thing was a setup. It was a cult whatever you call it. They were going to wash our brains of the cult that we were in.

They actually, literally, set us up that, "We are going to help you get out of this. We are going to take you and the kids," but it came on gradually as they started talking to us more and more. Then we realized, we were like, "What are you guys talking about?" "You girls are in a cult. You are brainwashed. You need to get out of here." They did all those little spooky things that cult busters do. We literally had to take the kids. They tried to take the baby, the little boy and girl. They said, "Well if you are not going to get out of the cult, we are taking your children out of the cult."

Phil, Roc, Sandra, Ashaya, Taylor, Stacee (front)
MJ, Chill, Geronimo, Trina (back)

She took one child, and I took the other. We literally had to run out of the Chicken House. That's how crazy they were. In front of everybody, they didn't care. They caused this big scene. That's how much they wanted to take us out of this cult, and that just caused more strife. More problems.

Then, Geronimo working with the music people all the time, Stacee had been a dancer also along with the other dancers and involved with the singing, but now she's got another baby. So time went on, there was suspicions. I talked to him about it, because I was concerned. "No, it's not true," the whole thing, lying. It ended up where she was going through some of his stuff and found something that she said, "Okay, this is it. I know you are messing around with this other girl." She was already going through turmoil, so she was like, "Okay, I'm out of here."

It was the saddest thing in the world. Because the two little babies, the little girl was probably 3 at the time, she knew. She was raised there. So my husband said, "Okay, if this is what you've got to do." He had one of the guys give her a ride to wherever she wanted to go. She insisted that now she believed her parents, that it was all a cult.

JIM BUCHANAN on the Davis family and Pastor Oden Fong: They were fundamentally un-scripturally wrong in the first place. Why are you chasing somebody else's sheep? A family comes to them, man or woman with a problem - I've done a lot of family counseling. When I sit down, I don't sit down with the wife and hear the husband bad mouth. I have the husband and wife sitting there. I have all the pertinent parties in the room. To me, that was unscriptural, and it was just plain bad taste and bad form to presume, to listen to one side of a story.

You've got to realize that we had thousands and thousands of people going through serious life issues. I'm talking about life, death, birth. I mean serious issues by the thousands. And shock of shocks, a family is disgruntled. They go to another church, talk to a junior pastor, who I think - I won't go there. They talk to a junior pastor, and he goes, "Oh, tell me more. Oh, and then what do they do? What else do you know?" They began a witch hunt.

I don't want to go any farther, but senior pastor should have put a squelch on that. They should have squashed that immediately and said, "In the first place, I'm going to go talk to that ministry." And we've worked with that ministry. I've personally sat in a room and worked with him on the Olympics in L.A. We worked with the pastor over there at Calvary himself, and he's got to know that we all had a heart for God. To listen to that BS was bad face at the beginning, but then to compound that without any further investigation. To go on a vendetta that lasted for years, it brought down a lot of people.

SANDRA on Pastor Oden Fong: In church on Thursday nights, we'd have Bible study. We noticed a lot more people coming to Bible study. A lot more young people coming to Bible study. So we found out that they were coming from Calvary churches, because they heard about this new movement at this place called Set Free and that we had a Thursday night Bible study. We would do Thursday night and Sunday mornings. So the hype of it all. The music, the rap, the testimonies, the message, I could never get enough of it, and I was there every week. So they would come on Thursday.

All of a sudden, this Oden Fong person who I guess worked with youth maybe at Calvary at the time. I'm not quite sure. He got wind of it, and he wasn't happy about it because he started saying that we were prose-lytizing - when you take people from other churches and try to get them to go to your church.

Nobody looked for anybody, they just came on their own. So he got on this bandwagon of - he wasn't actually calling him a cult leader at the time, but that he was using all these worldly things to get people to come to church. Then, eventually went into the cult leader thing. That all started with Stacee's parents, and they went out looking for cult busters. They found the Alnors and Ron Enroth, and they just went on a rampage. They nit-picked at every little thing that we did. Everything that we did was cultish. We were getting attacked constantly, and then they started putting it out more in the Christian world. Then it got more and more and more to the point where my kids were older now, and they were understanding more things. It was horrible for us because all of a sudden you have cameras. We are walking into a restaurant, and all of a sudden reporters come up with these cameras. It's just too much. It was just too much for a family. Way too much.

I couldn't understand it, because I'm like, "We are not a cult." To me - cult comes from the word culture. Everybody has got certain cultures, right? We are this culture. You are that culture. Some people are into just natural things. Some people are into not natural things. But you are in a culture.

So we were a cult in a culture world of our own, but then I thought about it. They are not in a world of their own. We are not living in some camp. These people go to work everyday. They have children, families. The percentage of people that went to church there did not live there in the houses. It was just ridiculous, the whole thing.

PASTOR PHIL on the rumors: Of course, it's easy to say Pastor Phil is controlling. I've got almost 400 people living in our homes, 30 homes that we leased at the time. The majority of them come from a heavy drug and alcohol background - many gang members, many of them straight out of prison. That's why Jan Crouch as you can imagine says, "Would you take these people in your home?" We have to have rules. We have to have guidelines. We have to have accountability.

A lot of people don't understand that I'm dealing with a rough crowd, and we have to have a curfew. Or, "if you do this, you have to go to the ranch", that's just all part of the necessary things when you've got that. When I take one grandkid to Disneyland, I let them run wild. When I take 12 of my grandkids or more, I say, "We got some rules here." And that's what I had to do to tighten it up like that.

While all these accusations are going on, I've still got a church with literally thousands of people, I've got ministry going on, I'm traveling, and I'm doing all these things, but now I've got this cloud coming over. I've got sections being written about me in major newspapers about how I am cultish or a cult-like leader.

ELIZABETH AGUILAR BUCHANAN on accusations of Set Free as a cult: The doors were not locked. There were no bars on the windows.

People were always free to leave. I say that was utter nonsense. It was not a cult. It wasn't. I really never understood why people have said that about - because it wasn't, right? We told people. We didn't hold people in. We didn't.

PASTOR PHIL on people leaving the church: One of the things about Set Free is through all our major beginnings and through our end when I finally said goodbye to everybody, the core group that started Set Free was part of that beginning and never, ever left until I left. They were there until the end. As people came in and people would want to leave, one of the things I tried to teach people - when you go out, don't take anybody down with you, because misery loves company.

So one of the things I would say is, "Hey, that person is going out. They want to use drugs again. They want to go get drunk again. They want to go party again. Watch out for them. We are who we hang out with." People always left, and there were always new people coming in. You've got to win a lot to keep a few. That was just part of the revolving door process.

Whenever I knew that there was somebody trying to pull somebody out of our midst, a love triangle or a relationship, I would tell them, "Don't hang out with that person. Stick in here, get discipled up." Because these people had very troubled lives when they came in. The majority of them didn't have homes, didn't have places to live, strung out on drugs, alcohol, rough lifestyles. This isn't your momma's church. This is Set Free.

If you looked at me back then, I've got a long ponytail, I'm wearing sunglasses all the time, I'm riding a Harley with tattoos, and I'm wearing all black. I'm looking like a tough guy, but at the same time I'm just doing ministry, trying to not let it bother me, trying to keep my focus on Jesus. But my son and my daughter-in-law have a child, boom. Then they have a second child. Now, this got the in-laws really heavy, because they want to see their grandkids, and my son's not letting them go there, because he wants his family with him.

I get put in the middle of it, but I'm not going to say, "Hey, do this or do that." It was just a rough, difficult time with a lot of misunderstandings, bitter feelings, and then some people jumped on board with the Davis family, the in-laws, and joined a little crew like that.

BILLY AGUILAR on leaving Set Free Anaheim: I put 10 years of my life in that church, and I actually had a job where I worked 40 hours, sometimes 50 hours a week, and I still devoted a lot of time to that church.

PRESSURE MOUNTS

Then, seeing it fall apart was heartbreaking. People were just back stabbing each other and saying things. I bailed before a lot of people did.

My brother told me when I first got there, he goes, "Hey bro, check it out. This can be a great church. It can be a good movement, but if I stop reading from this Bible and you see things that aren't right, be the first guy to take off." I never forgot that. I always listened to him. I always listened to my brother. It saved me a lot of headaches a lot of times from not getting locked up because he already went through it.

I was in my tenth year, and I see people coming up to me saying, "Hey, you know why is that band member hanging out with that chick when he's married?" And then next thing you know, we were like a sober church really. Clean and sober, we didn't even have people who smoked cigarettes, because he came from that Baptist. All of a sudden things started changing. People were drinking, and I believe some people were doing drugs. There was people cheating on their wives and wives cheating on their husbands. Typical churches, typical things that happen to all churches, you know? But when it happens to your church, man I was heartbroken. I was bitter.

You don't really go up to Pastor Phil and tell him what time it is. But I went up to him and shook his hand and said, "Hey bro, I don't think things are really going the way they should. It was great ride, and I'll take everything that I've learned here and I'm going to move on. But I still love you, I'll see you at Christmas or whenever, if you'll still allow me to come by." So I parted ways with him. He said I was crazy. He just defended the situation. You know, like a rabbit going down a hole, he was just defending. He knew back then it was going sideways, but he was fighting to keep it going. Because at that time, Set Free was the fastest growing church in the United States.

Phil and I are blood brothers, but the difference between my calling to God and his calling with God is he's anointed with God - I'm not. I'm a blue collar Christian, but Pastor Phil was anointed by God to start a church and thousands of people were saved through that ministry. Thousands of people changed their lives through that ministry, and that's because Pastor Phil got up in the morning.

People didn't realize that Pastor Phil would go to church, and people in the church that he's helping would sneak out of the church and go to his house and rip him off. Steal rings and steal jewelry, steal stuff out of his house. I knew all this was coming down, and I knew he was upset that I didn't stick it out, but I had to focus on my walk with Christ that I was taught by training to serve Jesus.

139

PASTOR PHIL on the cult experts: I've got all this drama trauma going on from this, and then along comes a couple named Bill and Jackie Alnor who were Christian apologists. They called them cult finders, the cult seekers. They were the people that tell you whether you are cult or not a cult. I'm getting them writing these articles and telling people that I'm like Jim Jones or this or that. All this kind of stuff is going on. I've got a guy named Hank Hanegraaff who is another cult guy.

Bill and Jackie Alnor

I've got this guy named Ron Enroth who wrote a book, *Churches that Abuse*, and they've got a chapter of me in there. Here's some of what he says, "Pastor Phil Aguilar of Set Free Christian Fellowship has been known to say, 'You need to trust God through me.'" I probably said that. I know what's best for you. Well, I'm telling you, when I'm dealing with a little baby that is just growing in the Lord, I probably do know what's best for the baby.

It continues, "That same attitude was communicated in one of his sermons when he was discussing his own responsibility as a shepherd of Set Free." I'm an under-shepherd for the Lord. I'm always discussing Jesus.

"People in this church, don't you say anything about each other." I'm sure I was trying to say, don't be judging each other. Love on one another. I don't remember saying anything like that, but maybe I was guilty.

"I can call you anything I want because I have the responsibility and the accountability according to God's word for each and every one of you. I can say what I want." Well if you can say it, I can say it.

"You don't know the scriptures. You don't have the responsibility and the accountability, I do. So when I get in your face, receive it from the Lord or let your tail wag and go home and cry." I never talked like that in my life.

"Go try and find a TV pastor so you can turn him on and off anytime you want." This guy, whoever this guy is, does not know me. Wagging tail? Come on, I'm a street character, a biker for Christ. Nothing like that. All I got to say is - he needed some story lines and couldn't find anybody else.

I'm going through all this drama, and I'm getting invited to churches. I'm on TBN. I've got my face everywhere I go. People are, "Hey, Pastor Phil. Thank you Pastor Phil. Love you Pastor Phil." I got all that going on, and at the same time I got all this trauma going on.

Now, I'm getting a little prideful though, because I'm going, "Things are going so great here. So much is happening, I don't even know if I need Jesus anymore." Every time I get up to give an altar call, hundreds come, and the church is filled. We had to lease another property. We put a thousand young kids over there.

FRED HUNTER on Set Free as a cult: Even before I was Mayor, I had heard folks downtown talk about this cult - Set Free. "Look at these people riding motorcycles, they have tattoos and they wear funny clothes and they are not fitting in. So it must be a cult." You know, here is how I looked at it, and it was because of my background of being a preacher years ago. People know

Pastor Phil and Mayor Fred Hunter

if you see a car going down the street, and it has a little sticker that says, "I'm not of this world." That's what Christians believe - that we are not of this world.

It's not a cult. They are Christians who believe in Jesus Christ, and they do it more outwardly by the way that they dress and the way that they might have services where it gets rather ruckus, like rock and roll. That must be a cult. I just totally disagree with those folks because establishment religion. What is going on in politics right now. Enough of establishment and the same thing with religion. There is so many establishment religions.

You go to church, and they are half empty or three quarters empty. The pews are empty, because they are not preaching the Gospel. That is what Pastor Phil was doing, but he was preaching it to the down and out people. And that is not a cult with me looking at it from a religious point of view, going back to the Bible and the Book of Acts, the first church. And I think a lot of the religions today need to start looking at the four Gospels and the very first chapter after the Gospels is called the Book of Acts. Those are the first Christians. They were first Christians.

I think Pastor Phil had to be a disciplinarian in order to control. You get people coming out of prison that are down and out, that are coming off of heroin or whatever drugs or whatever situation they are in. They might be suicidal. If you are not a disciplinarian, he could not have put Set Free together. It would have been chaos. A lady gets out of prison, and she is on the streets and Pastor Phil takes her in and protects her and gives her food and tries to get her on her way, you had to be a disciplinarian. There has to be a boss somewhere. That is what he was. I have no qualms about that, not at all.

MJ on Set Free being a cult: I look back now and can see some of the people's concerns for sure. If you don't know the world that Set Free was, at that time especially, then you can look from afar and think everything and a lot of bad things because you didn't know. Or because your son or because your daughter or your loved one was transformed in this radical way, which I believe they were. Our family was able to be used to help with that. I think it was hard for that parent or loved one to understand, because it's almost like not like they want them to be messed up or be hurt or homeless or anything like that. But they also don't want them to in an environment that they felt was controlled or one person had that control to say when you can leave and when you can go. With Set Free with Pastor Phil, it was like that.

He's like, "Yeah, I'm going to love you. I'm going to help you and feed you while you are here. But you've got to go with my flow. You've got to go with my program." And if he didn't believe someone was good for them or if that person didn't want to kind of go with our program but wanted to come on the property, he's not going to let them come in and poison the well or sow some discord or whisper to other people to get them going.

I respect that part more than ever as I have a family or I run a business or I work in a lot of the same way that he did. But I can see the concern from the outside for sure. Because it was without having walls up in a compound, it was just a few houses in a city called Anaheim, but in what is probably in a way that will never be done again. I don't even know if it has been done. Because usually you have to go to a ranch or some smaller community in middle America, but this was a known city in a regular boulevard. But it was its own. Separate from everything else where it was hard sometimes for someone to get a glimpse over the gate. But if you wanted to come in, cool, everyone is invited. But if it crossed something too, then he probably wasn't going to have it. And probably even more than I knew at the time, because again I'm still just concerned about sports and music and girls. This stuff is going on. I would hear it.

A lot of ways I would know that it was a difficult time or maybe the end times for that part of Set Free. It was also people leaving, right? People were jumping ship at a certain time when these were people that to me they were - I called them uncle. I called them friend. They lived in my house. So when they left, I didn't even know the reasons why, but it was a little more maybe the normal. That's kind of when you hear stuff. Or friends of mine that were close, and they couldn't really talk to me and that was tough because that's not a normal thing. Maybe it is, maybe it's not.

But their parents were like, "We're not going there anymore" or "You can't hang out with him anymore" or "You can't go over there anymore". Maybe they still go to church, because it was so different and fun and they liked that. But as far as going to our houses and property, maybe there was some parents that weren't as comfortable with that. Which again, I can kind of put myself now as a parent and an adult and look back and be like, "Yeah, I have questions." You should have questions.

KELLI MORENO on the culture of Set Free: It's what I needed. And I'll tell you what, my kids know when I tell them - they are like, "Yes, ma'am." They are taught, and they are respectful, and I think that's what our society is lacking today. We need more of that. That tough love. Because it's genuine. I was just like, "Why should I be throwing a fit? Why should we be letting them throw a fit?" It's just unacceptable. But the thing where people said Set Free was a cult or where people would complain when they lived in that home. I thought, "You don't have to be here. The front door is right there."

Some people would get mad. We had a rule - you just couldn't get in the refrigerator. I get that. We got 300 people. If everyone is just helping themselves to the fridge, there wouldn't be the food that needed to be prepared. And people would complain about that, I'm like, "Are you kidding me? If you are hungry, then go across the street and buy something from the little Mexican store. But the bottom line is, at the end of the day, you don't have to be here. The front door is unlocked, and its wide open. Either be grateful and be thankful or adios." You know? It was not a cult at all. It's crazy for anyone to say that.

PASTOR EDDIE BANALES on Pastor Phil's leadership style: He's got a very strong, charismatic personality. That's for sure. He lights up a room when he walks in there. No doubt about it. He could jump on any subject, any topic, and he would be on point. But I think with him you just never know if he is really wanting to do that or not wanting to do that. It's almost like I'm going to leave you to figure that out. So you are kind of left ambiguous as far as what direction. There is sometimes it's a clear point

- everybody is going to be here at this time, we are going to leave at this time, or we are going to do this at this time. And then, sometimes you feel like he's making it up as he goes along. But the good thing about it is, even though he might have been making it up as it goes along, it always worked out for the most part. It always worked out.

TRINA on Pastor Phil's reputation: I think that Pastor Phil has a reputation with a lot of people of being a control freak. What's the word people use? A narcissist. You know all the sayings. He does have a lot of traits of those. I'm not going to lie. He does. So I think people don't know how to deal with that. And then, because of all the problems that have happened, the ones that possibly could have overlooked certain things are like, "Is this real or is he a fake?" Blah, blah, blah.

But if there's one thing I can tell you about our family for sure is - what you see is what you get. He's the same all the time. All he does everyday is work with people, help people. That's really his whole life. Now it's at a treatment center, before it was a ministry home. But he spends - I'd say 80% of his time with other people still to this day. He definitely has a unique way of what he does, and some people it works for and some people it doesn't.

CHILL on infighting at Set Free: I started sensing that things weren't going to well at Set Free when I just seen the whole crowd, thousands of guys wearing pony tails. I was about 12 at the time, but I was smart enough to know. I've heard the Bible so much and stories of guys who've fell then made mistakes. So I seen pride take over. Not just in my dad, in a lot of people there. I've seen people start fighting with each other, arguing. Girls caring about how they looked, name calling. Just as a kid, you knew it wasn't right. Even as a kid.

People started changing. People started acting funny, acting weird. People started getting titles. "Hey, well I'm a pastor here. I run this. I don't have to listen to Pastor Phil. Pastor Phil doesn't know what he's talking about" or "Hey, this girl is in charge. I'm not listening to her." It just became chaos. At that time, I think my dad mentally had already checked out. He was already done with - we didn't know for sure, but we could kind of tell. We knew our dad. He was kind of tired and kind of tired of the people talking about him. The different things.

So yeah, I started seeing a lot of chaos and a lot of arguing. People leaving. I watched good people leave that were good members, that were good friends of ours. I watched them walk out of our lives and I begged them, "Please don't leave. Please don't leave. We need you. Pops needs you." They've be like, "I love you, but I can't 'tell you why." So all these secrets. As a kid you are like, "What the heck? Why won't nobody tell me what's going on?" I think that drove us more crazy, all my brothers and sisters. We didn't know what was going on.

KELLI MORENO on gossip and complaining: Nobody could come to me and gossip and complain. I was a closed door for that. So if there was people that had issues, I would tell them, "Rejoice in the Lord. Be thankful. If this isn't the life for you, then move on." But honestly, I never gave ear to any of that. And, I believe that's the way it should be, because I was there for one reason, and that reason was to serve the Lord. I dedicated a year of my time to the ministry for God.

And if there was something there that I thought shouldn't be right, I would have left, but there wasn't. Because everyday I had an opportunity to share Jesus to someone. Because of what Pastor Phil did, he opened the door of his house to me, and he supported me. If I needed money for something - which I do have to give props to my mom, because I wouldn't have been able to survive that whole time without my mom. She bought me shampoo, conditioner. If my car needed tires, I was pretty blessed, because I had a vehicle. But those people - if anybody was complaining, they didn't complain to me, because I wasn't an open door, a recipient for that.

ALEXA TEJEDA on the challenges at Set Free: I think that people tend to put pastors on a pedestal, and they want them to be perfect. They want a savior, one they can touch, feel and talk to. One they can rely on 24/7 as well. He's just a man, and I realized that after everything was over. It's like we all just idolized this man who was reaching out to people that no one else cared about. Out in the street, people that were ex-drug addicts, were into alcohol - whatever it was, the past - we all came from different paths in life. Most of realized that we were all one, and he made us feel part of the family, but eventually it got so big. It went from 300 within three years, to about 5000-6000. The growth was exponential. It was crazy.

I think that once we put a person in that place, the fall is a lot harder because he's just human. Power corrupts, money corrupts. When you lose sight of your vision, then what happens is you lose your way, and I think that's what happened here. Pastor Phil ended up I think - in the beginning he was very loving, very open, very fun, exciting. He just had something different to offer everyone that we had never experienced before.

Eventually, it just got so big that he started - I believed started getting a little selective. He would be a little sarcastic with people and maybe short with them. And I can understand, because they were always at him, always. He had no moment's rest. He lived with the people in his home, so that means he didn't have any private time. He didn't have a sounding board in order to say, "Hey look, I need some help here. What direction am I going?"

You can lose sight really quick, and I believe it kind of got a little cultish, dictatorial. If you don't do the Set Free way, then you just weren't that accepted. But I think that was towards the end. And I started hearing gossip of course, never verified it, because it wasn't my business. It was between him and God. Women and money, misappropriated money that wasn't used for the church and things like that.

The rumors and the gossip and everyone getting together outside of the church to meet and talk about what was going on and what the - because now Pastor Phil was hanging around a lot of the young people with his son, Geronimo - but we were wondering what was going on. And so everybody would get together outside of the church and start talking and tell their stories and compare stories.

So I attended some of the meetings, because some of my very close friends were going at the time. I would listen to people, but I really didn't want to be involved. I understood that he was a man, that we all make mistakes and that I was not there to judge him. But I no longer could vouch. I could no longer put my signature on something I didn't no longer want to support because of what was going on.

PASTOR PHIL on problems at Shiloh Ranch: The next thing you know over in Colleyville, Texas, on this big, fancy 60-acre ranch that Jan and Paul gave us, I have a problem. One of my overseers there was accused of giving drugs to a 17 year old in exchange for sex. I'm going, "Did you do it?" He says, "No, I didn't do it." Paul and Jan get a hold of me and said, "Man, we got to get the attorneys there, because we can't let this happen. The scandal can't happen." I go, "Well, let's fight it. Let's go against it." The attorneys go, "No, you don't understand how it works when you are in the big leagues. You've got to make a settlement as fast as you can." At the same time, the big newspapers are coming to do interviews with me. They are telling me, "Hey Phil, you are one of the board members of TBN?" I go, "I'm just a figurehead." I was meaning that it's just for show but believe me, they took "figurehead" and turned it into "I'm just a setup man" - just a yes-man to them.

PRESSURE MOUNTS

I call Oden Fong, and I say "let's have a meeting together", but I never heard back when the meeting was going to be. Then I get this letter a couple months later on February 26, 1991, that says, "To Whom It May Concern; Several months ago, one of our pastors received complaints regarding Set Free Christian Fellowship. Not wanting to believe the hearsay, the pastor asked for proof and received numerous testimonies and signed statements. He proposed to send a letter and a list of the compiled allegations to our affiliate churches. He decided to contact the pastor of Set Free first with the allegations before sending the letter to our churches."

"Upon contacting Pastor Phil Aguilar he received testimonies to the contrary of the allegations. My suggestion is whether we just put a lid on it and to let the Lord take care of whatever problems might exist. Therefore we did not send the letter. Previous to contacting Pastor Phil, copies were given by the pastor who was first contacted to the other staff, pastors and to the originators of the complaints. He did not send out any letters of the allegations, we have heard that some copies have gotten around and it was not our intent to have that happen. Paul, the apostle, rebuked them for judging another man's servant. Paul said before his own master, he either stands or falls, and God is able to make him stand. Pastor Phil Aguilar is not our servant, thus he is not responsible, nor does he have to answer to us. But the ultimate responsibility is to the Lord and before the Lord that he stands and falls, and we pray that God will enable him to stand."

It concludes with "Sincerely in Christ, Pastor Chuck Smith, Senior Pastor of Calvary Chapel Ministries Worldwide."

Chill, Pastor Chuck Smith, and Pastor Phil (years after the letter)

Later, I found out that Bill and Jackie Alnor were part of the group that spread copies of these allegations all over the world - not just to Calvary Chapels, but everywhere. I was being booked to speak all over the nation, and then all of a sudden I had pastors calling me up and going, "We have some concerns. There have been some rumors. There have been some allegations." This letter coming with Pastor Chuck Smith's own signature had a lot of clout.

PASTOR EDDIE BANALES on Set Free as a cult: Let me tell you something. Every pastor has the potential to be a cult leader. Because you have sheep in your church that either want you to tell them everything to do in life, or you have those in your church that don't want to do nothing you tell them in life. And its up to that person that's going to give you the response. I have never seen him nor have I ever witnessed - and I was part of some heavy, serious leadership meetings and teams - that I ever have him dictate somebody's life. If you wanted to leave that door, leave that door. But if you are going to be in Set Free, you are going to do it the Set Free way. That is clear. That is absolutely clear. Including myself, you know?

When I took over for the time being, they would say, "This is not the Set Free way." Well then you call dad, which is Phil, because I'm not signing that paperwork. I'm not doing that. I'm still my own man, and that's why I was able to maintain friendship with him and continue to be his friend. Because as far as I'm concerned, me and him, there has never been him ever forcing me to do anything I did not want to do. I was always my own man. When he was with me in my Set Free building in Pomona, I'd wear a suit every Sunday to church. They would come in their little biker garb and all that stuff. He would say, "Man, when you going to give up the suit?" "When I feel like it, but I'm not feeling like it today." To this day, every once and awhile when I feel like wearing a suit, I wear a suit. That's just me. If I don't, I don't. So I'm my own man.

But, I would say again, you've got people that get hurt. I've dealt with it. People that get hurt and try to not always make this right. I'm sorry we disagree. I'm sorry we don't have the same understanding. But you get people especially in church that are emotional, and they want to blame somebody else. You tell a man, "Hey, pick up your cojones and be a man at home," and the wife says, "Well he told my husband to start being different, and now that he starts to hang around Pastor Phil and now he's being mean and he's telling me to do this and do that." Well you know? How do you interpret the story? I've dealt with that - not on that big of a scale, because I've learned how to use my words wisely on how to counsel people.

There's patches where he got himself in trouble by just going over the edge with maybe some truth, but a Donald Trump moment. I understand what you are saying, but you are saying it wrong. He's just speaking his heart. But like he said, you are here to listen to me. I'm not forcing you to come here. You must like what I'm saying. You like the truth.

There was one time we were in church meeting, and this is before I became in charge. He was still running the Set Free ministries. He had an open mic night, ask the pastor a question. One lady said, "I want to know what happened to sister so and so. I haven't seen her in six months." You know what he responded to her, "Well then, you need to find out what happened to her, where she's at, and you report back to us if you are concerned." That kind of stuff. See that rubs people the wrong way, but there was nothing wrong with that. I thought that was a good answer. Save the pastor some work.

MJ on Pastor Phil as a cult leader: I'll go from just my whole kind of career of just being a son, a partner working side by side my whole life span. I wouldn't say cult leader. Those aren't the words or the term that I would use is cult leader. Leader? Yes. If you want to throw in what some people would consider cultish ways? Possibly. But I also saw the many people that if they didn't like something, they would leave. So that doesn't sound like a good cult to me. I'm not a cult expert and I know some that claim to be or would consider Set Free to be one. Especially at that time. Or at least my dad to be a cult leader. It didn't feel that way. It didn't feel anything like that.

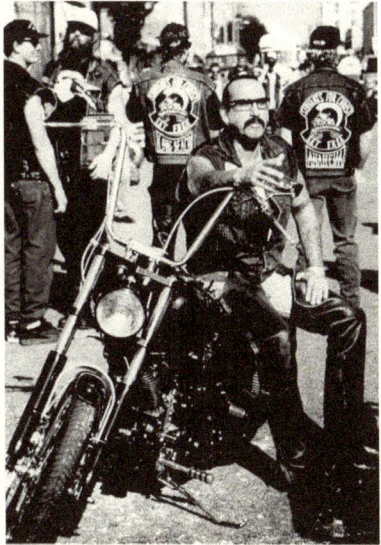

Pastor Phil

There was definitely an idea. There was definitely a brand. There was definitely something that was being preached and taught and maybe sold in some ways to people. And people were eating it up. I'm not just talking about the ones who were homeless. I'm talking about the ones who came from Anaheim Hills and different parts of nicer areas. Orange County has a lot of them. They would be right there next to the one who was on the streets last night. That was the wonderful part about it. To me, there is too much of that to be a cult. There is too much the things I saw - I was in the house. I was there. It was too much love. It was too much forgiveness.

If someone didn't like the way - a lot of people didn't like what it was for whatever reason - or not even didn't like it but just wanting to go somewhere else. I'm not saying there wasn't times where someone had made a comment like, "You are a baby," because they couldn't keep up with our style of Christianity. Which isn't right to say or do. I agree with that now, and I can look back how sometimes someone could be hard on someone like that. You don't know their story. You don't know what they are going through.

I think my dad learned that, and he passed that on to me too. Love people on the way out. You are probably going to see them again. Whether it's you needing them or them needing you, you needing each other. I think a lot of times he might have even said that back in those days, but he probably wasn't practicing it for sure. Because there wasn't a lot of mercy or grace on your way out. Because a lot of us came from a culture too that was like, "If you leave, we accepted you. You are in the family, but for you to leave, come on how dare you even?"

PASTOR WILLIE DALGITY on Set Free as a cult: Well, I would say this. I would say if a cult, if you really define it in a biblical term would be a group of people who say they are followers of Christ, but they deny the deity of Christ. So I believe that's what a cult is. Now I understand where they are coming from - those who accuse him of that, but it's because of his leadership style.

I came from a Southern Baptist. Their polity, their way of governance is congregational rule. Phil came from a Baptist background, probably congregational rule. But his is more on an elder type thing, where just he and few people, they call the shots. I believe that it's caused some problems for him. Because it has for us, we are the same thing, elder rule. But the other thing that people don't see is this, that in discipleship, when you have ranches and you have homes where you are trying to disciple people, there has to be a regiment put in place. Because everybody that is coming in off the streets, there is no discipline in their life. They are just doing their thing.

So when you have to begin to tell people, "Hey man, you got to do this. You got to go by our rules and our regulations." Sometimes people look at that and go, "Hey man, this is cultic, because these people are trying to control us." The people that are there in the program, they are digging it because they got a place to sleep, a place that is safe and all that. But you see if somebody gets pissed off, they go out there. That is the kind of the stuff they start talking. I understand it. We love them, but it's going to be there. The same thing with us. People trying to control relationships, when you are just telling people, "Hey, that's not good right now for you two. Are you still married? Probably ought to finish that project before you start another one."

PASTOR PHIL on Lois Trader's book entitled *Christianity's Executioners: A Woman's Story of Survival*: When people started talking bad about me, it was like they were talking about Lois, too. It was affecting her kids' life, her future. You messed with Set Free, you were messing with her. Lois was always aggressive. Aggressively working hard, aggressively taking care of business.

Lois Trader

When people were coming against me, a lot of times it's a lot easier for us to want to protect somebody else more than protect yourself. I am telling you, she was a pit bull for Jesus. She became that way because she loved Set Free that much. It was her life, her breath seven days, seven nights a week. At the time, I didn't really know that she was writing her book called *Christianity's Executioners*. A lot of people talk, "I'm writing this." I had no idea what she was compiling, but she was that type of person. She was a multitasker, doing things on the side. I was so involved in ministry, in the world. You imagine if you've got ten kids you are going to have problems. When you've got thousands of them, multiple problems. Like I said, I lost focus, and she took care of all the dirty work. I got to just show up, be there and speak. So I wasn't really that familiar with the book or her side of the story.

Here's part of what she wrote, "This group of so-called ex-Set Free members now had Oden Fong's backing and the Orange County Register article and Ron Enroth's book, *Churches that Abuse* to use against us. Don't forget, Bill Alnor, Hank Hanegraaff and Calvary Chapels all over. In our monthly newsletter, we had always made the practice of announcing in detail every single place that the church and our Set Free Posse would be visiting. We put in the newsletter their exact locations and phone numbers. Not wanting to lose the opportunity of communicating with our dear friends all over the United States, we continued this practice. Even though every church, school, or organization we were going to visit first got the packet from Oden Fong, all the allegations, the newspaper articles, various testimonies from ex-Set Free members. It was really beginning to take a toll on all of us in leadership. It was an enemy we couldn't fight. It was horrible. Now every church, city, or state where we were going to do an outreach to the lost was stopped by a group of stalking so-called

Christians. Pastor Phil would not defend himself, nor would he let us defend him. He kept teaching that if we keep our hands in our pockets, God will do the fighting for us. If we take the hands out of our pockets, then God won't fight for us."

I've always taught that. I've tried to practice it forever. I said, "If we try to do the fighting, it will be in the flesh. We need to put our hands in our pockets and let God do the fighting for us. He said that no weapon formed against us will prosper." During this time, it was a tough one. I was getting railed on. Some stuff was true, some stuff wasn't true. But it reminded me as I think of King David as he said, "It was good that I was afflicted." When this guy named Shimei was throwing rocks and talking trash about him, all of David's men wanted to go beat that guy down, to go knock him out. David would say, "No, this is good that I'm getting that because it keeps me eating humble pie."

That was where I was at in that time in my life. All these accusations coming around the Calvary Chapels, Oden Fong, Bill and Jackie Alnor, the ringleaders of all this stuff. Hank Hanegraaff was kind of just hanging on, just half in, half out, but it was a rough time.

TRINA on reading Lois' book: When I was probably in my early teens is when I seen Lois' book that she wrote about all the stuff that was going on. Court cases and accusations and all that stuff. A lot of the stuff, I don't know about a lot, but some of the stuff I knew because of what I knew and what I've seen is true. And then other stuff, I knew really just wasn't true because we were there. We've seen everything. We really were. It was like our own world for sure. So I definitely thought, "How are all these people Christians and this is how everybody treats each other?" So that's why Christians are kind of a turnoff for me because church is kind of a turn off. Just because it seems like Christians are the most vicious, mean people when we are supposed to be all about love and forgiveness.

We had a lot of damage done. I know my dad did it to himself but I think because nobody knows how it affects the kids and my mom. Just because they get so - I think at Set Free you become like - back then you become a star, you know? And then once that's over, you are mad. Or then people who never felt like they were part of the top team, so they get angry or whatever. But nobody ever thinks about how anything affects the kids. And as much as my dad bugs me sometimes and we get into arguments, it's still my dad. So I don't want to hear bad stuff about him all the time.

PRESSURE MOUNTS

MJ on the negative attention: Okay, in my eyes at this time, keep in mind I'm still pretty young. I'm occupied with whatever cassette I'm listening to that week. But I still was able to see a lot, and I would say a lot of it was the busier. It was really the busier because there is always that rise before it actually tumbles. So my dad was busier than ever, going places more than ever. I saw him less than I ever have. He was just moving. I'd have to wait in line like everybody else to see my own dad.

We'd go to lunch, but again, it was just a crowd of people. We would go in public, and there would be cameras and people following us from back in the days. There was this show called *Inside Edition* and *Current Affair* and certain shows that pretty much want to dig up stuff and call people out. True or not. They would do that, and they don't care. Those kind of people and programs didn't care. So they would really catch us with our family, and we'd be on the way to the car. They would come out almost like paparazzi, and I haven't even thought about that for a long time, but in a lot of ways, it was crazy and scary and exciting, too. "What is this? Is this good press or bad press?"

Pastor Phil (far right) with the Set Free Posse

When they started asking certain questions, they aren't trying to hide it - those kind of programs. They were asking stuff about - let me think of some of the questions, probably some were money related. "What do you do with the church's money?", timeless questions per any church. I guess at the time, we were considered a megachurch. People say that you won't let them have their food stamps or that you take their welfare checks or something like that. People that lived in our ministry home, they are not allowed to see their family. "Is this true that they are not allowed to see their family? Or that they can't visit with them?"

So those are the kind of things, I'm thinking in my young mind, "We don't live a wealthy lifestyle, we never did." Again sometimes I'd tell them, "What the hell is wrong with you? You could have saved and held onto to stuff. I think you have the right to do that, not for you but for us." But he didn't, so when it came to that I was like, "If there is, I don't know where that's hidden at when it comes to money or anything extra." Because we didn't have anything extra, I didn't think so.

As far as abuse, verbal or things like that, I'm trying to kind of understand it in my mind and play with that a little bit. Not seeing your family, I was trying to - I don't know there is a lot of people around. I felt like anyone who is allowed to and who is good for the area and is not an issue is always welcome to come around. But again, do they want to come around? Is it against what we are teaching, preaching, sharing with our people? Especially the ones that live with us, they are held to a different standard or accountability.

PASTOR PHIL on looking for a replacement: The church was growing and doing, everything like that, but I was starting to get my critics. "I think I can do a better job than Pastor Phil." So I put it out kind of as a sarcastic comment. "Pastor Phil looking for a replacement." I always have done reverse psychology, so I put that on there, looking for a replacement. I just put a list so people could see, "Hey, you sure you are cut out for this? Twenty four hours a day, seven days a week and not have compassion fatigue?" So yeah, it was more in jest just to get people. I've always been a little bit of a shock jock. I like to carry a spiritual taser around - get people to see and make sure they are listening.

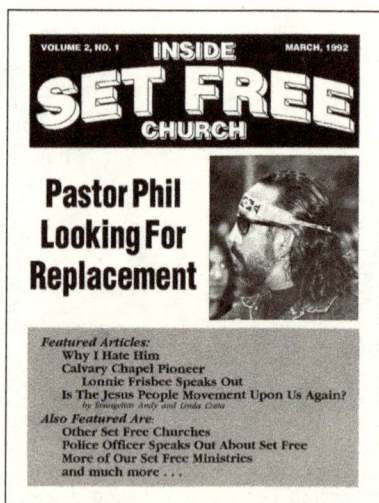

VOLUME 2, NO. 1   **INSIDE**   MARCH, 1992

SET FREE
CHURCH

Pastor Phil Looking For Replacement

Featured Articles:
  Why I Hate Him
  Calvary Chapel Pioneer
    Lonnie Frisbee Speaks Out
  Is The Jesus People Movement Upon Us Again?
  by Evangelists Andy and Linda Colca
Also Featured Are:
  Other Set Free Churches
  Police Officer Speaks Out About Set Free
  More of Our Set Free Ministries
  and much more . . .

Cover of "Inside Set Free Church"

Before I met Christ, I was just a loser. I had never really built anything before, so I was even shocked that Set Free happened and that I'm on TV.

PRESSURE MOUNTS

This was my first time pioneering and adventure. I had Lois in my corner and a few other people who had never done a ministry like this. Never done a TV program. So I didn't really have anybody to talk to. It seemed like that at the time. I'm sure there were people around, but I just didn't notice them.

During all the midst of this turmoil, it was heavy. The stress was on me. People see this guy on TV and say what a wonderful guy I am. Then, the newspapers are coming out saying that I'm like a cult leader. I make a meeting with Pastor Chuck Smith and Pastor Oden Fong trying to work out something. I went to Christian Conciliation. I'm trying to work out a peace agreement here, and I guess I just didn't make a good enough effort. Then, I've got the Davis family, Geronimo's in-laws. They are mad, and now they got a crew. They are talking smack. I'm just not happy at all. I'm pissed off at life - pissed off at everything.

MAYOR FRED HUNTER on Set Free's challenges with the City of Anaheim: The big warehouse downtown, I think it at one time was more of like an auto repair shop. I believe even back then, Bill Taormina owned that building, and Set Free leased that building legitimately. That's where he had a lot of big Gospel meetings - not just for Anaheim, but people would come from all over and have the big Gospel meetings there.

Some people complained, not knowing specifically, but they would call certain council members who wanted Pastor Phil out of Anaheim, out of the houses. They wanted him out, and that was a struggle while I was Mayor. And Pastor Phil knows while I was Mayor, they stayed there in that warehouse. And I can remember they had a Mayor's Night where you could come listen to me and the other person running for Mayor and other people running for City Council, and the place was packed by a lot of people in the neighborhood and a lot of Set Free folks.

And of course, me being an ex-Gospel preacher, I was preaching to the choir. And I think that my opponent did not like that, and he wanted Pastor Phil out. I know eventually they moved up to a large building in Fullerton of which I attended and the Crouches from TBN attended. There were thousands of people there, and I was very impressed with what Pastor Phil was doing up there. Once again, the complaints came in from the political folks that were actually against Pastor Phil and what he was doing. I look back now. He was preaching the Gospel, going to all the world and preached the Gospel to every creature. "He that believeth and is baptized shall be saved. He that believeth not shall be damned." That's what he was doing. I was a councilman at the time, and Tom Daley was the Mayor, and he had two other votes besides himself. And at that time, the

City Council was five, it still is, they are changing it now. And I think Tom Daley, along with some other folks again wanted Pastor Phil out of downtown Anaheim, and I really don't know how they got an injunction through the city attorney to have Pastor Phil and Set Free vacate that building. Anaheim, at that time, was going through a revitalization process again, and the city was buying buildings to sometime in the future tear down buildings and start building condominiums or houses. So I believe they were premature. They were using that as an excuse to kick them out.

PASTOR PHIL on Anaheim mayors: When I was starting Set Free and we were meeting downtown there in our first big building, I needed some help. I was reading the Book of Nehemiah and it said, "Nehemiah went to the King." So I asked my wife, "Who do you think the King is of this city?" She goes, "I think the King would be the Mayor." So I go not knowing this guy, Mayor Don Roth. Next thing you know he goes, "Hey, we have some empty houses we can let you rent. Help you out." So I had the Mayor on my side. The Mayor came on TBN. The Mayor

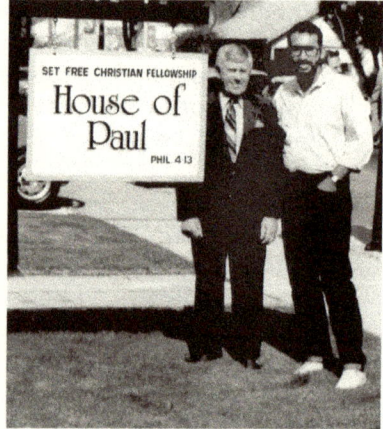
Mayor Don Roth and Pastor Phil

spoke, Christianity and all that stuff. It was just wonderful as could be. Then the next Mayor that comes on, Ben Bay. It was the same thing, that Mayor friendly to Set Free helped us out.

Then, I had Mayor Fred Hunter became a speaker at our church. He was on fire for Jesus. He was the best. Then, the next Mayor that came along was Tom Daley. We had been there for years. I had won every community services award, Disneyland community services award, houses beautiful award for having the most beautiful places. We had almost 400 people living in our homes. Church was thousands of people.

Everything was going great, and we leased another property, this old Baptist church building in Anaheim that we got. So we had all this going on, but then there is a new Mayor that came in that knew not Pastor Phil or didn't care for Pastor Phil. At the council meeting people by the thousands are pleading, "Let Set Free stay in this old Baptist church building."

Mayor Fred Hunter stood up and fought for us and said, "Hey, why do you got to take this building? We got other properties that somebody else could use. Why you gotta take this one? I think there is something going on here." Mayor Tom Daley and councilman Irv Pickler goes, "We don't warm to that biker leather image of downtown. We want a remodel downtown, and we don't think all the Set Free biker look is what we want in downtown." That was all BS, because I'm telling you they remodeled nothing down over there. They just had something going on. Tom Daley, love the guy, but I'm telling you he had an agenda. They were out to get Set Free out of downtown, because we were just getting bigger and bigger, and we were all over the streets of Anaheim.

We had a big protest downtown. Peaceful protest. I think some of my characters did go in front of Tom Daly's house. I can remember at City Hall meeting saying, "Tom Daley, I think you better watch out because I just might move next door to you." I did say that. I had a little holy anger going on. I was a little upset. I asked for forgiveness for that. That was a good day.

PASTOR WILEY DRAKE on supporting Set Free: Well, the way I first met Phil was we were working here, and the city was saying ,"We don't like what you are doing. We don't want you to do it. Don't bring all these dirty, smelly homeless people. We don't have homeless people in Buena Park." And I said, "Yes we do." And so we were ministering to them, and we were getting in trouble with the city.

Low and behold, I began to hear about another guy who was very different from me. Tattoos, long hair, earrings and here I am conservative, Southern Baptist, suit wearing - totally different people. But, we had one thing in common. We were trying to tell people about Jesus, and the authority didn't want us to. And so I began to say, "Well, wait a minute. I'm not the only guy getting in trouble," and I found out that Phil Aguilar and his family and their group were getting in trouble as well. Because they said, "We want you to come as you are. God has set us free." And that is where he got the name for their group and so forth.

So I began to hear about what was going on in Anaheim, our neighboring city. I found out that he indeed was being harassed and trying to be driven out of town. I said, "Hey, I want to stand up for this guy because he is fighting the same battle I'm fighting." So that is when we met and got together, and he had reservations about me. This guy in a suit, yada yada. And I had reservations because even though I used to be an old hippie, I didn't have any tattoos or long hair. So we sort of walked around each other, looking and saying, "Who is this crazy guy?" But then we realized that we both had the concept of the Lord Jesus Christ being Set Free. Yes, I'm a Baptist, but I'm Set Free as well.

So we began to follow him a little bit and see what the city was doing. And in all honesty, he didn't ask me to come, but I began butt in because I could see the media. And a lot of people said, "Well, the reason why they want to go over there and help Phil is because he gets on television." And I resemble that remark. That's true. At the same time, I thought it was a good cause. They were being criticized. They were being ostracized. They were being kicked out of town.

SANDRA about inappropriate situations: I started sensing unraveling with the whole situation with Geronimo. Geronimo was like I said, he's a very charismatic guy, fun guy. So there was this group of young people that were apart of the Posse, the dancers and all that. So then it ended up where they were asked to go to a lot of places and do a lot of different shows. They traveled a lot. Most of us, like myself, we did Christian school. My kids - I couldn't travel as much as they could. Stacee couldn't travel as much even though she was younger trying to travel more.

When you start traveling with a lot of young people, you start taking on that young also. You start going down to their level. You are free person, you are just having fun, you are out ministering. You don't have any of your obligations around you. It wasn't good, and I knew it wasn't good. Then I would alway pray, "Lord, please send somebody with them." My husband would go a lot of times also. Well before you know it, he would be going even more often. So now, he wasn't a part of the Posse, but he was the minister involved. So he's going more.

Then, little by little, I'd hear little things, inappropriate things. Something somebody would see. Or flirting going on. So I could see where it was unraveling, and I knew as much as God was using that group to minister to others, that the devil was just right there in the middle of it all. Just laughing and knowing that "Hey, you guys are so blind to what is happening right now. You are all going down." I was arguing with him all the time about inappropriate situations. Then of course, he would tell me, "You are just acting like a Baptist." There is a fine line between that, and yet I would always share with him, "I'm worried about Geronimo. Too much attention." My husband got too much attention.

So here you are busy mom and wife and teacher, and you are not running around with all these people and either is Stacee not running around with all these people. So our husbands are off just basically doing all the things they do. So before you know it, rumors start. Then also I know that they liked it. They liked the attention. They liked feeling that they are cool. They like feeling like someone thinks they are cool looking and attractive or whatever. So it was unraveling quickly, and I could see that. Because some of the people who had been so great, young people, were now getting a little off track in their attitudes. We've got the worship team and that's a little bit older people - people that I loved and worked with all the time. They are starting to go on the trips also. I'm thinking, why would they want to go? I think what happened was they got dragged into, "I want to be young again. This is fun. I want to be single." You could just see nothing changed in the way people were coming and they were ministering, but things were changing internally without a doubt.

PASTOR WILLIE DALGITY on rumors of Phil's infidelity: I have no clue on any of that. I've heard the same things. I've never just gone to Phil and said, "Hey, is any of that true?" I really doubt it. I think that in the work we do, there is a lot of that stuff that comes with it. There can be accusations. My whole thing is going back to the Bible. We are not to entertain an accusation against an elder but by two or three witnesses. And those will be eye witnesses. So if you don't have that? I'm not sure about all of that, but looking at his relationship with Sandra, I just don't think so. But that's my opinion.

PASTOR EDDIE BANALES on accusations against Phil: No one has ever came to me personally. Because here is what I said, "If you didn't see it, don't repeat it." If you heard it, you are talking about gossip and rumor. So I've always made that clear. I don't want you to tell me that somebody told you that they told your cousin over there when they were there. There was one incident where Phil - and I'm sure he'll probably tell you himself - he was in a nightclub, and he was going to the bathroom and the guy goes, "Pastor Phil, what are you doing here?" Pastor Phil tells him, "The same thing you are." That's just kind of the man he is.

If you are not willing to sit with me and to go to this brother and say the Matthew 18 story, there is a Bible that we are supposed to go beyond. But unfortunately, these rumors get so hot and spread like embers in a fire. You weren't there when that fire got started, but yet you want to catch an ember. You want to tell a story. Well you were not there at that bonfire. Again, not that I was ever trying to deny or not hear, but I made it clear. Unless you were there and you saw it or you got people that want to sit and talk and reconcile. Most people won't do that. I do the same thing in my church. I've had a few complaints at my church.

I've heard the accusations. I've heard everything from his biker ministry going to 1% biker club, going to affairs and women and everything. A smaller group of him that went and did private things. But by these kind of times, when I gave him back the baby, I was pretty much - we were always friends. Whenever we connected and talked, it was always like we've never left. To this day, it's like we've never left. But again, just like he's a grown man, if he wants to share something with me, then he shares it with me. If I want to share with him - as a matter of fact, a couple of weeks ago I asked him a question. We are talking about something. I said, "By the way Dr. Phil - ," because I call him Dr. Phil sometimes. I said, "Dr. Phil, how many children did actually Mary have?" I'm thinking this guy has been a pastor a lot longer then me, he knows. He goes, "You know what? Let me call you right back." And he gets on Google and calls me back and goes, "She had these children. These were their names," this and that. Because it was just kind of a curious question.

You think him and I have been pastoring long enough. You think we both together could answer a simple question like how many children did Mary have in total. There were questions like I said, but I always told people, "Does that person want to talk to me? Do they want to come? Do they want to see me?" And a lot of times they would say, "No, I don't want to do it." Then, why bring it up?

PASTOR PHIL on looking for love: I just knew that I needed to work on my life - that I'd taken my eyes off of Jesus, that I was a spiritual wreck, and that I needed help. I've got some pride problems big time in my life. I got my eye on something I shouldn't be looking at. I'm starting to see my personal character, my morals, start to fall apart in the middle of everything. It's that pride now I realize, pride goes before the fall. Everything else is just symptoms, but I had a problem going on. It's just coming down on me. I needed some relief somewhere, and I was looking for love in all the wrong places.

Pastor Phil in Israel

Kind of like King David, that one day when he didn't lead his people out to battle, my state of mind came to that place. I can remember I was taking a group every year on a trip to Israel. I just love Israel. I love the Jewish people, even got a Star of David tattoo. I can remember walking up to that bus, saying goodbye to the whole group of 50 of them as they were getting ready to go to the airport to go to Israel. I can remember how it related when I read about King David. He was supposed to lead his people to war, but he decided to stay home and took a walk on the balcony

160

instead. Well, I stayed home, took a walk on my own balcony and I saw my own little Bathsheba. I took my eyes off of Jesus. Got myself in a bad situation, and next thing you know I'm wanting to tell our church in the nicest way I could, didn't know how to do it. You know what? I'm done. I got to go. My life is not right. I couldn't hide it anymore. People knew I was falling apart. I tried to hide just like Adam did behind the trees, and that didn't work. I could hear God walking through my garden in the cool of the day saying, "Hey, where you at?"

No matter what I tried to do, I had people in leadership, they wanted me to tell them some juicy facts. I said I wasn't about to do that. I don't want to hurt other people. I got myself involved in a relationship, and it went downhill so quickly. I might have been on top of Mount Everest, but I'm telling you, I hit the bottom and here I was still standing.

SANDRA on whether an extramarital relationship motivated Pastor Phil to leave Set Free: I would say that wasn't his motivation to bail. I think people had all their different ideas and different things. I don't think you really know a person unless you live with them and I lived with him. There was a lot of things. The cult thing devastated him. It threw him through a loop. Then you've got leadership leaving. It all happened at the same time. The Geronimo thing, this whole thing with the cult thing.

Funny because Vern Jackson and his wife Sandra, great people. Vern actually became famous on TBN, because God used us as a tool for that. They were great people. They had a son who was a heroin addict off and on. That's how they started coming to our church, because they brought him to get help. At the time, he had a girlfriend, this girl that was his girlfriend. I know people don't believe this but from the first time I saw her, I said, "This person is trouble." I could just sense it immediately.

There was something about her that before you knew it, trouble was coming. It was funny because she had this way about her - tiny, little cute thing - and she had this way of BSing people. Her personality. You know how some people just love power? That's what she loved. She loved power. She wanted to be with people with power. So little by little she got more involved with Geronimo, more involved with my husband. She started to do dancing with the group. Started being a helper. Started doing this, started doing that, and forgot all about this boy that she came with.

Lois would go crazy if anybody got my husband's attention, because they had to go through her first. She was like the president's secretary. Lois had her own weird emotional relationship with my husband. It wasn't anything else but emotional. She owned him, and nobody could besides me could

161

get near him unless they had her permission. Literally, anybody will vouch for that one. You couldn't be his friend or close to him unless she said it was okay. Then, because she did such great stuff and had such confidence that she could get something done, that was great for him, because that was a great tool in ministry. So things get webbed together.

The situation with this girl became worse. It started off where Lois made such a big deal about it all the time in a lot of different ways. To the point where my husband is the type of person, "You are going to tell me something, I'm going to do more." It turned into that. Then it was like, "Oh, I want her to help me with this, and I want her to help me with that." Then before you know it this person feels like, "He thinks I'm special."

So of course, as I would talk to him about it, we'd talk about it and everything. He would go, "It's just emotional tie." There was an emotional tie. Do you believe it, do you not believe it? You want to believe your husband. I thought, "Do you really want to throw all this away? Do you really want me to just take the kids and leave and you can just go do whatever you want to do?"

Pastor Phil and Sandra

SANDRA on whether Pastor Phil talked to her about leaving for another woman: Never. Never. He never - it wasn't like he was really taking off with this person. It was all speculation, it was all people. Because of the attention. The stupid things, "He is up there talking, but he is just looking at her," or ,"He's making motions towards her." People were starting to talk more, because it was already in the rumors. So it got more and more and more.

Lois was having a breakdown, so we had to help her. It was always like I was always helping somebody else who is having a breakdown. So finally it go to the point where I just said, "If this is what you want to do." "Not a chance, that is not what I want to do." In those days, there wasn't cellphones. People wrote notes. That's how this kind of came about. Somebody found a note that he had written and interpreted it the way they wanted to interpret. It wasn't anything sexual or anything like that. It was just something else, and they took it and went with it. Lois went with it a lot, because she was so angry that it was something that she could not control.

I even said to him, "Go ahead. We've had a great life ministering." He said he had no desire. The greatest part of all is God is so great. He shows me things. I tell people it's hard to understand. We were just at a bad place, because so much tension going on with everything that I just wanted my kids to be happy and have as normal of a life as possible. So I just went on as normal and never would argue in front of the kids or anything like that.

One night, when I was sleeping, I literally woke up being choked. I couldn't breathe. I felt like I was being choked. So I'm thinking - he's choking me, right? He was sound asleep. He wasn't choking me. Then, all of a sudden, I could breathe again, and it was like the Lord told me, "You need to pray over your husband right now. Because it's either now or never that this is going to happen." I remember praying over him while he was sleeping. Just praying and praying and praying.

And then, the very next day, it was like the sun shined in my life, and he came to me and he said, "I need to change a lot of things in my life. I need to get back on track and you need to help me get back on track." That's really how it all started getting back on track. Never planning on moving at that moment, but you have to remember the cult thing, the cult thing, the cult thing was bothering him. The city was bothering him about getting out of town. They don't want us there anymore. The deacons were bugging him because they wanted to get a million dollar place, and he was fighting with them. Because if you get a million dollar place, we don't have the money to house people and use the money for that. He didn't want a million dollar place. Fighting with them. Fighting with Lois, his secretary. This person who was getting my husband's attention - I still believe she was totally of the devil - just would not stop. Just bugging all the time. Just so many things that I believe that we had this opportunity in Visalia. Our friends had a home there, and our kids had ministered in all the areas around there. I think he just thought, "Let's just start afresh somewhere else." Not running away from the Lord, just doing different ministry for the Lord.

MJ on Pastor Phil's affair: At that time, I knew her well. She lived with us, which obviously is part of the problem, because it was too close. It was just too close. We had a lot of females and co-ed. Some people met their soulmate, and some not so much. So it was tough, because you see someone who is - this girl in particular was more closer than others to me. We were friends. We hung out. She was a few years older, but super friendly, cool. She was one of the females that I was closer too at that time. We had a cool relationship me and her more than maybe the hundred others that lived with us. Super cool.

So for me, it was rumors and things were heard. And even later in the years, you've got names. Because at the time, no one is giving you names. I'm still a teenager. I'm young, and my parents are doing their best to keep it from you or figure things out. It was hard enough just to do that in our house, because it's filled with so many people. And a lot knew what was going on or thought they knew what was going on. So it wasn't like during that time - it kind of sucks and probably wish someone would have addressed me. Nobody ever did.

Not once did my family, brother, mother, father say, "Hey, I know there is some stuff flying around. I know there is some stuff that you might have heard or that you might hear. Lets prepare you. Let's set you up for that. Let's talk about this. We know this person is close to you. We know this person is nice to you. We know your father is father, and I'm your mom."

Whatever it is, not once. Not once. I don't know if that's ever happened to this day. It's more just that it came up in conversations or over time little bits kind of leak out. That's how it was at the time. I heard stuff, but you don't want to think or believe it. Not everything your dad did was an outreach. It wasn't a meeting. It wasn't building a new church. It was other stuff. Or that he would spend more time with females maybe. Or too many females at least that weren't his wife. That was a big one. Because over time I saw that I can look back now and again you always trying to, "Nah, not my dad. Not this." And if you know my dad's story, that's what happened to him. The same thing.

PRESSURE MOUNTS

So you don't want to believe it. You just keep playing your football and keep playing your video games and keep hanging out with your buddies. And while all this craziness is going on, you are just trying to make sense in your young mind, but it's always there. We know that. It's always just a cover, and it's always there.

So when I would see that my mom would be around less, she wasn't around us more, but she was around him less. He was doing so much or other things where it was now where he wasn't - it wasn't like he was just hanging out making up for that vacation that they never had in the last 12 years.

It was, "Well that girl is around him and that girl is around him." He's got a team of females and some closer than others that even me at a young age, you know that's my mom's job. That's my mom's. That's a wife's job. That's a mother's job. That's something that I felt like even at that age I knew that was her role, but there were other people that were in that role. People that would act a certain way with him, talk a certain way with him, that I knew that's not okay, but it wasn't enough for me to ever say anything.

I'm not going to say, "Hey pops," and have a little sidebar. Of course not, that's not - I wouldn't at that time do that. And my mom, I don't want to make her feel worse even though she sees it all. If I see, she does. So I didn't want to bring that up to her. So with everything and everyone that was around, I had no one to talk to. It's one of those moments where you would just be like, "Who would I even begin to open up to and talk to?" And if this girl who is a friend of mine and family, but now is kind of rumored to be having some stuff going on with my dad who is a leader of us all and a parent to so many of us all not just me and my siblings - I'm not going to talk to her either. Tell her to cut it out or friends of her that live in the house, because who is in on it now? Maybe there is other people.

And at the same time, there is stuff with not just my dad, but maybe another person, another guy. Stuff that I would maybe know or see and I was like, "Wait a minute, is that what you do at that age? Is that okay? Did your wife sign off on that? Did your husband sign off on that? I don't want to get into your business."

I'm living around a whole bunch of females, too, that are older than me - that know more than me. That like my long hair, too. Whatever it is, you know what I mean? And dealing with that whole part of it. You have people in your house and all around your children. But my dad at that time especially was so deep into himself. He was so wrapped up in himself and everything that came with that. There was no talking to him. Probably not

165

even no stopping him at that time. So it was a very confusing time. And even over the years as it's continued to play out, probably we'll say that was '92, '93, so ten years later you are getting bits of pieces of evidence and discovery.

You are like, "How come we aren't going over there?" or "How come we don't like that person?" Or that person showed up and my mom is furious and my dad is trying to make it cool now because he's changed his ways but your scars and mistakes from the past just because you are better don't mean people still aren't bitter, and it doesn't mean especially your own wife or spouse that they've gotten over it because you have to. Or because we are doing things for God and God has taken Pastor Phil or Set Free from that rough time of the early to mid '90's and revived it in so many cool ways, but there is still those people that are walking this earth that we haven't had maybe the best relationships with. And maybe both parties have moved on, but it's still weird.

My dad is like that. He'll try to bury the hatchet and move on, but that doesn't mean that lady's husband wants to or your wife wants to or the people involved want to. For us, as kids and siblings, as we found out more, it's like, "Cool." Not cool, but that's done. That was a time you made some big mistakes that you are going to have to figure out as a husband and a marriage, but I don't want to hang out with that person. I don't want to see them at my church even. You know what I mean? I think a lot of people would feel that way, and I understand exactly why.

JIM BUCHANAN on Pastor Phil's fall: You take what you hear with a grain of salt, and you compare what is said with what you know to be the facts and you come up - it doesn't outweigh, you know what I mean? We all fail. We all fall. I can't think of a Bible hero that hasn't fallen and to think that somebody with the attacks that Satan has to bring over all those years. That there's got to be problems. There has got to be failures. There has got to be disappointments. You've got to bring tears to God's eye at some point. But our God is all about restoration. That is the key right there.

What he did or didn't do as far as a peccadillo is really irrelevant. I can think about a million things I've done. I can think of a million things this saint has done that would bring shame and dishonor to the name of Christ. Nobody, nobody can serve properly, especially when they are under the intense attack that you know the enemy is going to bring that somebody, that an organization, that is actually doing something for God. We started something. Nobody was doing what we did. No one was taking in people just to help.

PRESSURE MOUNTS

BILLY AGUILAR on addressing the situation: I was taught early in life - my mom had a little sign in our house that said, "Your friends know your faults and don't give a damn." I don't know what the story was, but I rolled with a guy named Danny Barrios, Mike Baraza, and different structured guys in the club that didn't know what was going on. Big Danny came up to me as my vice president and goes, "You know what, bro? We were so busy rowing the boat that we didn't have time to rock it." I didn't ask Phil about his personal life. That's none of my business. You don't ask me about my wife and I - we'll get through it. Whatever him and Sandra or whatever games that were going on, I don't know. I never asked. I really believe that you should check your own house, before you start trying to clean somebody else's house.

But I knew - I sensed it. I sensed there was a woman. I sensed there was a man. The Bible tells us that the devil is not going to knock on the door, he is going to destroy from inside out. That's what happened to Set Free, it got destroyed from Pastor Phil. The guys that brought the girls are just as guilty as the guy cheating on his wife. The guy is giving money to go on a date with a girl is just as guilty as the bank robber that is driving the car is just as guilty as the guy robbing the bank. So it wasn't really completely Pastor Phil's fault, but if ask a lot of people today, they blame everything on him.

I run into these people everyday. I run Anaheim. I'm from Anaheim. My mom was born here in Anaheim. We call it 'Klannaheim'. So I run into people all the time, and they ask me that question, "Hey man did you know what was going on? Did you know what happened to Set Free?" I go, "I sort of bailed out, because I knew something was up, and I took all my knowledge that I learned and I applied it to my marriage, my children, my job." Set Free made me a better Christian. It made me a better husband. It made me a better father, and it made me a better employee and I ran with it and I didn't look back. I miss my brother dearly though, the years that we were apart and not serving the Lord together, but I had to do it man. I had to do it for my sake, because I'm the blue-collar Christian. I wasn't the anointed by God to be a Christian like he was.

ELIZABETH AGUILAR BUCHANAN on the unraveling: I didn't have a sense of it at all. I was just in lala land, a young mom, raising my kids, being happy at our church. I was pretty devastated when it did start to unravel. It got big so fast and to me, I don't know if it just had gone to his head as it has with other preachers and people in high authority like that. I have no idea, but it was heartbreaking for me to see it happen.

TRINA on noticing what was going on: I was younger, but I'm not dumb so I noticed stuff going on. I was a kid so what is anybody going to listen to me? So there was a lot of stuff I knew I didn't like at the time, but there was so much good stuff going on that it kind of outweighed the bad stuff. Then, my dad and my brother got away from Jesus and what it was really about. We became so huge that I think maybe there heads got a little too big and forgot that Jesus put them where they were, and they became like young kids. It was weird. They started acting like young people instead of - well my brother was young I guess, but my dad started acting like my brother if that makes any sense. So I think men - you know men are just prideful and get all this attention and start changing. I think it's most men that I know do that. I guess anybody in power can have whatever they want, so they - I don't know. I think that's what happened. They lost sight of what we were doing.

CHILL on the fall of Set Free: Well, I don't think that my dad was the main guy who made Set Free go down. There were times in my life I thought that, but the reality after doing my research and growing up and being a man and just looking at it from different angles, I think other people played a part in his downfall that caused him to get weak. I'm not blaming them, I'm just saying other people - I know my dad fell into sin like most men do. He chose whatever his sin was at the time over the church and whatever else. And he did it. He did what he did, and it was a long, long time ago, and I was still really young so I didn't know all the details or facts.

I knew that something wasn't right, and I knew that my dad probably was definitely in sin because when you are in sin - for all of us, when we are in sin, we don't want to answer any accusations. We don't want to talk to anybody. We just want to, "Oh, I didn't do nothing. I'm good."

So I'm sure, yeah, people played a part in his downfall. You probably will never hear about them or they will never be blamed, because my dad really doesn't talk about them. He doesn't want to put their life on blast. But yeah, I definitely think that my dad just didn't blow it up himself. I think other people, consenting adults, people that were saved put their eyes on Pastor Phil instead of Jesus, and they fell.

MJ on open dialogue: It's like it's almost one of those where you brush over it or you - I don't know, there is nothing humorous about it. But it's so long ago, and I guess again you try to put it out. Whether that's me or one of my siblings talking about something, there has never been a moment where - my dad don't really do that. Again we didn't - there wasn't the birds and bees talk. There wasn't the, "Hey there is some rumors flying around and going on in the church. Do you want to talk about your favorite baseball cards?" "Hey we are going to be moving, lets talk about that." "We are going to be moving again to another location, let's talk about that." "The church is closing, let's talk about that." "Me and your mom, some stuff is going on in our relationship. Let's talk about that."

That never happened and over the years, as much as he loves to talk and as open and transparent as he is, I think it's just been too difficult for him to maybe admit it or accept it - or he felt like they know enough. And because kind of the world that we lived in, there was a lot. Maybe we didn't get it from him, but we got all this other stuff, and we came to our own conclusions. Now as adults, especially now it's kind of like - and my mom is like that, too. Obviously, they are still married and after so many years and so many ups and downs, she loves him more than anything else and supports him over anything else. I'm not even mad at that. That's her husband. She should and she has.

She is not the one to open up and say, "Hey, I just want to sit down and talk to you." She never has and neither has he in that way. I don't even know if I want them to. For what? What is it now? Definitely now. Back then? Sure, it probably could have helped me out as a young man or a boy. I've learned quite a bit from them not saying anything and how to apply that to my life and how to again add up the puzzle over the years that has made up my life or made up my relationship with my father and my mother and parents.

Again, while I'm still looking for pieces and things like that or some I don't mind, because I can still see the picture without maybe certain pieces. That's enough for me, and I'd rather have a relationship with them now while they are all here on this earth than be so busy looking for all the pieces and answers that I miss out on in this life.

TRINA on wrestling with the situation as a kid: I think that's part of the reason why I had so much anger towards my dad growing up probably. Especially because you in your mind you think people are supposed to act a certain way. Especially pastors, Christians, and as you get older you realize they are just as messed up as everybody else, but I didn't get that as a kid. I think those are feelings of resentment that I carried on for a long time, and I think that's why we butted heads so much, because I didn't really respect him because of the things that I heard or saw or whatever it was. You know? Until now, becoming an adult, is where I really appreciate all the good parts about him that I took for granted growing up, because I just held onto certain things that I didn't think was right or whatever. I'm really close with my mom, so I was being protective for her, too, because she never would say anything - well, at least not in front of any of us. I know one time I got caught because I was like, "I can't believe you stay with him," telling her. And then he walked in right behind me, and I'm like, "Damn it." He's like, "What did you say?" I'm all, "Nothing, I'm out of here." Yeah, so I think I was really hurt for her too, because even whatever is true or is not true, nobody wants to hear that about your husband. So I was definitely more angry at him for that.

My mom is my best friend so we talk about stuff. Nothing that I would give details about. But, we definitely have had adult conversations about situations, and then my dad now I've become where I've made it like a joke when I joke with him about stuff. Not today, because it's so long ago, but when I was finally at that place in life, yeah I made jokes about it. But me and my dad never had a serious conversation about it. I don't think I'd feel comfortable having that conversation with him. That would be awkward.

PASTOR PHIL on moving forward: I had thousands of people telling me to keep on keeping on. All I was doing was looking for a way out. I was looking for a place to hide. I was looking how to get out of this. But I had so many people that were willing to go to the Adullam Cave with me. They were willing to go anywhere with me, just because they loved me. People call me a cult leader, but people usually obey their cult leader. Most of mine didn't listen to me, so I wasn't that much of a good cult leader. I had those people that wanted to stay with me.

I had a couple of fellows come up and say, "Hey, you need to turn it over to somebody." One of my brothers, Billy, and another guy came over and said, "You need to turn the church over to Bob Nixon, one of your loyal, faithful guys that has been with you ten years. You helped him and his wife through divorce. He'd be the one to do it." Because I was thinking the natural one would be my assistant who helped me

Pastor Wayne Palmer

start Set Free, Pastor Wayne Palmer. I figured Wayne Palmer would rather just stay with me and not take over the church. Little did I know, that wasn't what he was thinking. So, I turned over Set Free Church in Anaheim to Pastor Bob Nixon who became pastor.

PRESSURE MOUNTS

As I'm going through my difficulties there, I'm going on the road trying to basically actually run from God or look for a place. I was confused, dazed, messed up in my head. But I knew pastor Willie Dalgity had Set Free Church in Yucaipa, California, going on. He was doing a great job. So I asked Pastor Willie, I said, "Hey Willie, will you take over the Set Free Worldwide Ministries to give it a covering?" I wanted it to be somebody who I know has the best interests at heart of Set Free Ministries. I can remember Pastor Willie taking it over and having a gathering of people together. I was just letting other pastors know, "Hey, he's taking the wheel for now."

TRINA on whether Pastor Phil's affair contributed to the end of Set Free Anaheim: I don't think that had anything to do with the end of Set Free to be honest with you. The day that Pastor Phil decided to say he wasn't going to be doing church no more, the whole stadium was packed. It was like 3000 people there, and nobody knew they were coming for a last service. (Editor's Note: Pastor Phil indicates there were 6-7,000 people in attendance.)

I really don't think that relationship had nothing to do with it. I think there is a lot of people who didn't like it and didn't like what was going on or whatever they thought was going on or whatever. But I definitely think there was way more people who weren't even thinking about it for sure. The only people thinking about that situation was the inner crowd or the deacons or elders or the people maybe who were trying to look out for Pastor Phil, and he wasn't listening. I don't know, you know?

That was adult conversation at the time. But there was way more people I think Set Free could have continued on if Pastor Phil did not step down that day. A lot of people really were mad that he did and hate him for that. Yeah, I don't think the relationship between them was a downfall. I mean it's his personal downfall, I guess. But not Set Free's downfall.

PASTOR WILLIE DALGITY on the timing of Pastor Phil's departure: It's kind of strange in a way because we hooked up in '93 of May, we got our own storefront building on Yucaipa Boulevard. Just a little 2,500 square foot building. And Phil and one of his guys came up, and they did a little - we did an outreach. They rolled in 50 motorcycles right in Yucaipa. Then, right after that, it all goes kaboom, you know? He's gone. It was kind of weird, but again I kind of knew. I was in communication with him. But before he left he went over to Fullerton, they opened a building up there ,but code came in and popped them. So really, from then on for a while, Phil was kind of out of the deal.

It was awkward, but I'm going to tell you I wasn't angry. There was one thing through all these years is that people told me from the beginning when some of that controversy came down, "Hey, you need to take the Set Free name off." And I said, "Nah, I'm not going to do that because Set Free works." The model that Phil had laid out in just a beautiful way and reaching people right where they are at. We said, "Hey we're not going to drop that. I'm not dropping the name."

Now I'm going to tell you, 20 something years - Phil, anybody can ask him, he knows, he's been up here. He says, "Hey Willie, when I was in rehab, you drove the bus for Set Free," so to speak. But I wouldn't do it, because I know the heart of Phil Aguilar. He is one of the only guys I know that can reach what the Gospel to the outlaws, to the deepest. He wins them to Christ, so I know his heart. All the other stuff, whatever. I'm a pastor too, so I know about people shooting you down. Just go with it.

PASTOR PHIL on hitting the road: In 1993, the turmoil from all the accusations, the allegations coming to me, and my family made me just want to say farewell to ministry. I wanted to get out of there. People are hurting, and people are asking me questions. I got inner turmoil going on in my life. I'm just not right with Jesus at the time. I'm out of my mind.

The next thing you know - when it rains it pours. There were posters being put up all over where I lived. My mom's car, my mom's front door. The posters said, "Beware of these people." Posters showed Lois Trader, her husband, Tim, and myself. "They are not real Christians." I knew the people that were putting them up. They were people that helped me start Set Free. They were people that were leaders in the church.

Paul and Jan Crouch stayed faithful, wonderful, loving friends through it all. That's when I started going to Visalia, going to Pismo Beach, Venice Beach, and all that kind of thing. But Paul and Jan were always back there. They wanted to support me. I ended up at Pomona Set Free doing ministry, and the TV cameras came to me again with Hal Eisner, Channel 13 News. They had Oden Fong saying that I was like Jim Jones or a cult leader.

While that was going on, Paul Crouch decided to have me on TBN again to support me. He pointed his finger into the camera and says, "Calvary Chapels, you better straighten your act out." He knew that the Calvary Chapels were saying all this stuff, putting up posters and doing all this stuff to destroy not just my life, but my family's, my mom, everybody. Going through, and I can remember just like it was yesterday Paul Crouch going, "You know what? I don't know if they are acting like Christians.

We are not supposed to sue our brothers, but I don't know if they are our brothers. If I were you, Pastor Phil, I'd sue the bastards." He came back to say it again, "I would sue the bastards."

HAVE YOU SEEN THESE PEOPLE ?

PHIL AGUILAR / TIM and LOIS TRADER
OF
Set Free Tribe, Set Free Christian Fellowship, Set Free Church
Beware of them!!
They will do and say anything in order to have people join their
Cult like group!!
They speak about Jesus Christ and they claim to be Christians,
but be warned... THEY ARE NOT REAL CHRISTIANS
Phil Aguilar has been run out of every town he's gone to.
Yet, he continues to move from city to city.
He is now attempting to get a foothold in your city
Huntington Beach!!
Tim & Lois Trader hold what they call a "Bible Study.
You may also notice them walking around the pier area... trying
to get people to come.
The Traders are closely tied to Aguilar and have been
instrumental in hundreds of abuses committed against
hundreds of people. Lois Trader has and continues to make
serious threats against ex-Set Free members hoping to silence
us. Both Aguilar and Tim and Lois Trader are not normal people.
They are very dangerous. Please take this as a serious warning!

ELIZABETH AGUILAR BUCHANAN on the animosity toward Pastor Phil and Set Free: We were shocked. People even put flyers in front of my mother's home saying negative things about my brother. She was heartbroken. Yeah, we were shocked, and I have an unconditional love for my brother, there is no doubt about that. But I just saw a man with a heart after God, and I don't know anyone to this day who has taken in the amount of people he has taken in and loved them over and over. Even my own sons. So I was angry. I personally was angry at the people that did that. I was hurt.

To be honest, there are a few of them that I have a very hard time having to see in public to this day. I don't like to see them. I think what they did to our ministry was horrid, and of course we are supposed to forgive, but Set Free is such a wonderful ministry. Phil made mistakes, but I feel like the mistakes could have been forgiven and then moved on. But the way that they did it, people would come to my mom at work and come and tell her what a horrible person my brother was, and no mother wants to hear that. So, it was shock. And to me, that a man from Cavalry who was supposed to be up in the church, high person up in the church and to not really have any solid information would do this to my brother. Yeah, I had a hard time with that.

Pastor Phil and Paul Crouch appear on "Praise the Lord" Trinity Broadcasting Network

174

CHILL on being unaware of the problems with Calvary Chapel: We were very kept away from all that stuff. All the cult busters and the Bible Answer Man or whatever he is, Oden Fong. We never even knew what they looked like. My dad and mom did a pretty good job. They didn't want us to hear all that stuff and see the negative that they were saying or whatever was going on. So we didn't see it. We didn't see it until church was already moved on, and we were in Pomona.

We saw that video of Oden Fong, my dad, compared him to Jim Jones and stuff is on fire. We snuck out and watched it. From then, I think I was about I want to say 15 or 14, somewhere in that area, that changed my life forever. I was angry, I was pissed. It was like something switched on inside of me. I was a pretty loving kid, but I made a point that I'm never going to let nobody disrespect my dad. If I ever met Oden Fong, I would beat the crap out of him. I was so angry, right? I couldn't do nothing for my dad. I watched my dad go into kind of a depression.

It was dark for a lot of years after Set Free had closed down. My dad went on the tour. I always call it the 'manure tour'. We went from city to city, and we were getting chased out. They are putting flyers up of my dad at my little brother's elementary school. The principals are making him leave. Just stuff that we weren't ready for. You don't know how to take that in at 14 or 15. Those are crucial ages to take in that type of stuff. My dad never talked about. Never talked about. Never brought it up. Never said, "Oh yeah, did you see the news? Did you see that?" Never talked about it to us. So we were just all wondering what he was thinking or feeling.

PASTOR EDDIE BANALES on working with Set Free pastors: When Phil decided that he was going to take his little time out, there was five of us at the time that he felt were - he called a big ministries meeting. There was about - I remember it was at my facility. He called a big meeting, there was probably 60 or 70 ministers there. And he just made a suggestion, he said, "Look, I'm done. I need a time-out." I don't remember the exact speech he made, but we all knew. He goes, "I want to nominate five men that I think could continue this journey." I remember I was one of them. Pastor Mike from Bakersfield. Rob Sheltman, God bless his soul, was another one. There was I think - Willie was one of them. I forget who the fifth one was, but there was five of us - Mike from New Jersey.

There was five of us that he pretty much - and then he says, "Because of Pastor Eddie's experience with Assembly of God organization and the little administration knowledge, I'd like him to be kind of like..." He called me the 'Little Pope' at the time. I said, "Well, I don't know if I want to do that," but right away, everybody started clapping and everything.

The next thing I knew, I was kind of like the lead guy of what was going to take place after his little time out. And so I just ran with it the best I knew how organizationally, and that kind of was the beginning of a different journey for me. I didn't realize that there were different lawsuits for properties or different things like that. They didn't come right away.

I definitely ran into a problem where ministers were calling me. I was all over the country checking on churches and pastors - realizing, "You got no business being a pastor. Shut this down now." Some of them were incorporated, some of them were not. Now a mother church - if you become a mother church, there is legalities if you decide to sponsor somebody, you are responsible for them financially and anything else that they do. I wanted them to incorporate, because if you incorporate it's your business and your boards business, not our business. It's like I knew the denominational function. I knew the hierarchy.

So I was known as the hatchet man, because I would not renew licenses and they go, "Well, I'm going to call Pastor Phil." Go call him. If he wants to do it, then let him do it, but I'm not going to renew your license because right now you are living in a garage, calling yourself a pastor in a church. You are living in your mother's garage. That's just not happening. We are kind of falsifying what we are doing here. It looked good on paper but it just wasn't reality. Those were my convictions that I kept pretty strong.

We started going through lawsuits and everything, and I realized that at that time there was everybody after him legally. From personal to people with vendettas - most of them were frivolous, but they were still out there. Once people start circling, there was one lawsuit with a building lease or something like that. They seized my account. They thought he was on it. Praise God, I won the suit and everything. Because Phil was never - again there was five of us that were incorporated individually aside from Set Free Anaheim.

So I decided maybe it's a good time that we don't have to worry about getting tagged every time there is a lawsuit after him. So we changed our name to Center of Hope at that time. My board was tired, I was tired. The fighting financially, legal stuff. Even though they are frivolous, you still have to fight them. I just wasn't at a place at that time to do that.

By that time, I had gone through so much, not to the bad part but try to get it squared off. By that time, he was resurrecting and ready to go. "Here is your baby back," is pretty much what I said. But we always maintained friends. We've never wavered our friendship and our commitment to one another, because I know the man's heart and his family. Our kids, we spent time together as a family and our kids together. They are the same age pretty much. So that's kind of how that transition went.

PASTOR TIM STOREY on the struggles of Pastor Phil: I think what a lot of people felt is in 1993 when things looked like they were imploding is, "See there it goes."Meaning that what happened with Phil Aguilar was probably too good to be true and that he probably did not have the foundation to handle this new fame that he had. And the way I saw it is that, "Wow, now I really want to get to know Phil Aguilar." Because I love people who are working through something. People who understand that we are going through recovery and discovery at all times. So, whatever version of the Phil Aguilar story that somebody bought into, I bought into the version of, "Men of God, women of God sometimes struggle and let's see what this man may need." Not to get back to where he was, but just to get to back on track to what God has for him now.

CHAPTER SIX
THE MANURE TOUR

With a bus load of people and cars trailing behind, Pastor Phil led a team to Visalia, California, to start a new ministry, and the remnant of Set Free splintered into multiple churches - including two congregations founded by assistant pastors Bob Nixon and Wayne Palmer. With pressure from local Calvary Chapel churches, Phil moved his family and the dwindling ministry team from city to city trying to find a place to minister - what Chill has termed "The Manure Tour".

With most of his followers gone, Pastor Phil was on the move once again as his family and a few team members landed in Venice, California, a place where they had ministered on many occasions in the past. At one of Phil's lowest points, Pastor Tommy Barnett reached out to seek his assistance in starting the Los Angeles International Church and Dream Center alongside his son, Matthew Barnett. Phil rallied former Set Free members to move to Los Angeles to start the Dream Center, and his own family was the first to move on the property. As the ministry expanded, so did the friction between Phil and the Barnetts, which resulted in the departure of Set Free from the Dream Center.

After leaving, Phil and his family started "LA Center for the Broken" and hosted school assemblies throughout Los Angeles County in an effort to dissuade drug and alcohol abuse as well as gang activity.

PASTOR PHIL on moving to Visalia: Set Free Anaheim dwindled down to a group of about 300 people meeting in a place called the Training Center. A lot of people were just upset and didn't want to go to church anywhere. They had abandonment issues, because I left them and said goodbye. It was just a small group of a few hundred people, but Bob Nixon was a loyal, faithful servant who said, "Hey, I'll do this." And so he started meeting with them, and I was on the road. I was on the run. I was doing my thing. The last thing I could have cared about was what had happened. I was just trying to get my own life back together.

Now I'm on the road to Visalia, Kern County, trying to run away from my troubles, because all northern California loved Set Free. They were always saying, "Please come back, please come back." I headed on over there. I've got about fifty people in our bus, and I got about a hundred more people following in their cars. They are just following me wherever I go, because one thing that God was doing in spite of my ugly self was he was winning people to Christ. He was touching people's lives in spite of my actions. He was just showing favor for their benefit.

We get up to Visalia. I've got a church that hooks us up with a house. We start doing events at high schools and middle schools, and I mean miracles are happening. Lives are being changed, and then Calvary Chapel Pastor Bob Grenier makes a phone call and says, "Hey listen, if you don't come clean with this, I'm going to have the TV cameras over at your place. We are going to get you out of this town. These accusations, you've got to address all of those to us." I'm going, "Who is this guy?" First I didn't believe it, but the next thing I know, TV cameras are at my house. I said - I'm tired of fighting, and I'm out of here.

Next, we took off to Pismo Beach. The crew started dwindling, and I can remember my wife in Visalia saying, "What's going on?" I shared with my shortcomings with her - my affair - and I let her know, "I'm so sorry I don't even know how to get out of this now. I'm so jacked up. I'm such a mess. I don't know what to do." She was loving me through it or whatever was going on, she loved me, hated me through it. But, we headed up to Pismo Beach, and I was there for a little while. I'm trying to hide out. I'm trying to do ministry at the same time, and then the next thing you know I end up in Lake Elsinore, because I had another friend who had a big property. So I said, "I'm going to set up a Set Free training school up in Lake Elsinore."

I put a little flyer up, and then I got this guy Duncan, Pastor John Duncan. "You are not setting up over here, you're evil." He started passing out flyers around town telling all the pastors, "This guy, he'll get your kids. He's evil. He's a cult leader." I go, "You've got to be kidding me. What's going on here?"

TRINA on Calvary Chapel: When the whole Calvary Chapel thing was going on, I was old enough to know. Especially because everywhere we moved, there would be flyers put up, and we kind of got ran out of all the cities we were in. They were all from Calvary Chapel so it really affected our life, so obviously I knew about it because of that reason. We kept having to move place to place, and basically they didn't physically kick us out but you kind of get forced out because it's just so - they make your life miserable there.

MJ on moving constantly: So just in Anaheim itself, I'm talking about from a young boy as early as I can remember until I'd be 14 years old, we moved through the city of Anaheim a couple dozen times. Different houses, yards, friends houses, trailers, homes, first floor, top floor, first bunk, top bunk, whatever. Just Anaheim.

Then, when Set Free started crumbling and people were left and right leaving, my dad decided to relocate to up north a little bit to a place called Visalia, California. And so we took a small crew which was pretty crazy because again no warning. I didn't know anything. Like, "We are really going to move?" I heard some stuff, but I was just doing outreaches, doing music, traveling at that age. My two younger brothers and sister, we went to a place called Sturgis - which is a big biker rally, probably the biggest in the country - to go ride there, to perform music, and to just have a good time of outreach. We drove on a school bus the whole way there to South Dakota and slept on some speakers. It was a blast. I was a kid, so I didn't mind. While we are there doing that ministry or what I thought was ministry in my mind and heart, it was and still is, my mom was moving my siblings and probably about maybe a dozen other people to Visalia, which is about 3 hours north from Anaheim.

I didn't even know. Maybe didn't even care. I'm with my dad, still all this stuff is going on. The turmoil, the issues and my parents are both literally on opposite sides of the country. Who does that? Who moves like that? Who doesn't talk to their kids about something like that? So while I'm here she is going there. That was the beginning of moving outside of Anaheim. We bounced around. I got them all in my head, but we moved I would say every few months. Everywhere from Lake Elsinore to Pomona to Venice until we landed in Los Angeles. I think we even went back to Anaheim once or twice more before we landed in L.A. working there and starting some new ministry. But we moved a whole lot. It just became what we did.

It also became where people during that time less and less they are like, "Yeah, I think this is my exit." Looking back I can't believe you stayed that long. I mean it was crazy. Who does that? Who moves with 70 people to a city three hours away? Because so many people were still on board. Even though there was so many people that weren't, there was so many people that this was their life. This was all they knew. This was their family. This was their home. My parents were their parents. We were brothers. We were close. But then the next stop and the next stop and the next stop, it really was just our family.

The reason we moved so much - I believe the same issues that were going on, they follow you. I know that. I know my dad knows that, knew that probably more now than then, but you don't like to admit. So I guess we were running. I guess we were on the run in some ways. Looking back on it, I'm trying to think of a more spiritual way to put it, but we were like - it was like we took the show on the road for sure. The circus is moving, we lost an elephant here, a couple people kind of left off, or we took out the trapeze because that was too dangerous.

Now we are kind of just back to some bare stuff which again was fine by me, but my mom wasn't around. Some of my siblings weren't around. There was a core crew, but it was just a different time. So looking back now, I'm guessing it was just, "Hey, that didn't work out. Let's try this spot." "Hey we always had a good relationship over there because we tour and travel to all these places, so let's go to this part of town because we've got some people that have always shown us some love there." But it's different when you are visiting, than when you are staying.

Some of those same people that invite you into their home or their church home - doesn't mean they want you in town every day all day. Especially our crowd. It might just be a little too much. That's why people do those events once a year, because we are a once a year group for them. Not every day. So we were looking for a place probably to rest, too. I'm thinking my dad was just at this time - I'm thinking we are just vagabonds and roaming the earth. "Wait a minute, we've never not really had a home," and now we are looking for one, and in the meantime, people are figuring out what their purpose is. So as they kind of dwindle off, by the time we moved to a place called Venice Beach, California, it was slim pickings. We had a few people, and I'm sure you have or will talk to someone about that. It was a pretty difficult time.

SANDRA on moving: Well, I would say when we went to Visalia and uprooted my whole entire family, my children - that is all they ever knew was that corner of the world. Their cousins and their friends from Christian school. That was the hardest thing to do, but it was the right thing to do. Because he was not in a good place anymore, and he needed to get back on track. So going to Visalia was a godsend. It was very sad, because we were only there a few months when they destroyed it, the cult busters. They destroyed that.

Once again, my children in a humiliating situation had to be uprooted. No finances, because obviously all this money that we had was really nowhere. So no finances. I think we moved to Pismo Beach at that time. Then we were selling stuff just to survive. Then, I got a job with a friend of mine, Anaheim Hills. Pismo Beach and Anaheim Hills is quite a drive. But anyways, so we just went through so many tough times, and we can look back now and laugh.

THE MANURE TOUR

At Christmas, we were just watching this video of one Christmas that we had at this little house that our friend had that let us live there for a little while in Cypress. It was in between Pismo and all that. But literally it was Christmas Eve, Geronimo was there. No more Stacee. That was it, we were a shell of people there, my kids.

They went out for Christmas Eve and brought back tacos or something. My kids are excited about opening gifts. We really didn't hardly have anything. We were laughing because my youngest son - we had these G.I. Joes - you get donations at Christmas time. He kept opening it, and it was the same G.I. Joe - the same G.I. Joe. We went through some really hard times, but the best part about all is we stayed a family unit. My kids saw that I never strayed away. I looked out for them first, and I never let on even when I was in my darkest time - I never let on.

Trina (seated) selling incense at Venice Beach

TRINA on moving: When we first moved out of Anaheim, we moved to Visalia, and we still had tons of people living with us. So it was kind of just normal except different stuff. Like all of a sudden, we opened up some frozen yogurt shop, and that was weird because we never had that kind of thing. And then, each place we moved to, less and less people were with us. That's when I started noticing, "Okay, something is off." Every move we lost people.

Then, when we moved to Venice Beach is when we lived like a lot of people in these two apartments. We lived in the ghetto there. My dad used to have us make incense and sell it on the boardwalk. Seriously. My brothers used to rap out there, that was pretty funny. That's when my oldest brother Geronimo left in the middle of the night one night there. Then, I was like, "Okay, this part of our life is over for sure." Everybody is gone.

183

My dad went through a bad time of not wanting to do church or anything like that. That's when he became 'Chief' when we were there. But honestly, those times never bothered me. I don't mind moving me and all that. That stuff didn't bother me. We had like no money, no nothing. I know everybody thinks we are so rich, but we really had nothing. That's why we were selling incense literally. We had people that this guy John Tully who owned a house Cypress. Every time we were heading over to Cypress, he would let us stay there. But really, we had nothing for awhile.

CHILL on the lack of conversation about the challenges: I don't think my dad talked about a lot of the stuff that was being said about him at that time, because I think maybe he was afraid to approach us with it because we'd be shocked or we'd be like, "Wow, why are they saying this?" We asked him questions, "Is it true dad?" He didn't maybe want to be confronted, and I don't think honestly I just don't think he thought it was appropriate for a 14 year old kid.

These guys forget - all these people who ran their mouths or did that stuff, the kids suffered in all this. It wasn't like they were just hitting my dad. We were kids. I would never do that to people's kids. I wouldn't want to do that. To hurt people intentionally. But yeah, I think he tried to protect us, and that was his way of protecting us, but it kind of backfired, because we started seeing news clippings and hearing about it.

You always hear your parents. Kids always sneak in, and you listen to what your parents are fighting about or arguing about, and we heard the conversations. It would break their hearts - my mom's heart. You can hear her crying. She'd go to her room and cry for days. So you knew that stuff was going on. Everything is falling down around you at the same time. Does that make sense? When it rains, it pours. So it was just from the time my dad told the church, it was just like the rain didn't stop for a decade or two decades. It let up some days where it was shiny, but it's pretty intense times.

My dad didn't even really talk to us. You'd see my dad - he'd look at you and go, "What's up?" "Sup." He was going through it. He was trying to figure out a way. He had a bunch of kids, and he had still people following him. He was trying to take care of people still. He has 200 followers. He was trying to figure out a way to take care of them and feed them. He had nowhere to go. Somebody would say, "Oh, you can come stay here." They would kick him out because they heard - it's weird, weird stuff.

Kelli Moreno selling incense at Venice Beach

KELLI MORENO on moving: I was with Set Free the whole time we were in Anaheim, and then we switched buildings and I don't know what was going on with the city. I was kind of young and naive. I just knew that they didn't want us there. The fire marshals were coming. We had restored this building, and they were going to cite Pastor Phil and, "If you have another service, we are going to arrest you." I mean craziness. We were having church service, and they are going to arrest him. So anyways, so then we ended up doing a lot.

When we left Anaheim, we were I think donated a house in Visalia to live in. It was a gorgeous property on an acre with I don't even know, I want to say we had 60 people maybe. It was a huge house with a huge finished basement, and then we were starting a church there. So I'm not quite sure what happened. We were there for a little while, and then for whatever reason - oh, we opened a skater shop in downtown Visalia, so we were selling skater clothes. Just reaching out to the community. I don't know exactly what happened there or why we moved.

Then he just said, "Okay, we are moving." So the next spot we moved to I think was Grover Beach. I'm not quite sure, but the crowd just kept getting smaller and smaller. So, then we ended up in Cypress, in this small house, and it was probably just 18 of us. Which was his family, which consisted of seven or eight people - all the kids. And then, there was just a few of us. And then in Venice Beach, there was a pastor who had a three-unit place. Then that's when we just ended up moving to Venice. At that time, he had a few people there. Pastor Chip was there, Pastor Jeff and Pastor Phil, there was probably about 25 to 30 of us there.

So we were in Venice Beach for quite a while and then Pastor Phil had told me, "I'm moving to Lake Elsinore. We are moving to Lake Elsinore." I said, "What? Lake Elsinore? No, not Lake Elsinore, right? From Venice Beach to Lake Elsinore." I was like, "Pastor Phil I love you and I love what we are doing, but I don't think I could move to Lake Elsinore." He said, "Alright Kelly, you stay here. Get a place. I'll leave a crew with you, and I'll let you run the incense booths."

I was like, "Alright, okay. I can do that. I said, I need a car though because my car was dying." He goes, "Alright, well you keep a third of the money. You bring me two-thirds of the money. You make sure everything is paid for. You make sure everyone is fed, and we'll make that happen." I said, "Alright, cool. Thank you Jesus." So, that's what happened. He moved to Lake Elsinore. I ended up staying in Venice Beach, and that was kind of it. That was kind of where we parted ways and I did that for awhile and then I ended up moving on with my life, going back to being a hairstylist in Long Beach, and he just kept going from there.

PASTOR PHIL on moving to Venice Beach: Where do I have to hide now? I want to do ministry all the time, but where do I have to hide? Where can I go? A place where I did ministry all the time, where there are thousands, there is multitudes of people and I can just blend in.

In those days, I had a van with a sticker that said, "Trained to Serve Jesus at Set Free." I took that off, and I put on a sticker that said, "Shiznit-faced and pissed off." Then, the license plate I used to have said, "Biker Pas," and then I changed it to, "Chief." Then I had painted underneath, "Of Sinners." I was feeling like the chief of sinners - even the church people were wondering about me. I didn't want to keep defending myself so I was on my way to Venice Beach. Nobody will find me there. By the time I got to Venice Beach, I moved into this gang neighborhood. There is a war going on over there, people are shooting each other, but God was just saying that's what's going on inside of your heart - so look at it.

Then, the Northridge earthquake happened in 1994, so everything's shaking. God is reminding me, all this stuff that is happening on the outside is happening on the inside of you. So there I am, now I'm down to about 30 people. I've got people coming up to visit me. My bikers were coming up to visit me in Venice. They are trying to encourage me and help me. I'm in a public bathroom there in the middle of Venice, and somebody is knocking on the door going, "Pastor Phil, is that you in there? Can you pray for me?" The last thing I wanted to do was pray for anybody. I couldn't pray for myself.

I was as low as you could get. I hated my life and the people that were with me. I felt sorry for them. "Why are you even with me?" I was Johnny Victim. Poor me, I was next to suicide right there. I went from a successful ministry to four of the girls I had with me were selling incense for me on the boardwalk and patchouli and all that kind of stuff.

CHILL on ministry in Venice Beach: You know what? There is always good things that happen even in our darkness and in our madness, in our terrible times and in our ugliness. God still always shines, because we are still His kids.

I always tell people - you gotta understand one thing about my dad and the way he is. He can wake up on the Jesus side of the bed, and the dude is going to win people to the Lord all day long. He is going to help people. Help sick, broken and take them in his home. But if he wakes up on the other side of the bed, which I've seen many years of my life too, on the devil's side, if he wakes up as the Chief and not Pastor Phil, it's on and cracking. He's a very gangster, angry, hardcore, manipulating guy. Just like all of us, we have two sides of us. It just depends what beast you are going to wake up in the morning.

The reality is - even in my dad's darkness and brokenness, the dude still was being used heavenly. He would be there - he was in the bathroom at Venice Beach trying to hide from everybody in church and they'd be like, "Pastor Phil, is that you under there? Can you pray for me?" He was still ministering to people despite of the ugliness and brokenness and the hate in our hearts and his heart. He still was going to start ministries, to pray with people. See God never - just because people are finished with us or Him, God wasn't finished with him yet. So yeah, still had some great memories of being in these places and God doing stuff in dark places.

TRINA on calling her Dad 'Pastor Phil': That's always what I called him. Just he never really answered to dad. I get his attention quicker if I say Pastor Phil, so then it just stuck. I've just always - now I always call him that. And now that he made his name Chief. I don't like that name so I make sure to call him Pastor Phil. He's a pastor, so he should go by Pastor Phil. That's my opinion.

MJ on Pastor Phil's faith at the time: At the time, there was still a good front. I say front, because we were still doing the ministry and the outreach, I don't think he could ever fake helping people or loving people. That's what we were taught. So that was still going on, but it did get less and less. It did get kind of few and far between where we weren't doing the things that fed us, that made us, that even probably gave us all our purpose in life, especially his.

When that came, where he didn't have that and probably his own ego too, the crowd, the numbers, the calls, people weren't looking for you like they used to. I can only imagine in his mind and heart - I know for me it was like, "Alright," it was going maybe backwards in a way. Our calendar was booked and now we are just like a few homies hanging out in front of a house in Pismo Beach, California. I don't know how we landed there - or Cypress, California where we had this little house for awhile. We are sharing a room with six people, and yeah we are doing some stuff still but nothing like we used to. It was pretty crazy at that time. Again you find fun in it, especially at a younger age, because you don't know all the realities yet.

But, his faith was decreasing. His drive that he always had, he was the leader. He was always the mover. The one getting everybody going. Hyping us all up. That was kind of fading away, because the less maybe things to do or be apart of or the people that were super close to him that have signed off - there was a lot of people.

And I can see now because a lot of people were probably closer to his age that were like, "This ain't cool." Or, "That's not us. We don't approve of what you are doing." And the ones that were with us were probably more closer to my age. So yeah, they are easier to convince, to lead, to direct, to just go with the flow, because it's not like everyone had kids or anything like that. And, if they did get a person in their life or a kid, in a lot of ways it was almost like you're done. Your career was over in a lot of ways, because my dad was a mover, and he would leave his own life behind and family behind. So you might be on that list, too.

That was tough, but his faith by the time we got to Venice Beach, his faith was rocked. There wasn't faith. You know how it is - my faith was built on his faith. He's my Mount Rushmore of a guy and a man of faith seeing him have led so many. He got to a point where it wasn't even not going to church or not having faith, it was like the opposite. "I ain't even trying to be a part of that. That's not who I am. That's the old me." He was still running from all of that. So if he's running, I'm just not really caring, and I'm a teenager at this time. So I'm just trying to figure out what life is anyways. So I was doing my own running. My own playing.

I would see my dad at that time - we lived in Venice. We used to rap, and we used to hustle on the beach for change. That was how we made any kind of money. Because we lived in apartments, a two bedroom apartment. All of us. So that's how I'd make money. Just hustling, thieving. It was Venice Beach at that time too, so it's not like how it is now. It was pretty open to be just a kind of a young punk kid. There was a big gang war going on, so we had to ride our bike fast or take alternate routes to get home. We lived right in the middle of the war between Black and Brown. So a lot was going on.

I didn't see him. I didn't know where he was. I honestly don't know where my mom was during that time either. I really don't. There was so many nights where we just come home and be there. It was on us to get fed, or it was on us to make a couple of bucks to buy something or get something. My dad would come by and throw money in our bucket with his few friends that he had left that were probably not the best time at that time. They were like, "Whatever you do," at that time he became Chief. "Whatever you do Chief." It wasn't Pastor Phil anymore ,and that can be dangerous, too. But he would come by, show some love, and that was it. He'd keep moving, and we'd keep rapping. Maybe I'll see you later, and maybe I won't.

CHILL on Pastor Phil's faith at the time: How did I see my dad's faith change and grow over that decade? I really didn't see it. I saw my dad be more guarding his heart. A little more gangster. A little more ready - if somebody wants to take a jab at him, he's going to take one back - but still being a Christian about it. Because he had firepower to say stuff about people too, but he never did. If you watch, he was quiet. He knew that he had done some stuff. He was dealing with it. But he didn't ever like to blame or put it off on somebody or be like, "Well, they did this or they did that." He didn't like that, so we would always tell him, "You need to stand up or say your peace."

I didn't really watch his faith change, because I had so much drama and self-hate going on in my life. We didn't even pay attention. Me and my dad didn't really have any communication. We lived together. We did music together and ministry. But we didn't have no - like I couldn't tell the difference, you know what I mean. I respected he still was doing ministry and got back on the saddle again. But by that time we were so burned out, I only speak for me, but we didn't even care. We didn't even care. Ministry or not.

So I think we didn't really see the change. I saw him become more gangster for sure. More gangster, he was definitely a little more rough. He just went through hell. He'd just been kicked in the teeth by people that he loved. He did kick in, too. Don't get me wrong. He did his kicking. He did what he did, and he had to pay a price. The thing about it - I think he was

TRAINED TO SERVE JESUS

just more like happy to be in the ring again and helping people. But we thought in our minds, we were just over it. I think by the time we hit L.A. or the Dream Center - we were kind of mentally checked out.

PASTOR EDDIE BANALES on connecting Pastor Phil to Pastor Tommy Barnett: When Pastor Phil was ready to get restored, he came back. He was with me in Pomona for a long time. He felt his strength. He felt his legs. He felt his muscles. He was ready to go, and of course, I was the one that introduced him to Tommy Barnett. I said, "Hey, this man respects you. He respects you highly." Tommy was also where Phil - remember Phil had some TBN time. So they kind of knew each other. He goes, "Tell him to call me."

So I happened to meet Tommy. I was sitting outside his office. What they didn't know is that I've been to Pastor's School in Phoenix for 7, 8, 9 years. I happened to be sitting outside his office, looking which class I was going to take. He walks out of his office and goes, "Hey bud, what's going on?" I said, "Hey Pastor Tommy, how are you doing?" He goes, "How long you been here?" I go, "I've been coming here for years. This is the first time I got to meet you." Because if you meet Tommy Barnett in passing in the hallway, you would think he'd make you feel the most special guy in the room.

At the end of the day, I said, "Can I talk to you for a second? There's a guy, Phil Aguilar." He perked and said, "Have him call me. Have him contact me." So I call Phil and say, "Hey, he's willing to see you if you want to contact him."

Phil was with me at the time. They opened up the Dream Center in L.A. the following year, 1995. He goes, I went with my Gangster Grace ministry, Phil took Set Free Ministries there. We connected there, and then a couple of years later I got the Dream Center buzz and changed my name from Center of Hope to Southern California Dream Center. I got a little letter on file from Matthew Barnett, thanking me for my support from Tommy, too. And also the thank you for - the blessing of being a Dream Center. Because they were starting them all over the country. Actually, people were calling themselves Dream Centers because of the vision and the mission. So that's kind of where that went.

PASTOR PHIL on getting a call from Pastor Tommy Barnett: After about four months there, I got a phone call from Pastor Tommy Barnett who invited me to come and be part of a place called the Los Angeles International Church and Dream Center. Here I am, off of my hate, and

THE MANURE TOUR

Pastor Tommy has invited me to be part of this place called the Dream Center. He had been a friend of mine for years, and he really respected my ministry and the biker ministry. He says, "Come out there." Little did I know what I was walking into, because when I went out to East L.A., the Echo Park area. He had a church called the Bethel Temple and about a dozen homes that were given to him by the Assemblies of God. All they had was his son and about 15 Filipino members, because all of his group, the Master's Commission, went back to Phoenix, Arizona, because L.A. is scary. Gunshots and all that stuff.

This kid, Matthew, bold young kid and just a teenager at the time - he was basically left alone there. Pastor Tommy was helping me at a tough time, rented me a house right across the street from the church. I just started doing what I do – reaching out to the neighborhood. I set up a basketball court, and I started working with the gang members. Nobody was coming to church much, so Pastor Tommy asked me, "Hey you got a band?" So I brought the Set Free band together. I said, "Hey Pastor Tommy, I got a rap group too, Set Free's West Coast Flava." "Well I don't know about that, but let's try it out." He saw it week after week as our band, our music started happening, and the place started to fill up.

It was about a 900-seat facility, and within 6 months, we had a revival where Pastor Tommy was preaching Thursdays. I was preaching Saturday nights. Pastor Matthew was preaching Sunday mornings. We were the three pastors. I was the Outreach Pastor of the church. The three of us got together, and it was a revival. It was God moving. Filled up. We had a Pastor's School there. The whole block we bought off. Now these homes that were there, I taught him how to do 'Adopt-A-Block'. I taught him how to do discipleship homes by taking people of the streets and putting them in there and put them as part of the working ministry. It was beautiful.

I can remember Tommy taking me to this place called the Queen of Angels, and the two of us looked at that building and he goes, "I'm not going to get this place unless you'll come in as a pastor here. If you commit to help me and my son Matthew here." I looked at that big ten-acre, 50-story building with about 40 rooms in it and I said, "Yeah, we can do this." The three of us made a commitment, and we pioneered. I was the first one to move on that Dream Center campus with my family. I had 100 volunteer staff to come on from Orange County from Set Free Ministries. We fixed the kitchens, the plumbing. I took the bus out to Skid Row, and we got it going.

MJ on the Dream Center: Yeah, we lived in Anaheim right before we moved or got the call to go to Los Angeles. I remember going over there with my dad on a little tour. He's like that - he doesn't say a lot. Every time even as kids, we'd drive somewhere and just enjoy the ride. "Where you going?" "To the moon." Crazy, all that dumb dad stuff. And he's still the same way, and he was at that time where I'm like, "Oh cool, L.A. Right on, we've been to L.A. for years doing some work and ministry, rapping, having fun." But we were walking around and he's like, "Oh yeah, this is going to go on." There was this old church called Bethel Temple that Phoenix First Assembly, Tommy Barnett and Matthew Barnett had. So they got that first before they got this big old hospital that they renovated called the Dream Center. So that was the beginning of it.

There was a house right across the street from this little church, right off Sunset in a cool part of Echo Park. He would show us around, but he never told us that we were moving there still. Then about a week later, we end up moving to that same place. Now we come from Anaheim, and the hood moved in with me. Usually you are like, "Hey don't go out. You are going to get - ." No, they all lived with me, so it wasn't about that. Drug addicts, gang members you name it. Prostitutes they lived in my house. So that wasn't nothing new, but here we went to Los Angeles which is where everything started. The riots happened not long ago and gangs and drugs and you name it. Its Los Angeles.

So we moved into the heart of it, but once we moved there, it was pretty cool because we were getting back into ministry though. We were doing more outreaches and rapping. This was like another kind of lease on life for my dad. He was very excited. Again, he was busy and gone doing a lot of stuff. But we did a lot more stuff together because I was a little older at that time. Very involved in music. Very involved in the industry. We lived in L.A. - so if you are into music, that's the place. It was pretty cool.

It was almost two separate things, because there was pastor Matthew Barnett and his family and all of them that would come from Scottsdale, Arizona. So they would come to visit or come when the church was, but then you wouldn't see him for the next week. We lived from here to across the street. That was our life. We lived there. So at that age I'm like, "Where is this dude go?" It seems like he just kind of shows up when the camera is on or shows up when there is someone to feed or a story to tell or a sermon to preach. Which wasn't the worst thing in the world. I wasn't mad, but I just know what we are doing.

That's why Pastor Tommy Barnett called my dad and our crew to do. He knew we had what some would call a ghetto past to be in that part of the street. Scottsdale is not the most ghetto place in the world, but we had that. That was one of our things that we've had for years doing ministry. That took us to a different part of the world. So that helped him, and he knew that would help his son because you can have a dream, but does your dream have security? Does your dream dodge bullets? So he brought my dad and crew in to protect his son and his dream that he had one night in Scottsdale. So it was very cool. There was a lot of cool things that I loved in that time in Los Angeles.

CHILL on the Dream Center: The Dream Center, some call it the 'Scream Center'. The Dream Center, man, Matthew Barnett was a little kid. They asked my dad to come, and we came. We are from Orange County so it was definitely a culture shock. Gang members on every street and corner, throwing gang signs at you acting hard. So we had to get tough real quick, me and my brothers. Because my dad was doing ministry and we dealt with the hoodlums. My dad made programs for the hoodlums and the gang members, which are now our friends. We made lifelong friend-ships with some of these guys until this day.

But yeah, Matthew Barnett, we just saw him as a white nice kid. Didn't know nothing about the streets, which was cool. We were all like a family for a little while. Matt and Tommy, they would hug me and tell me they loved me. At that time, I didn't really believe anybody when they said that, but it was very influential the Dream Center. Because we were doing ministry, and it was fun and we got to run through the hallways. It was like being a kid again. Like when we were eight or nine running through the church hallways and going through people's stuff to make sure they didn't have cigarettes. It was like living that again, but now the main focus wasn't my dad, and he wasn't the main guy.

It was these two white guys, Tommy and Matthew - they were amazing at - they were good salesmen. We had kind of already seen past the BS, so we were kind of joining another circus. Does that make sense? Doesn't mean that people weren't getting saved and God was using us, but I believe that they used my dad up and that was another rough thing to watch. My dad could have said, "Hey, I need this or I need that," but my dad is that guy. He is just happy to be on a team again. So the Dream Center was great, and a lot of people got saved. But I think that was really rough time again for my sister and my brothers and a lot of us started being attracted to the gang mentality. Started dressing like the gang members. I started being like, "Yo, wassup homes." I wasn't even a real Mexican, I'm half Sicilian, half Mexican. I was talking like a cholo.

TD Jakes would be there, Casey Treat, all these big shots. So I was like, man, pops is back in the saddle. There is a little bit of hope left in us. You wanted to believe, man, this can be our time. We are going to be okay now. We are going to be okay. And Tommy would be there, and I'd come up like a gang member walking slow, big old pants creased down. We attracted what we respected, and we respected the gang members at that time because they were kind of like our safe place. I know it sounds weird, but they embraced my dad, they didn't judge him. Because they were doing bad stuff, so they didn't judge him. They loved us where they are at. They didn't know about church. They just knew, man, these people love us where we are at, too. So it's equal respect.

So we would bring all the gang members to church and Tommy would bring me up there and be like, "We found this kid. He was in a gang." I'm like, "My dad is Pastor Phil." But he'd be like, "Just go with it. His dream was broken." Then the crowd goes crazy. And then again, I look around and think damn, I'm part of another freaking circus. I'm not getting paid.

So it was very fun time, but again I was 15, 16 at that time so I got a little bit smarter. A little more knowing, like, "Wait a minute. Wait a minute. Pops, why is he doing all the work and this white boy, God bless him, is getting all the credit? Why is he staying in Bunker Hill?" that's downtown L.A., rich area, "And we are here at the nuns' quarters on the campus and there is gunshots going off and gang members jumping up and down the street?" Jumping fences in Rampart District. It was like chaos.

I'm just grateful to the Lord that we survived. If it wasn't for the Temple Street gang down there, we wouldn't have survived, because they protected us many times. Because we didn't know where to stand. We are in our living room, they tell my mom - they call her Miss Sandra, "Don't sit in that chair, that's where the window is. They'll shoot you, drive bys." So the gang members saved our - God used them as our angels. But with that they taught us, don't let anybody disrespect you. Don't let nobody disrespect your dad. You throw punches and fight either way, win or lose. Don't let nobody push you around. So that was in our brain. And our thinking was to defend my dad.

TRINA on the Dream Center: It didn't turn around until he met Tommy Barnett whose son was going to start a church in Los Angeles for inner city people. Pastor Phil was the perfect guy to think about when you are doing something like that. We actually all moved to Angelino Heights which is right by Echo Park. We moved in there, and just did what we did best, started meeting the neighborhood people. We started church there, and we helped Matthew get the whole thing going. I know nobody gives him credit for that, but we were the ones who moved there. People from our ministry, that still liked my dad at the time, moved their whole families out there and everything to help it get going.

Then they got the Queen of Angels hospital and, we actually lived on the property there and got the whole church going. My dad's secretary was a big part of it. All of the people that moved, we had I think maybe 25 families that moved there with us. That's when we started performing at schools and doing part of the Impact Program. My brothers and we had a group of people breakdancers, and we started getting like we did back in the day. We started growing. And then I guess they didn't like it, because it was kind of becoming where people were thinking of the Dream Center as Pastor Phil and not Matthew Barnett. So I think that's probably why it didn't work out. Then, we went on a moving spree again.

PASTOR PHIL on his departure from the Dream Center: It was going strong, but Set Free started becoming pretty strong in the campus, and I think it just got a little bit mixed up on their stuff. Because Set Free has got a little bit different flavor than the vanilla flavor they had. We had a little Tapatío in the mix, too.

But, Pastor Tommy pulled me out and put me back on a good path, and I love him forever for that. Matthew is just the greatest young kid. It was a beautiful thing, but it was time for me to move on for many different reasons. So I've got much love for them, but it was time to go.

PASTOR EDDIE BANALES on the challenges at the Dream Center: In my opinion, Phil Aguilar is the type of person that he is like, "Look, I know how to get homeless people here. Drug addicts here. Homosexuals here. Street people here. But I'll catch them, you clean them." That was kind of what I remember. Now there are still to this day people in the church that think you can pray over them, lay hands over them, anoint them with oil, and they are fixed. That is such falsehood. I've been pastoring 25 years, three years as an associate, saved over 30. I'm telling you the truth. And in some cases, it does happen, there are those divine moments. But Phil was bringing them in left and right.

Well, guess what? They still had their cigarettes, they still had their little meth, they still had drugs that the men would sneak. Why do you think I have a men's home here and women's home somewhere else? Because men will get with women, and they are two wet noodles, but they will still try to get together even though they can't hold each other up. But they will still try to get together. So in that case, that's what the Dream Center became. They had hospital rooms. They had all that building there. So Phil was bringing them in. They were busing them in to feed them on Saturday. They were doing all this kind of stuff, but for a lot of people, it was just too chaotic. It wasn't churchy enough. Maybe it wasn't holy enough. And again, I don't judge nobody, but I've been in that situation as a pastor, and you bring in a bunch of people that are paying the bills want to know, "Hey, what's going on back there in that back pew?" It can be tough.

I saw that being a challenge where maybe he was feeling boxed or not feeling like, "What more do you want me to do? I'm bringing them in." And then again, at the same time, the establishment there had a responsibility to do whatever they wanted to do as far as - no, no, no. What do you want to do? Hire security guards? Thats kind of what in a nutshell. I think that Phil just felt like he was not free to do what he loved to do. He brings you to Jesus.

Even in me and his relationship he goes, "Eddie, I'll catch em, you clean em." But I was okay with that. I was okay with taking the time to counsel. I was okay taking the time to mediate and do that, because that's the true pastor's heart of me. And even where I'm at today, I'm more like an evangelist, and I take it to my staff now, "Hey, you clean em. I've been cleaning them for a long time." I love to witness and bring them to church. I got a men's home, I got a women's home, but guess what? I've got a staff now to deal with that. Where before it used to be just me. I was the staff.

So I just think it came to that point, where it just came to a head where there was just too much going on. I just think they came to an agreement. Probably after a couple of meetings, they came to an agreement or an understanding that, "Maybe this isn't working for me. Maybe this isn't working for you. It's time to move on."

Phil Aguilar, Benny Hinn, Matthew Barnett, Tommy Barnett

THE MANURE TOUR

MJ on why Set Free left the Dream Center: Because my dad is my dad. Because he's not going to change certain things about him and because it got divided. We know that division, especially in a ministry, a church, it's killer. So we were doing so much great work, but it was becoming known for Pastor Phil and Set Free. Yeah, it was called the Dream Center. Yeah, we knew the Barnetts were behind it, and they would come for Thanksgiving. We'd wave and give out turkeys. Him and Benny Hinn would bless the crowd.

That was awesome, but we were the ones who were - we lived on the property. We lived in the nuns' convent on the hospital property. We lived right there, so how could they not know us? The other guy goes to his apartments downtown, and we are there. I mean I'm talking about like every member of any kind of neighborhood in the area, and that's a pretty serious area as they consider it for gangs. Every homeless person, you name it. Everyone with need. Everyone from Skid Row. We had a big Skid Row bus ministry. All of them knew Pastor Phil and Set Free for what we did. We always tried to pump the name, Dream Center. But they just always know and see who they see.

So from that time, they were trying to bring in other people from their church - from other parts of Arizona and their things - to make their presence felt and do things. But things that work in Scottsdale or even at a certain church, didn't work in the heart of Los Angeles and this community. We maybe didn't mesh sometimes. Again Pastor Phil is Pastor Phil.

So it became divided, where we did a Pastor's School one time at Phoenix First Assembly, the church of Pastor Tommy Barnett. This is like the mother church. We owe a lot to them, but as a youngster I didn't really care. When the lights went out, we were just messing, clowning, pillowcase just bombing on people. I was young, so we were being punks, but it was divided.

All the work we do, and you guys aren't appreciating it. You are looking at it. I'm there in the streets and in the neighborhoods and in the schools, and these guys know our names, and they are at my house. I'm giving them my clothes and letting them be in my house and possibly steal my stuff - which happened many times. Let us just be, let us do our thing. It just got so much. So much conflict, and we are still sharing the same house. I think it got to the point where I think my dad was over it. Pastor Tommy Barnett, who pretty much called the shots, was over it and wanted to just not have to deal with it. As much as we did cool things, they just didn't want to deal with it.

CHILL on the end of their time at the Dream Center: Why did the Dream Center thing end? I don't know. I thought we were going to be forever. I heard Tommy and Matthew tell me, "We are family. We love you. You are the best." I don't know why it ended. Honestly, we never really sat and talked about it - me and my dad.

I know that they started letting a lot of cops and different law enforcement on the campus, and we were working with a lot of gang members and people that may be broken or have issues with the law that needed to go to court or they had tickets or whatever. So my dad's thing is - we don't want to let the cops on here full-time, because we work with broken people. It's like having a hospital full of sick people and saying, "Okay, you can't have any patients here no more." A lot of the patients would have ran.

So the cops, God bless them, they are doing their job, but unfortunately we had a crooked Rampart District scandal going on where they are beating up gang members, beating up people, planting drugs on them. So it made it very hard to do what we do when you got a bunch of cops there breathing down people's necks. I think it ended bad, because my dad probably didn't communicate with them what he wanted, and they didn't want him as - my dad started being the figurehead of the Dream Center.

Everybody that came knew my dad was the guy. My dad's church would have a thousand people on a Saturday night. Tommy's son, Matthew Barnett, would have 50 people. It started becoming pride. And everything they said they weren't going to do, they ended up being. "We love you. We are not going to get prideful" - and everybody gets prideful. I thought we were all on the same team, but as we started looking around, we realized we are there eating beans and rice, and they are eating five-star dinners after church with their big pastor friends. We started realizing, we are just the help. We are nothing. That's fine, but eventually I'm sure my dad got tired of helping promote their thing and not be supported by them. But, there is other things that happened between them two that they only know, so I don't know. My dad I'm sure was hard to deal with, too. I'm sure.

PASTOR WILLIE on his challenges with Pastor Phil: If I could, let me just share this. In 1997, Phil had pretty much had it. Lois Trader, who was his secretary at that time. She sent me a letter and said, "We would like you to take leadership of Set Free worldwide for awhile while Phil - ," they were kind of going in different directions. So, I agreed to that, and we also took leadership of Servants for Christ, their motorcycle ministry.

Phil, he came back in, he was in Hollywood. Doing that little place up there in Hollywood, you know? So he was just kind of feeling his way. This was really after he had helped pioneer the Dream Center. But it was after that time about a year later, Phil he took back leadership of Set Free Worldwide.

Me and him in about 2000 - there was some things going down, and we kind of didn't agree on some things. You know Phil. Phil is really just - he just says it like it is. So we kind of disagreed for a little while about some things. But even in that, I would never, ever jump on that bandwagon of attacking Phil. We were just like in any family, siblings can have fights and kind of be on the outs for awhile. But we kind of re-engaged several years ago where we really became again really good friends. But we never left the fold, okay?

Phil, he'll do some things sometimes and has done, they are really controversial. They hit the media. I know he doesn't do this purposely and say, "Well this is going to get on everybody else" - but it does. So anything that happened in Orange County, I have to deal with here. So there was a tension in that, because I was saying, "Hey man, I've got to take some steps and do this - ," but I wasn't jumping off the thing. But he thought, "Hey man, where you at? You need to stand with me." I said, "I am, but there are certain things we have to do what God's given us to roll on out here with." But as I said, before too long, we were back. He came up and kissed me right on the mouth at one of our events.

PASTOR PHIL on the lawsuit brought by three women: After the Dream Center, I was doing a ministry called "L.A. Center for the Broken" with Lois Trader - speaking to all the kids in all the high schools, anti-drug movement. Everything is going good, and then in 1998, I got a letter, a subpoena that I was being sued by three women from Set Free from back in the early '90s. I knew who all three of these women were real well. I'd taken care of their lives. I'd taken them on trips. I brought them out of terrible situations, but now they were suing me. So, for the next 18 months, me and two of my friends from the ministry were having these lawsuits, and we were just being sued for millions of dollars.

The biggest charge was that I was a cult leader and that I'd made them have separation anxiety from their children. Took away their belongings. Wouldn't let them go anywhere they want to go. That I was just a cult leader and that I got money from them. All of it was just so far from the truth, but here they are. I just believed that they thought they could get me to make a settlement or give them some money because of what had happened in the Colleyville, Texas, case with TBN. When that happened and somebody charged something against Set Free Ministry and TBN, Paul and Jan and them said, "No, we have to pay them. We have to make a plea agreement with them." I said, "Let's fight it." I wanted to fight it, but I didn't understand how it works when you are big ministry like that. You'd rather just do a little hush money to say the least.

I endured 18 months of going to trial, deposition after deposition, them saying all this negative stuff. During that time, one of the girls ended up in a hospital - she had an overdose. One of my nurse friends saw her there, and we saw what was going on with her life. Another one of the girls called my attorney and asked, "Hey, can you guys just give me $10,000, and I'll drop out of this court case." That wasn't going to happen. Then with the third one, someone I know said, "This girl that is suing you, she's a stripper in our strip club over there." By their lives, I could tell they were looking for money, and they thought that they could get it from me. I had insurance from the old days, but I didn't have any personal money.

After 18 months, finally we get in front of the judge right before they are getting ready to pick the jury. The judge asked the attorney, "Can you give me what your opening statements are going to be so I can see what this case is really based on?" She said what a bad guy I am. I'm a cult leader, because she followed up with all the allegations, the Jim Jones, the Guyana stuff.

The judge goes, "Now, does Pastor Phil let you leave if you want to leave?" They go, "Well, yeah." "Does he have electric fences where he keeps you in?" "No." "So you are there of your own volition? Your own will? He feeds you, takes care of you, but you can leave anytime you want?" The attorney for them says, "Well, yeah." He goes, "What's this separation anxiety from the children?" "Well at nighttime all the women have to work the telephones at TBN counseling people, and their kids are at home being babysat by other ladies." The ladies told the judge when they go to work at TBN that their babies cry.

The judge goes, "You mean the kids cry when you leave them? That happens at daycare centers all across America." So, the judge just threw it all out. There isn't any reason for this case to go forward and threw it out, because it was just for money. Later on, the one lady who was really spearheading the lawsuit came to my church on a Saturday at Buena Park around 2005-ish. At the altar call, I saw her walk forward with a bouquet of flowers to give to me and my wife. She says, "I'm sorry for that lawsuit. I just needed money. That's why we all did it. We needed money." She said she was sorry, and she ended up becoming a part of Set Free Ministries again.

I had people that saw her walk up to me, and they said, "That sad girl. She got you to court. She had these newspaper articles that you did this and you did that. Should we throw her out of here?" I go, "No, God has forgiven me for so many things. Those who have been forgiven much, love much." So, I just loved her right back in. That's the way Jesus taught me how to do it.

TRAINED TO SERVE JESUS

CHAPTER SEVEN
SET FREE SOLDIERS

Pastor Phil started a new Set Free Church, and after multiple moves, the church began meeting on Saturday nights at First Southern Baptist Church of Buena Park, California. With his sons, MJ and Chill, now leading the music and dancing, the church continued to grow under the leadership of Pastor Phil.

Meanwhile, Servants For Christ motorcycle ministry was growing older and losing steam in the eyes of some, so a new motorcycle ministry / club was formed under the name Set Free Soldiers. With great attention placed on this group of men, other Set Free members began to feel slighted. Although the church was outgrowing the space, Pastor Phil chose to move the ministry to a new location and host a gathering that was more exclusive and centered around the Set Free Soldiers. In addition, the Aguilar family opened a bar called Club Roc in Costa Mesa, California, where his son, Roc, could promote bands and host events.

The Soldiers caught the attention of other motorcycle clubs through their black bikes, unified look, and strong presence, and a prominent publication named them the only Christian 1% club in the nation. At the same time, A&E began production on a show called "Saints or Sinners" featuring Pastor Phil and Set Free Soldiers at the center.

CHILL on starting another Set Free Church: We were in L.A. and in 1997, we moved back to Anaheim, which I didn't want to go back to Anaheim. I was like, "Oh, heck no." We still knew a lot of people didn't like us there, too. But now we are a little bit grown, we've put some size on. I said, "Well, if we go back at least, we already know if somebody talks about my dad, I'm just going to punch him in the face." Forget all this, we are going to pray for them and all that. At least for me, I was so not walking with the Lord. I was so insane, so angry and depressed at that time in my life.

I did not want to go back to Anaheim, but we went. And then my dad started doing church again in his backyard. How he does. He went from five people me being in charge of doing music. This is terrible. Those are crucial years, too. My dad started doing ministry and the backyard started getting filled. I'm like how is this guy filling - this is 7 or 8 years later - how is he getting more people? The whole backyard was filled, so he needed a building. So we met at another building in Westminster, California. He packed that place out and God was doing it again. We were like, "Whoa, this is crazy." All new characters. Some older people that were from the old days, but a lot of the old regime was gone. New people, new fire. My dad was - I think he was still not the guy he was, but he still had some fight in him left. He still did what he did, and people loved him.

So from there, we went to Wiley Drake's. Wiley Drake is crazy. I have nothing - anything good about the guy. Try to love him like Jesus, but that guy is nuts. He probably know he's nuts. He lives off of people. That is his game. He knows he's crazy. He likes that.

We get there, right? First church service - he parks a big truck out front with an aborted baby on it. A billboard of aborted baby. I tell my dad, "What is this? This is nasty." It said, "Stop Abortion." Which I understand he is trying to stand for someone, I'm not hating on that. I was just like - this is not us. That's not Set Free. We are not trying to judge nobody - put nobody down.

Man this guy was nutty. My dad would be preaching, and he'd walk on stage, "Hey brother, I got something to say," and grab the mic. "Check my radio station." I'm like - what radio station? This was on the Internet, but this was before the Internet was real popular in like 2000. We'd be like, "Get this guy out of here." Me and my brother Turtle - we are going to grab this guy and choke him out, because he would get up on stage and it was his building, but my dad just rented it. So my dad is super nice.

My dad loves crazy people as you can see. He hangs around people that aren't all there in the brain. Wiley Drake is just a radical. I'm not saying he's a bad guy, but for us, "This guy is loopy." I don't get it. He would just show up with his pants real high and suspenders. Is this guy from the South? From the 1400's? He would come in, and he had that accent. I don't have too much good thing to say about Wiley Drake. I never really liked the guy. I'm just being honest. I don't have to love him like Jesus. But if we are being honest, I just don't get his whole deal.

We rented from him, and my dad blew up that church, too. We had 600 or 700 people. We were doing all the music now. So I was at least happy. Now this is our time. Me and my brother, we are running it. This ain't like the old days where we were just kids, "Hey, get off stage." We are nine or ten. Now we are in our 18, 19. We are men. This is our home, and we are never going to let anybody disrespect my dad again. We are going to stand up. We watch all these so called friends of his run away and not stand up for him. We are like, "We are going to stand up for him" - all my brothers made a pact and my sister. We are going to stand up. Then, we started bringing our friends. It was a whole new generation, but unfortunately it was a more crazier group of people that we brought around.

Pastor Phil baptizing in his backyard in Anaheim, CA

PASTOR PHIL on starting Set Free Buena Park: After my lawsuit was finished around 1999-2000, I moved back from L.A. and was living right in Anaheim on Katella and 9th Street. I had a friend called Wiley Drake, and I knew him, because he was a Baptist preacher - very outspoken and running for president all the time. Crazy, wonderful time. I saw Wiley had an open Saturday night, so I started Set Free Saturday night church, and the place just started jumping off. Got our band, got our Posse. Just got rocking and rolling again.

PASTOR WILEY DRAKE on inviting Set Free to host services at First Southern Baptist Church of Buena Park: It was pretty obvious they needed a place, and Phil said, "Wiley, I understand you are a pastor over in Buena Park, and you've got a church. How much do you use it?" And I said, "Well, we use it quite a bit." "Well, how about on Saturday?" "No." So that's when he approached me with a possibility. "Well how much would you charge us to rent your church?" I said, "We don't rent the church. It's God's church. If you want to come, come on down. Lights are on, and we keep the light bill paid. You are welcome to come." So they started coming. And I, in all honesty, didn't know really what to expect. The first Saturday night there were about 50 motorcycles parked here on the street, and I'm getting calls from the police department asking, "What is going on down at the church Wiley? You've got all these motorcycles, gang-bangers." And I said, "No, we don't have gang-bangers. We've got Set Free."

So we basically opened our church up about 2002 and said, "Ya'll can come every Saturday." They came once and awhile to other services, but by and large, they would come here. They would start showing up three or four o'clock in the afternoon on Saturday. Motorcycles would start coming, and then along about 6 o'clock or so they would do a worship service in our sanctuary. Packing it out. Our sanctuary seats about 300 comfortably, they would bring in 400 or 500, but they liked that, and we liked that. So that is where and how we started.

They were here up until 2007, that's the last year they were here with us. Contrary to what some of the media says, Phil did not get mad at me and leave. Nor did I get mad and Phil and run him off. We came to a mutual understand. He came to me and said, "Wiley, we are outgrowing your building, and we need to go somewhere else. We've decided that we are not going to try and find another bigger building. What we are going to do is go to a smaller building and sort of cut back and go a different direction." So that's what happened. Thats' where they went in about 2007.

REGINALD "FIELDY" ARVIZU on going to Set Free Buena Park: When I was growing up, I didn't have any type of anything period but running the streets, riding dirt bikes, and playing music. That's all I had in my life, period. When my family divorced and everything kind of fell apart, later in life my dad ended up giving his life to Jesus and he was really cool about it and kind of just laid back and didn't say much because I think when he did, I would kind of attack on him. I don't even

Pastor Phil and Fieldy

know why, but I'd flip out. So he kind of just put it aside and would just love me and hang out.

And then when he went in 2005 to be with the Lord, his wife, she's like, "Hey, do you want to go to this place that your dad used to go to?" She kind of played it all low key. I said, "Yeah, sure." So I went over there, rolled up with all these hundred bikers out front. I was like, "Whoa man, am I going to get beat up?" I didn't know what this place was, and I kind of walked through the line, and everybody was really nice and shaking my hand. It was just awkward for me. I walked in the door and they were like breakdancing and rapping, and I was like, "Whoa, this is crazy." I didn't know. I sat down, and I was listening. They were rapping, but they were rapping about Jesus and all these songs about love, and I just started crying. I was bursting out crying.

At that point, I thought I was the toughest dude in the world. Then Phil walks out. I didn't even know what a Pastor was. He came out, and he had sunglasses on and tattoos everywhere and a tank top. I was like, "What is going on?" He started preaching, and it was all love. If anybody knows anything about Phil - I've only in my whole life met maybe 5 or 10 people that are like him. They are like positive encouragers. I was blown away.

That's what his message was. It was very positive and love and I was like, "Whoa, I've got to meet this guy." I went a couple of times, and then I finally went up and introduced myself and he goes, "Oh, you play in that band Korn." I could tell that he didn't know who I was and I said, "Yeah." He then said, "Your dad used to come in here and ask me to pray for you all the time." I was like, "He did?" I remember walking up and thinking, 'My dad used to hang out here?' I was tripping out. That is part of my dad that I didn't know. That's how I met him. I just kind of walked up after a few times of seeing him and just said, "Hi."

JOHN "QUICKY" JUAREZ on moving in with Pastor Phil: A friend of mine took me there, a guy named Top Hat. He said, "Come on, let's go here. There is a lot of pretty women there." I said, "Church? Come on man." He goes, "Come on." So we went to Set Free, and I got to listen to this man share a story. And he spoke in a language that I understood. He wasn't like doing all that stuff, and he wasn't going to dunk me. He allowed me to listen to the message. He said something, he said, "Look, if the shoe doesn't fit, what I'm sharing, don't wear it." I got it.

So I didn't go back for a long time. That was interesting. I went through some trials and tribulations in my life, and I started hanging out with him a little bit. Getting to know him and going to church. And then I started bringing more of my brothers to church. We used to fill up three aisles with Vagos then listen to him.

I loved his message. I loved the music. He taught me just by listening. He taught me that I can be who I am and still have the love that I have for God, and I don't have to change. Changes will happen within. People tell me all the time when they meet me today, they go, "Man, you are not the same guy. You are not that guy that - ." I got a patch for my own charter, my own club, it's called "Scandalous," because according to them I was even more scandalous than they were. I just laughed about that. I don't know if I deserve that, but I guess I was kind of a devious little guy for a long time.

The more I went to church, the more comfortable I started feeling with myself. I went through a bad marriage. I didn't know what to do. I married - here's my best thinking, I'm 50 and I married a 23 year old, right? She broke my heart, and I didn't know what I was going to do. I moved in with Phil. He moved me in, and I hung out with him for close to a year, and I was celibate. I'd always pick a women to fill the hole, the God spot. I was celibate and from there, I learned a lot.

Like I said I lived with him close to a year, and in that year, I did things I never thought I'd do. I'd stand out there, and I'd go with him - because they would go places and share the ministry, and I was there and I did that. I worked at a place called V Twin City, and I rode my bike to work everyday, came home and was blessed. Things happened in that year that were magical. When I left there, I really had no place to go.

What happened after 13 years of being abstinent, after I got out, left Phil's, I went to a bar to watch some friends of mine play pool I thought. Somebody came by and said, "Do you want a beer?" See, I can't eat one potato chip, what makes me think I could have a beer? What happened was, I drank that beer and for me at the bottom of every bottle of beer like a Mescal worm is a sack of dough. So I drank that beer, I was okay. The next day I came back, I drank another beer. The next thing you know, I was drinking hard liquor. Next thing you know, I was smoking weed. The next thing you know, I was running. God saved me one more time. I did for about 5 or 6 months, and I wound up back in the rooms at Narcotics Anonymous. Then, I started going to church religiously at Set Free.

TURTLE on getting clean at Set Free: So in 1998, like I said a little history, I had a great family. I'd love to tell you my family was disheveled or I grew up in this whole gang life and that type, but it's not true. I had a great family. My dad was my best friend. He was my hero. He was my everything. We did everything together. In 1998, he was taken from us, July 26, 1998. That was the day that my life changed I used to say for the worst, but now I'm realizing what God had for my life, it was actually for the better. I just found myself in a spot, hooked on heroin, getting busted.

My mom kicked me out of the house. Running with the homeboys, that's what I was doing. I remember I was actually living on the streets in the back of my homeboy's car - the back of his truck. We were strung out like dogs. I remember waking up one day, this was in 2001 or 2002, I had overdosed multiple times. I just woke up and knew, "Hey man, this isn't the way my dad raised me man. I got to do something." So I told my homeboy, I was like, "Yo man, this ain't me man. I got to do something otherwise I'm going to end up doing a long stretch in prison or next time I overdose I might not come out of it." And he said, "Hey man, remember Pastor Phil?" I was like, "Yeah man, I remember Pastor Phil." He goes, "We could go there."

At that time, I had nothing so I was willing to try anything. Sure enough, he was right here on Archer Street, 305 South Archer Street. We pulled up, and he was in the middle of a house meeting, and one of their house managers came out, asked us, "What's up? What do we need?" I just told him, "I need a place to stay. I need a program. I need to get clean, and I need to talk to Pastor Phil." If anybody knows back then and anybody that's out there that knows Set Free, you didn't just talk to Pastor Phil. You sit around and wait. It could be hours. It could be weeks. If he was busy doing something, you just waited. And I said, "Go in there, and let them know that I'm out here," and my homeboy had a little more juice with him, because he knew him going to his church and stuff. So when they dropped our names to Chief, he came out like that. Boom.

I explained my story to him, and I told him I needed a place to stay and everybody else is giving up on me, and I need somewhere to go, and I'm willing to do anything. So, he told me to come on in right now. Well, me being a dope fiend that I was, I told him, "Hey, I got to go get some of my stuff." Everybody knows what that meant. I was going to get one more in me and so his words to me were, "I hope you make it back." Which at that time, it hits you now you know he knows what you are going to go do, and he knows he can't stop you, but he's hoping that you can make it back.

Sure enough, I made it back, and he sent me to the ranch in Del Sur. I was there kicking heroin cold turkey for weeks. Not eating, not sleeping. There was one guy down there at the ranch that used to sit next to my bed, and all he used to do was read me scriptures and pray. Scriptures and pray. Sure enough, at that point when I was well enough to get up on my feet, I accepted the Lord that day at the ranch in Del Sur, San Diego California, and became a member of Set Free Church.

GEORGE NATZIC on getting involved at Set Free: My wife had gone to Set Free a few times in the past, and she really felt that it was a great ministry. Towards the end of 1998, we were planning to get married and my wife said, "If we are going to get married, there is only one person that I would like to do the wedding." So it ended up leading to an introduction to Pastor Phil. That was early in 1999. We went over and met him. I thought he would be the right individual to do the wedding. So we were married in February of 1999, and that's where our relationship began.

From that point on, we became I would say good friends. I was really relieved to see his relaxed style. He was a very real individual. I thought it was just a great fit and like I said, I became very fast friends with him. I liked his style, and that's where we made the decision to move forward with the wedding.

Pastor Phil with Cheri-Lynn and George Natzic

After the wedding, he invited us to church, and yes, I had ridden motor-cycles for a number of years. So there was a great connection there. So my wife and I rode our motorcycle out to the church service that he had, and that was the first time. We really liked the service quite a bit. So going from there, probably a little bit of time had passed, and we went to the church again, and we began to become regular attendees of the church. So it really worked out quite well for us. We could ride to church, go there and get blessed, have a fantastic church service and see the next week thereafter.

Originally, it was out in the Riverside area. I believe it was at a rented school. But again in the auditorium, it was a very comfortable setting. The type of music that was appealing to us, rock type setting. Everybody in there was dressed in casual clothes, and there were quite a few motorcy-cles outside, so we were able to ride up and fit right in. Then, the church moved from the Riverside area down to the Buena Park area. At that time, we started to attend more frequently. I really felt the draw, and I mean the draw of the Lord had pulled us there. It grew stronger and stronger, and the ability to work with people on the streets was something that was always important to me. That was really the focus of the ministry. So it was really taking us to a place where we could go out and work with other people in the community that were in need.

TURTLE on meeting Trina Aguilar, his future wife: It goes back to the first day when I came into the home before I went to the ranch. Being strung out and this and that, Chief was doing a house meeting, and I remember Trina was eating some jelly beans. You know when you are loaded, man, there is nothing better than some candy or some sweets. I remember I leaned forward and said, "Hey, can I get a couple of your jelly beans?" And she poured a couple in her hand and gave me the bag. Which again, you are thinking, "Wow, I don't meet people like this. That was a kind gesture."

Then, I went to the ranch, did that. I ended up coming back and it wasn't nothing - I can't say like it was this time that just I knew that she was the one. She kind of grew on me, and I'm sure she can tell you the same thing. She didn't really want nothing to do with me at the time. But we just conversed. We just conversed, and she was part of the home, so obviously everything that went down went through Trina. So I had a lot of opportunities to talk to her and speak to her, and I just really loved her spirit. She had a gentle spirit, man. But you knew at the same time, she's a raw dog - she's a pitbull. So the combination of having that gentle spirit and also knowing at the same time that if this chick was with me, she'd have my back to the fullest. It's kind of how it all started, you know?

I had multiple relapses, and she continued to support me through those relapses. And then you know after some time, Pastor Phil took notice that me and her were exchanging looks and things like that. He, obviously being a guy that also ran down the same road that I ran, didn't want his daughter with a guy like me. And multiple times, he explained it and made it real clear, "Stay away from my daughter. Nothing is going to happen. Don't even think for a second. She'll never marry a dope fiend like you. It's not going to happen." Brothers were the same way. All three of the brothers who I love, Chilly, Roc and MJ, to the max, those are my brothers. They were the same way, very protective of their sister but then eventually as I continued in the program and finally got my life on track, I got Chief's blessing to go ahead and walk down the aisle with Trina, and now we've got a beautiful family. Two sets of twins, and I've been clean since 2010, so I think it worked out.

Fieldy and Pastor Phil

FIELDY on inviting Pastor Phil on tour with Korn: We hung out a lot to a point where I asked him if he wanted to go on tour with me. Because just being around him, he's such an encouraging, loving guy that it was kind of contagious. I wanted to hang out, and he would always help me say the Word or just small blessings, which I still like, because I'm a one-liner guy. I still am. My wife says I should make Hallmark cards. It's hard for me to write a page, but I can do one liners. So he's kind of a one liner guy, too, and that's why I think we hit it off. But, a lot of people love that just get to the point. I love that. I would go see him speak, and he'll get rolling his little funny joke. He'll be up there speaking, and he's all five minutes into it, he says, "I'm going to close with this..." And I laugh, because it's only been five minutes. But he'll keep making that joke, and he'll be up there for 20 minutes maybe, but that's what I liked about it. He kept it short and sweet.

I brought him out just to have somebody with me. At the time, I didn't really know this, but I think it was to keep me accountable and keep me getting rooted into this. I know he liked to have a good time all the time, so we brought a trailer behind my bus, full of choppers and took them out riding every day, and we just hung out. It was almost just to be around someone, more than worrying about, "Oh, we need to do this or that." When you can find somebody that can keep you accountable, it's just hanging out and watching them live. Not worrying about it - we didn't worry. We just went out and had a good time and just hung out. We went and rode bikes, and I would just watch him live, that was enough for me. When I brought him out, my band loved him, all of them. They knew what he was about, but Phil's not like that. People would meet him, and he would just walk up and love people. Shaking somebody's hand - forget about it. You are going to get a big ol' hug from him. He is just one of those people. I guess he's a people person I would say.

TURTLE on getting Pastor Phil's blessing in marriage: He had a lot of different ways that he dealt with certain things, and obviously, her being his daughter, he had us on a 40 foot rule, where we could not be within 40 feet of each other except for in large crowds. Which meant only at church. So he definitely had some ways of trying to keep us apart because obviously - I think back now that I have daughters, I wouldn't want my daughters marrying someone like me either.

I reminded Chief a lot of himself too in ways, so I'm sure that was a deterrent as well. But I do remember when I went and asked him. I'm from the old school like I said. I went and asked him for his blessing. Which nowadays a lot of kids and people don't do that, but I went and asked Chief for his blessing. I said, "I'd like your blessing to marry your daughter." He looked at me with those eyes he has, he said, "No way, no chance in hell brother. It ain't going down." And so I asked him what I got to do, "There's nothing you can do." And then like I said, people knew and like I said, I just continued to walk that path and continued to be a blessing. I remember eventually him asking me, "Do you still want to marry my daughter?", and I said, "Absolutely." And so I got his blessing, and we got married on October 9th, I believe it was 2007.

DR. RICHIE COLE on meeting Pastor Phil: I was aware of Chief before I actually met him, because he had already had an impact on the community in southern California. I had known people - it was probably around the first few years of Set Free that I had heard about it and stuff like that. But I had met him, I don't know exactly, but maybe around '91. He was going through a transition down here at Muscle Beach. I started working out here in '85, and when I saw him, his motorcycle club which is the only Christian 1% club in the world according to law enforcement and documented books and stuff like that. And they really looked cool.

They had it down - their patches. They just really look good and I've been riding motorcycles my whole life, so I went up and said, "Hello." Just mutual respect, great dude. He thought I was a drug dealer, but I wasn't at that time. We just started crossing paths in a lot of different ways and random things in motorcycle events and at my motorcycle club. Chief is always the highest of dudes in every motorcycle club, you know? Because he doesn't care about this, that, and whatever. He is just an alpha male, and he'll connect with leaders. He is a natural leader, so he'll connect with leaders. So he was hanging out with our motorcycle club for a long time with the higher ups, and we'd see each other and I knew his kids. You know it's radical, because attraction in general is probably something that is biochemical and electric that is beyond our ability to explain. But in terms of my conscious awareness, he just emanated coolness - and just a great guy - has helped a lot of people.

I'm a people person, so I say, "What's up?" to everybody. Like Chief said, I was the most polite atheist he had ever known. So, he is just an alpha male. I'm not really like a hardcore alpha male leader type as much, but so he was just one of those dudes that has that energy. So just say, "Hey, what's up?", and we just say, "What's up?"

I didn't know of course what the future entailed that we would inter-twine to such a degree, but then looking back, it's so radical because you see the crossing of the paths and all of that. My baby's mom had been through Set Free. Her best friend that she grew up with had been through Set Free. But they were believers. I was a hardcore atheist, so the Chris-tian aspect wasn't a part of our relationship for the first many, many years.

Set Free Soldiers

JOHN "QUICKY" JUAREZ on the impact of Pastor Phil and Set Free on his life: My wife bought a little home, I moved in with her and some-body came to my door and was hurting. I said, "Hey man, I'll give you a spot in my garage," because that's what I had learned from Phil. If you want to feed, give them food. If you want to clothe, give them clothes. If you want them sheltered, give them shelter. I started doing that. I've been doing it ever since, 2001. I've never not had a home with people that need help. I can say that God has helped a lot of them. I haven't done anything, I've just been that guy. I've been that guy that's here that they can come to and say - before you got here, I was working with a young man who is 21 years old. He's going through his own demons, and he was sitting here telling me about them. We are sharing that it's going to be okay. He's getting it. We'll see, but that's all orientated by Pastor Phil. He's my hero. He truly is my friend. Because of that we started Set Free in Hawaii, and we opened a home. We bought a home, had three bedrooms, we added 8 rooms to it and filled it with people needing help, needing recovery.

Today, as of right now, I have 7 people that live with me. What we do - in the morning we do morning meditation. We try to learn a little bit about our Higher Power and how God works in our lives. I don't push anything on anyone. I had a young man in Hawaii, and this is an awesome message for me. He couldn't get the God concept. He would go, "Screw God, come on man, I didn't come here for that. I want to get clean." People think they can get clean. You want to get clean, but guess what the bottom line is? You are going to have to find a power greater than yourself. God is going to reveal Himself in some kind of way, and you've got to look for that. If you open your eyes, you are going to find it. For 45 days, he couldn't get it. One day he ran out of the room, he say, "Hey, John!" I said, "What?" He said, "I found my Higher Power." I said, "What is it?" He said, "The positive energy in my life." I said, "Okay, we can go with that." Today, after that, God came into his life. It's just the opening of a door.

Like I said, I've got 7 guys that are here. We do meetings. We do a lot of Narcotic Anonymous meetings, because that's just what we do. AA meetings. We just survive. It's abstinence. They live here. They follow the rules. The rules are simple. Be each other's friends. Keep the house clean, and don't use. God is going to come into your life.

I had another friend here. He is going to laugh when he sees this. His name is Jay, who got here, and he hated God. Hated Him. He would say, "Screw God," and harder words. Screw God. My wife sat down there one day, she said, "Look, pick a color." "Purple." She goes, "Okay, purple is your God. Let's leave it at that for now." And, he did for a minute, but now if you talk to him today, he's got a God of understanding who is loving and caring. He's not the same guy, because this guy is a very intelligent man. "Why this? Why God? Why this?" If God is so big, the universe is so big, there is no explaining Him. Yep, you've got your answer. That stuff happens, and I love that.

Turtle as a prospect for the Set Free Soldiers

TURTLE on the allure of the Servants for Christ: Oh yeah, from the jump going to church and seeing those cats ride up on the Harleys, there is nothing like it. It brought an excitement to church. And those guys, I'm going to tell you - there is a lot of those guys that were very instrumental in my upbringing in the Lord. They loved on me man. Every time I messed up, they were there for me to pray for me. And I saw men that had that raw look, but they had that loving spirit man, and they were willing to reach out to a guy like me who had nobody at the time.

There was one cat that used to - when Chief used to preach, obviously he's very controversial, knows a lot of people from a lot of different areas, so they provided protection to the man as well. Which I felt, because of what he's done for my life, I owed him that. You know, so there was a guy that used to stand by the door, and he made sure nobody came in. They had to come through the front. I remember telling my mom, "I want to be that guy." That definitely drew me. Then, talking with my brothers-in-law and a couple other cats that were in the homes, a lot of these guys that were in Servants for Christ, they kind of grew stale. It was kind of stale.

We brought this idea that we need to bring some youngsters in there. We want to change it up a little bit - do it a little bit different. So that's when we asked. We actually showed up to a Servants for Christ meeting and basically asked to be apart of the club, and some people jumped and were excited with joy that now some young cats, young bloods getting in the club. But, there was a lot of them that thought these guys were a little too radical, especially that Turtle guy. "We don't know what he's going to do." But like I said, I had some great brothers step up and lead the way. That is actually how I started out with Set Free was in the Servants for Christ.

PASTOR PHIL on starting the Set Free Soldiers: We were doing our Servants for Christ motorcycle ministry at the time, and a couple of the guys said, "Hey, let's get a club that is a little more committed. A little more like the green berets." So, we started the Set Free Soldiers. Still had Servants for Christ. Christ's Sons, our first biker ministry was kind of just put on hold and retirement, but here comes the Set Free Soldiers. We didn't let everybody come in, because we wanted to be a really elite group. A committed group. Just people that we know were ready to ride, ready to go for it. Ready to go behind the enemy lines. So we started the Set Free Soldiers. It started out with just a group of men. We were going to be hardcore soldiers for Jesus.

What started happening, the Soldiers started growing, and the Soldiers started becoming kind of a priority. So lots of other parts of the church didn't feel they were that important. I ended up moving our services over to another place located by the Anaheim Angels baseball stadium where we started meeting. It was literally invite-only. I just wanted to deal with people that I believed were a good investment and were serious about God. They wanted to get involved and do it Set Free Soldier style like we were doing. We had all our motorcycles all black, black and white patches. We started becoming a real exclusive group like that. I wasn't looking for just big numbers anymore. I was looking for just a tight group.

DR. RICHIE COLE on why someone joins a motorcycle club: Its multiple factors. First of all, it's the most natural thing in the world to want to be part of something bigger than yourself. As human beings, we are a social animal. Now, the type of guys that end up getting into motorcycle clubs, there is generally four or five different schools of guys. It was started by guys after being in combat, and they didn't really fit into mainstream society. They were a little rebellious, so they just rode motorcycles. That was probably around World War I or after that. But then, also dudes who have been to prison. So guys in motorcycle clubs, a lot of times, they are loners, but were loners together.

First of all, we love to ride motorcycles. It's a thrilling thing. I've been riding - I used to race motocross. But then, there are guys who are from neighborhoods or various, so they are used to that thing. There is the militant structure or the organization, and then there is guys like me who just sex, drugs, rock and roll and rode motorcycles my whole life. Never been to the joint, never been in combat, never been in the military, never been in a gang.

I just love to ride motorcycles and a lot of my friends have died from heroin overdoses in bed, so there was a point in my life where I was just hanging out with whatever woman I was with, and as men we need that male bonding, that camaraderie. Because, if we are just hanging out with our lady all the time, we start going cuckoo, you know? So you need to connect with another man just for some sanity, because we are wired differently. So, different motorcycle clubs are different. There is the Christian club thing, and his brothers have started a lot of them, so that was their angle. Then, there is our clubs, there is family clubs, there is black clubs, there is woman clubs. So it depends specifically which type as well.

Pastor Phil with Set Free Soldiers

MJ on the start of Set Free Soldiers: Well, motorcycles and riding bikes, just the whole biker lifestyle, has been apart of my family since I can remember. Part of my dad's roots. So as a young kid, I was on the back of a bike, and I always loved it. It was just normal to me. My uncles, everyone had a bike. Growing up sitting on them and being around it. So again, that being part of my dad's roots was a big part of our ministry and a big tool. It was always music and bikes. And a lot of times the hip-hop, the rock and roll, and bikes. Those were probably the two number one soul winning tools that we've ever had and probably still have and ever will I think for our crowd.

Roc Aguilar, MJ Aguilar, Dave Bermeo, Glenn Schoeman, Ron Riddle, Erik Bryant (from left)

So, with bikes being around all the time, there was a ministry all the time - a club, a group of men that developed Servants for Christ many years ago. In the Set Free Church, there is a lot of men that still want to ride and ride for the Lord, but still look a certain way. You still kind of crave that brotherhood and that camaraderie that the biker lifestyle gives to so many. So, Servants for Christ were around since I was a little kid. I remember being there, when the guy drew up the first patch that they still wear today - this guy named Chato. He spelled it wrong. Instead of "Servants for Jesus," it said, "Servants for Jesse." And he wasn't the best. He didn't finish school or anything, but he was a good tattoo artist so we loved him the way he was. But it was cool. So a lot of history with Servants for Christ.

Over the years with Servants for Christ and the way it transitioned into the Set Free Soldiers - it was a big move for a lot of people. Especially those that just loved the old wineskin and love Servants for Christ for what it meant to them. And because many of them were still wearing the Servants for Christ patch. So they are like, "Wait a minute, you've been about this forever. We are all wearing it and we've prospected or we've moved or we've got a bike or we've got a new patch maybe last week that said Servants for Christ," and now Chief and some of his crew are kind of starting. It started as this - Servants for Christ was like a branch of the military. So after so long it kind of got, in my eyes too and to a few of us, diluted. It got watered down. It wasn't what it started out to be.

There was some clowns. There were some people at the time who we wouldn't pick or choose to wear that patch. Even though, yeah, we are all saved and love God, that means something to a lot of people. So, when they see that, it represents all of us, I don't want that to represent me. I don't want to wear the same thing he's wearing. Again, I'm not saying that's all Bible. I'm just saying that's where we came from, so that meant something to us and still does in a lot of ways. So it was like the Set Free Soldiers was the elite. Kind of like the Navy Seals maybe. Or the elite of the Servants for Christ.

So, whatever was kind of hand picked, Chief had conversations and some other men had conversations with some of the guys that were in Servants. Like, "Hey, we are going to start this up, and we want you to be apart of the founding members of that." There was many that were honored to do it, and then there's ones that are like, "No, I'm Servants for Christ. I like that." So that time right there, some people left. Some people dropped out. Some people just didn't understand it. I can look back and see why, because that was over a dozen years ago now. Because Servants for Christ meant a lot to a lot of people. But that was it. It was becoming something else, Servants for Christ. So it almost kind of squashed that, put it to rest.

Anybody now that wanted to wear Servants for Christ, "Hey, oh cool. You want to be a biker? You don't even have a bike?" Because that's what it came to, most guys didn't even have bikes. So, for people again even though you are a Christian, how are you going to be a biker without a bike? But that's where it came to when more guys in Servants for Christ around us at least didn't have a motorcycle than did. So, you don't want that, you know what I mean? Its not the way its supposed to be.

Its supposed to be MC, motorcycle club, and it turned into MC, mostly cars. You know? That became just an ongoing joke, and people don't want to be apart of a joke. They want to ride for a cause and a purpose and next to men that they feel like really love this lifestyle and culture. So Set Free Soldiers came out of that. It was like that elite group of men that wanted to ride and have fun. All that good stuff.

DR. RICHIE COLE on the difference between motorcycle clubs: Well, I'm not authorized to speak for my club or any other club. But just in general outlaw clubs versus Christian clubs, it's like a microcosm of society. So if you are saved and that is your belief system but you are a little rough around the edges, or whatever it is - even within the Christian motorcycle club there is such variations. Then there is family clubs, so those are people that probably love to ride motorcycles, but they have their wife and their kids that can be part of the club. And then the outlaw clubs - usually those guys are a little bit more off, or there are a few marbles loose or a screw loose. Anybody in one of those kind of organizations, a lot of times there is tremendous strengths, tremendous intelligence, but there is a little something off that is hard to articulate with each one of them.

TURTLE on how Set Free Soldiers evolved: Basically in a nutshell, Set Free Soldiers evolved from within the Servants for Christ, and it became a group of guys that were wanting to take it to the next level as far ministry. Back then, Chief used to go on some really long rides, and a lot of cats couldn't hang with him. And you know Chief, he does a lot of things, and there is a lot of action. When you are hanging with Chief, you've got to

Turtle

be ready at the crack of dawn, and you've got to go until midnight sometimes. Basically, the Soldiers evolved as I would say more of a hybrid club that we really wanted to reach the down and outers like ourselves, and we also knew that we wanted to roll with Chief. We just had a loyalty to Chief, because he's done so much for everybody, and that's kind of how that branch started off.

It was always a ministry-minded club, and it was always set forth that way per Chief. But I can only speak for myself, yeah, I got sidetracked. We got into some other things. We actually recruited a bunch of people, maybe that should have been more trained up in the Lord. And we kind of went away from - you know what I mean? But, we were still always a church. We were still always doing that, running with Chief. It just became - Chief got a lot of haters at that time. So yeah, I would say for me personally, I downgraded away from the ministry, and it became more about the club and more about riding motorcycles and stirring shit up. I mean that's what it was.

JOHN "QUICKY" JUAREZ on his life as a Vago: It's my life. I am capable today. I am an excellent husband. My wife loves me unconditionally. I don't have thoughts of anything. I don't cheat. I'm trustworthy, because I'm trustful. I trust my wife, because I'm trustworthy. I'm a good husband. I'm a great grandfather. I'm a great father today to the grace of God. I'm an excellent Vago. If I can help carry the message to one person by being who I am, then I've accomplished my goal in life.

See, we can be anything we want to be, anything. And, we don't have to be that guy you were talking about, that outlaw killer level four yard on the one yard guy. I see people all the time, they get here, and I tell them one thing, "Be who you are. The patch doesn't make the man. The man makes the patch." So you don't have to - there is no cookie cutter Vago. They come from all walks of life. We have attorneys, we have doctors, we have me. And we love to ride together. We all stand for each other. And yes, if you attack me, if you and other people attack me, then we'll stand together, because that is just the way it is.

If people are attracted to me, there is something they see in me. Listen to me. I go to a lot of meetings. I do a lot of things, and if they like what they see, then it's a program of attraction. They are attracted to me, and they get to know me. Once they get to know me, that persona they had of me is gone. Because that's not who I am. It trips them out when I go, "Hey, you want to go to church with me?" "What?" "Yeah."

I'm a teddy bear who loves Christ. That's who I see. I don't see that other guy. People tell me that, but I don't see that. I see who I am. I see that I'm a vessel for Christ, bro. I'm that guy. I'm that guy that maybe the normal guy can't reach. All of these guys in here, the normal person couldn't reach him. But the fact that for whatever reason, they are drawn to me because they think, "Look at that old guy. He's cool." They get here, and I'm able to share a message with them. A message of recovery. I think it's pretty awesome that that's what God - that's my job. Some sow, some reap. In this world, we all have a job. As long as we are doing the next right thing, for the next right reason, the next right thing is going to happen.

CHILL on the history of Set Free Soldiers: The transition between Servants for Christ and the Set Free Soldiers motorcycle club was this. My dad was a rider - his whole thing is a biker. He loves bikes and ministry, all that stuff. Now his kids were older, and we are all just came through the whole gang mentality life in L.A. We are very intense. We are with my dad at a biker event. We didn't like to go to many of them, because usually bikers just try to stand and act hard. We are like, "This is dumb, we are from L.A." We were living in L.A. These dudes really are the serious. They don't talk, they fight, or they do what they do.

My dad had a bunch of his Servants for Christ around him, supposed to be his brothers and down until the end. "We are bikers, we are tough," I guess that is their whole thing. Us, we are all standing in the corner, me and about five or six of my partners, Turtle, my friend George Natzic, and my little brother Hebrew fresh out of high school. We had our own little crew. We decided to roll with my dad that day. This is probably 1999. Somewhere around there, 2000. Something had happened. Some guy that used to be apart of somewhere or whatever is about to get beat up by some other guys. And this guy was now with my dad, and my dad led him to the Lord. He was Christian, his life changed. But I guess he was going to get smashed from some old stuff. I don't know. I don't know the politics.

Set Free Soldiers and other motorcycle clubs

I was just standing against the wall. I think we were drinking a soda or whatever. We were just watching. We would just laugh at old bikers, act hard. We were making fun of them. So, all I knew is one of the Servants for Christ came and told us, "Get all the Servants together. There is a bunch of dudes surrounding your dad right now - some hardcore guys." I've seen my dad surrounded a lot of times in my life, and he is gangster. He'll talk his way out of it, or praise his way out of it. He manipulates his way out. He gets out of it. You don't throw no blows. Misunderstanding, miscommunication. But this time, I don't think it was working.

At this time, my dad was a lot more not the Jesus - he probably woke up on the - not the Pastor Phil side of the bed. He woke up on the Chief side. So if you wake up on the Chief side of the bed, you know that dude - he can be a little bit intense. We run over there, and we tell all the guys, we tell all the Servants for Christ, "Get off your butt!" They were lying under a tree eating a hotdog. "Get over there, one of our guys is about to be beat up. Get over there. My dad wants everybody over there to at least be there and show a presence that we have some guys." A lot of guys - they put the hotdog in their mouth, "Not me brother. I didn't sign up for this. I signed up for church, Jesus."

So me and Turtle were furious. We started saying not the Jesus words. A lot of them got on their bikes and left and left my dad and maybe eight other guys over there to deal with a situation that my dad didn't even - it wasn't even his fault. He was defending a Christian brother. A guy who - he was defending one of his brothers in Christ that he loved. He didn't want to see the guy hurt so he tried - he worked it all out. So we ran over there, all us youngsters, and we were like, "Oh, a fight? Yeah, let's do this." We are right behind my dad. We are talking smack and cussing and my dad is like, "Shut up!" He's trying to talk about Jesus and diffuse it. He's not trying to - he's not that ugly, but I think he saw a sense, that was the day it all changed.

Set Free Soldiers including Chill (second from left) and George Natzic (third from left)

We never even wanted to ride bikes or anything, but I told all my home-boys, about seven or eight of us. Some of them were from low rider Nazi gangs that got saved or from different southside gangs that got saved. They were all down. They changed their life, and I said, "Hey, let's do it for Jesus now." Sold them on - we are going to do it for Jesus, and you get to go to heaven. This is okay to be gangster a little bit and pray for people. So we started doing - we started riding. We didn't even know how to ride. We couldn't stand bikers, right? The whole biker scene - my dad's friends to us were just like kind of the guys he rolled with were kind of loppy, they called it. Like they didn't dress cool. Their jeans were dirty, and they smelled. It wasn't our scene. We wanted to look good. We want-ed to impress women. We wanted to get girls, and we wanted to back up my dad. We said we are never going to let that happen again - where he is alone there about to be smashed, and he didn't even do it. It was on something lame that he backed up. So long story short, I think that is where the Servant and Set Free thing changed. Because the Servants and the Set Free Soldiers changed.

There are great Servants out there. They were doing their thing but the ones we were with - that was a big thing to leave your brother. You are born for the day you can lay down your life for your brother. All the scripture they talked. Then, when it came time to just be there to back up your brother, right or wrong, they weren't there. So we joined, me and my brothers and a few other guys. Actually just me and Rock, MJ didn't join until later. Me, Rock, Turtle, a group of us joined, like eight of us. Didn't even know how to ride bikes, and then we kind of pushed out the older group, and they got mad that we were in there wearing shorts and vans. We weren't wearing biker jeans and boat boots. We didn't smell.

We were getting in people's faces. So our thing was, "Hey dad, I don't want to wear a Servants for Christ vest if I'm going to be going to a club and trying to pick up on chicks. I know you are about ministry," because it would always touch the back of their vests and in the biker world, you don't touch their vests. The back, the patch. Servants were known to get - "Hey!" Touch their patch. "You guys love Jesus?" and be all in their grill. We didn't want that. I'm just being honest. So they made the Servant for Christ thing - it was cheesy for us. We were like, "This is dumb, I don't want to be apart of this."

So long story short, the Soldier thing happened, and they changed the patch. We were more making it, at least us - my dad was still believing that it was going to be a Christian club. We thought, "Cool, now it's our time," we can be a full - I don't want to call it an outlaw club, because we were even different than that. We were just a bunch of brothers who wanted to ride together, and we didn't want to be put in that position that we were going to be judged if somebody had a cigarette or a beer with their patch on. We felt like it was - that was an oxymoron type thing. So we didn't want to be a phony, does that make sense? With a Jesus on our back, trained to serve Jesus, and then we are there not acting Jesus-like.

JOHN "QUICKY" JUAREZ on the competitiveness between the Set Free Soldiers and other motorcycle clubs: You know I can't speak for them. That's their internal workings. I don't know. All I know is that the Vagos have always respected Pastor Phil, because he's done a lot of good for a lot of us. My international president back then used to go to church with us, which is interesting. My international president that just stepped down, and he doesn't mind if I use his name, his name is Tata. He started his spiritual walk with God through Pastor Phil, and now he's awesome spiritually motivated gentleman. It all started there at Set Free, so that stuff works. It does. There is no competitiveness with Set Free. They are a total different branch of the service, like the Navy. They are good men. They are good strong men, and they carry their message. They attract people to Set Free because of who they are. There is so many churches, everybody attracts whoever. I have a friend of mine who I went to see him because he wanted to talk to me about his spiritual program, and he started preaching at me. I'm sitting there talking about it says this in Job and Jacob and Corinthians. And instead of talking to me, he was preaching at me. And I said, "I appreciate your friendship, and I'm glad that you found - ," he was a Vago this young man. I said, "I'm glad you found a place that you're content with. You've found Christ. That you are good." That's it, and I just left.

Because, you know what? I don't want to be preached at. That's what Phil does. He doesn't preach at me. He teaches me. As far as other clubs are concerned, they all think they are the best. I don't care, they could be from a mom and pop club. We are 50 years old, so we've been around for a minute. Hell's Angels have all that - they have the notoriety, because they just have the notoriety. In the beginning, in California, there wasn't, but maybe 10 motorcycle clubs, and it's grown to hundreds. In the past, the beginning clubs used to try to stop other clubs from starting. Its got to a point where it doesn't matter anymore. We are just who we are, and we'll let it be.

Pastor Phil (right) hanging out with members of Hell's Angels

GEORGE NATZIC on Phil's house as a Set Free Soldier hangout: Yeah, Phil's house in Anaheim was really just a central location for us to meet as a group prior to going on runs. We would meet there, and then we would go out, do a particular event, and then we would most generally come back to the house there and then wrap up our day and go home. So in regards to the neighbors, I could imagine how that could look at times. It probably could look intimidating for sure, especially if there is 20 to 30 motorcycles outside on a routine basis. I think that could raise people's concerns. So, the work that was actually going on there, compared to what people may have interpreted, were two different things for sure. I think there was hearsay that the neighbors were concerned about the type of people and all of the motorcycles that were to congregate over at Phil's house.

Set Free Soldiers

MJ on the culture of Set Free Soldiers: Being a certain age at that time now, because we are talking about last maybe 10 to 12 years. You are old enough now, for me, I know what's going on. This isn't anymore of that stuff where you can turn a blind eye or pretend it's just my youth or I didn't get it or no one told me. You see what's going on. And Set Free Soldiers was in a lot of ways, so many good times and good moments and a lot of men and relationships I'll cherish for the rest of my life. But as you are apart of any kind of specific group, club - that is all that matters, and everyone else began to not matter. And when you are about Jesus and when you are about the ministry and you do know better, that's not a good thing all the time. We stopped reaching out in that way.

TRAINED TO SERVE JESUS

Our runs and our rides weren't to so much proclaim the name of Jesus, but to proclaim the name of Set Free Soldiers. And that was really all we kind of cared out. Did they know that we were there? Did they know we had so many members? Did they know we had the nicest bikes? Did they know that we looked good? I don't know - whatever. At least, those were my thoughts. And it did. It became about us. It became about me. It became about how cool and maybe how hard and even at times how tough we looked. Because there was a lot of times where we would roll in and be deep, and we had our crew.

I felt we always represented well, which Set Free was always known for doing. Our bikes - we had some of the nicest bikes. We were into it. So a lot of men around that same thing. The purpose from what it started out to be was now secondary, and our primary focus was now kind of how cool we were. The pride slips in and being in the middle of it, I didn't realize how quick and how it overtook us all.

PASTOR PHIL on interacting with other motorcycle clubs: When the Set Free Soldiers were rolling, we were a great group of men. Great club. A lot of good things. We helped a lot of people. But in the world that we do ministry in, addicts, gang members, people that are violent, we don't work with your regular church kids. We get into places, we pull in and sometimes there are haters, people don't like us for whatever reason. Sometimes, there is even somebody that might want to do wrong or do violence to me. I'm the father figure. I'm the father of a lot of the kids there. I've heard that there were times that one of my family, church family had to stop somebody from saying something or give them a little instruction, "Maybe you better go now." That's just part of family love. You hear about it all the time. Like I said, you go out with my daughter, you better treat her right or else. I'm just a dad figure to a lot of different people. I'm an older guy so they want to protect their dad.

I grew up with bikers in my house at a young age so, I've been familiar with the bike scene and all the big clubs. I've had the opportunity and the privilege to do weddings and funerals from just about every club there is. I've always tried to get along and be at peace with everybody. My club has always been a Christian club, but when you are working with other club members and other different gangs and people who are involved in violence, every once and awhile you cross paths where somebody doesn't like you. That's just how it is. But my motto, my decisions have always been as a peacemaker. I've never lifted a hand one time - in all these years I've been saved - to anybody in any violent kind of way - not one time. It's always been "coming in peace, coming in love". At certain times, it's been really nice being able to work with all these different groups of

228

people that maybe didn't like each other. But God has allowed me a lot of freedom and privilege to be able to minister to all kinds of groups, because I love them all, right where they are at.

During this time when the Set Free Soldiers were rolling heavy, A&E wanted to do a story on us called 'Saints or Sinners'. We started a pilot project, we are rolling everywhere, we are getting popular. People are going, "How cool, Set Free!"

Filming of "Saints or Sinners" for A&E

We went to Arizona where we had another chapter of our Set Free Soldiers over there. While we were there, we had some visitors from another club, and they saw that we had a bottom rocker that said, 'Phoenix". They pointed out to me that we are not allowed to have "Phoenix" because that is claiming territory, "Would you please remove that?" I said, "Definitely. We will remove that." We did that, because we like to get along. Just as simple as that. We respect the rules that people have in their different cities and states. In the biker world just like in any other world, you wear certain things to show you belong there. For example, some people in Wall Street wear certain types of suits, certain churches got the hipster skinny jeans or the torn-up pants and stuff like that. In the biker world, when people are part of a 1% club, they have patches, and they'll say a certain county or they'll say a state. They just like to represent where they are from.

They are motorcycle enthusiasts having a good time riding and doing their thing. So my bottom rocker said, "Heaven" because I'm representing heaven, and Set Free Soldier means I'm a soldier for the Lord. Different people put on different things for different reasons. We loved to be kids in the neighborhood that wear red and think that means a certain thing or blue that means a thing. It's all up for opinion. But just bikers out there whether it's Christian motorcycle association or any club, they are just representing for their cause. They all believe they have a good cause.

JOHN "QUICKY" JUAREZ on how Pastor Phil connects with multiple motorcycle clubs: Because we understand that that's the message he carries. I don't think because he talks to Hell's Angels that he's talking to them about me. Nor if he talks to a Mongol who I have a lot of friends, that he's talking about me. He talks to them individually for whatever they need to be talked about. So he is carrying the message himself to those people the way he carries it to me. So it's just that simple. He's best serving all of us by staying who he is. If he had become a Vago, become a Hell's Angel, become a Mongol, become anybody, there would have been a separation, and he couldn't do what he does right now.

PASTOR PHIL on starting Club Roc: I was having a good time, and then my youngest son said, "Hey dad, I'd like to get a nightclub. Because I'd like to work with bands and do all that stuff." And we open up a place called Club Roc in Costa Mesa, California. A nightclub and bar. My youngest son's nickname is Roc, and they have a rap song called R.O.C. - Running Orange County. It's kind of like the young people in their raps, "We be running this stuff. Running O.C." It's an attitude. It's a swag. It's a feeling like that. This be our place, that type of thing. It might seem kind of crazy. Some people go, "Pastor having a nightclub bar?" My son wants to have bands, so I started having services there on Sundays at that place. But, other biker groups saw that we had a bar, and people started looking at us while we were doing that. I started getting judged from all over the place. "What's a pastor doing with a bar?" It's a good question. I look at it now, and it looks a lot different than when I was going through it. Didn't think that big a deal of it. That's kind of how I just got soft or weak around my convictions and things like that. But we had Club Roc, we had a bar. Biker bar, bands, punk rock bands, mosh pits, the whole works. It was a trip.

TRINA on Club Roc: My little brother always wanted to own a bar. I'm not really sure why, but he wanted to be an entrepreneur or whatever. So my dad was trying to help him make his dream come true, and him and a few of the guys bought a bar. They used to have bands play and stuff like that, but it didn't really turn into anything. It turned into a money hole. We had church there a few times. We had a few weddings and definitely knew that people were definitely not going to like having church there. We lost some people through that time for sure.

Performance at Club Roc

CHILL on the start of Club Roc: Club Roc, that started - man so many memories, 2005. I want to say, 2004. Club Roc was probably the worst things that we ever did. The worst idea. It was between a church - getting a church building or Club Roc. Somehow, the vote turned to a club, because I think everybody was just tired. My little brother wanted to run a nightclub and wanted to do it - wanted to make something happen. But we ended up taking over, me and my wife. My wife was an esthetician, but she bartended and knew the business. We took it over, not really knowing nothing about how to run a club. Man, we did good for the first year. Then, it just turned to chaos.

I would say it like this, the further you get away from Jesus, the more sin creeps in and the more your life becomes a freaking wreck. I didn't care about church or Jesus. We went in full mode of, "Hey, we are a club and we ride and we are brotherhood. We know we are going to heaven." That's a dangerous place to be when you know you are going to heaven, and you know it's already been paid for. You can do whatever you want - grace. Which it's true. It's there, but you take advantage of the grace and we just started - the club was just rocking and rolling.

We had hip-hop nights there - Snoop Dogg, guys from Korn. It was just debauchery and craziness, which wasn't us. We let sin in, and it started transpiring. My dad wasn't even around the Club Roc scene much. He was doing whatever he was doing. Me, Turtle, and my wife - we pretty much ran the place. It just turned into a battleground. The hip-hop nights there - we were the bouncers and security, so we have 30, 40 guys in the street challenging five of us, me, Turtle and other guys. We are getting beat up, but we are still fighting. It just was everything that we weren't, but we now had turned into everything we actually respected, which sounds crazy. It had nothing to do with Jesus. We started the club and trying to make it a cool club, and it ended up being just a battleground.

There was a church that happened for a minute there - my dad did on Sunday mornings, but most people didn't want to go to that. I understand, and I respect them now. Some of them were alcoholics. They couldn't be in a bar. It scared them. So yeah, the church went for maybe a few weeks or a month. People think it went for a long time. It didn't. My dad wasn't doing church at a bar for long time. He didn't even want to do it no more. He would rather ride on a Sunday. So the bar was more just for nightclub, music, parties, events. It wasn't made for really doing church.

Chill, Roc, Trina, MJ, Sandra, and Pastor Phi.

TURTLE on working at Club Roc: Yeah, Club Roc was some good times. It started off obviously the name Club Roc, one of Chief's kids, Roco, wanted to do a night club. He wanted to do some type of club for entertainment purposes. He was a big time promoter back then - did a lot of work with a lot of live bands and knew a lot of people. So that was an avenue, something that he wanted to do with his life, and his dad always being a great supporter of all his kids found an opportunity down there close to Costa Mesa to do that club.

And at the same time, Chief wanted to do church there. See you know he's always looking for a different fishing hole to reach different people. We started off doing church there on Sundays, and some people were coming. Some of the church members that we had here were coming out there, and they got into the religiosity of stuff where, "I can't be serving my Jesus in a bar." That's how it really the big split happened. A lot of people were like, "There is alcohol here. It's a night club ,but we are doing church." The legalism comes in, which is a terrible thing, but we were doing church there for a minute.

After that, basically it was the club. Everybody would go down there at night time to support whatever venue was going on. We met a lot of great people down there - a lot of live bands. It really became just a place where obviously alcohol being served and I was a bartender there at the time - just to support. Me being the kid that I was, I was nipping back every once and awhile. It became more of a relaxed party atmosphere where everybody could be themselves. And those that didn't like it, left. And those that were all with it, stayed.

We even became a tighter knit brotherhood where nobody was judging nobody. It was, "Hey, if Johnny boy is having a drink, hey, he is still my brother." All the legalism that came with church, I feel for my life was disappeared when we got Club Roc. So for that, it was a great thing. Basically, we just went there all the time. That was our hangout. That was where we did a lot of meeting in places like that. People would ride in from everywhere. So yeah, it was a great time for me, that whole venue. I think then what happened - I think they had some issues with the property or the coding enforcement out there, and they ended up shutting the doors on that place. But yeah, it was a great time.

Anytime you have a bar or nightclub, there is always patrons that come into the facility and end up having too much to drink. Certain things happen ,and you have to ask them to leave and a lot of times a lot of people don't want to leave. But if they are being disruptive to the whole facility, you've got to get them out. So yeah, I took on that role as well. Kind of the bouncer type thing, and we did have to forcefully remove some people from that club. But yeah, it was a learning experience. That's for sure.

CHAPTER EIGHT

THE FIGHT, THE RAID, AND THE TRIAL

On July 27, 2008, a number of the Set Free Soldiers were involved in an altercation with members of the Hell's Angels at Blackie's by the Sea in Newport Beach, California. After years of surveillance by the Anaheim Police Department, this altercation gave them reason to conduct a raid on homes occupied by the Aguilar family and other Set Free Soldiers on August 6, 2008.

While Jose Enrique Quinones was sentenced to eight years for attempted murder at Blackie's, MJ and Pastor Phil were given probation, and Turtle was sentenced to a year in county jail.

The impact of the raid, arrest, and trial on the Aguilar family was not only financial, but relational as well. Soon after, Chill and his family moved to Virginia to be the worship leader at Richmond Outreach Center where Geronimo was the founding pastor. While on staff, Chill became aware of Geronimo's immoral behavior, confronted the situation, and ended up leaving the church to travel as a worship leader.

GEORGE NATZIC on sensing a shift in the Set Free Soldiers: I would say after a handful of years, my spirit began to change, and I think there was a time in which our focus began to move away in my opinion from full time helping others in the ministry. I think I would sense that we would do a lot more riding and a lot less ministry. To me, that began to be a signal that probably it was time for me to move on. It began to take more and more time away from my family. That was a huge thing for me. So as we continued to do that, I had to delegate my time

George Natzic

in different areas. It was more important for me to spend time with my family, and ultimately, that lead to my decision to go ahead and leave. When I decided to leave, I had told Phil that I was going to leave, and he was sorry that I had made that decision. He seemed to understand, and there was really no input from any of the other club members, because I had a conversation with Phil himself.

Set Free Soldiers

CHILL on surveillance by Anaheim Police Department: The Anaheim Police - they were always watching throughout our whole lives. I understand part of it, because we dealt with a lot of crazy people. People that were on meds and out of insane asylums. We dealt with a lot of edgy, crazy people that were back and forth out of jail. So I understood, and I respected the fact that they had to do their job. It got more intense as we got bigger, got more bikes, more club members. We saw undercovers across the street waiting for us to do something wrong and bad, but we were pretty legit.

We weren't selling drugs or any of that stuff. We were just riding, brotherhood. Did we back down from a fight somewhere? No. If somebody puts their hands on my dad or somebody I love, what would you do if it was your kid? Or, if it was somebody you loved or your dad or relative? You defend them. It's your first instinct. If somebody messes with their kid, you are there.

We probably could have went about things different, but at that time, we were in sin a lot of us, and I can only speak for me. You go off your flesh. So yeah, Anaheim PD was always watching. We didn't do good to be good Christian brothers. We were flipping them off. At that time, we were in sin. We would ride by them fast on our bikes. We had one brother named Lou - he would do fast wheelies down the street and stop traffic. So were we doing things that were irritating them? I can only speak for me, yeah I'm sure, but nothing that would cause to be what kind of happened to us at the raid.

PASTOR PHIL on the incident at Blackie's: All I can say that happened at Blackie's is, it was an unfortunate situation, and I'm sorry that it happened. I'm glad that nobody got seriously injured. Other than that, I have no comment on that history.

TURTLE on the Blackie's incident: The Blackie's thing, as far as that goes, the incident, I really can't comment on due to political reasons and that nature. Man, we were riding down - we actually went to - they were doing some surfing down in Dana Point. So down there in Dana Point, they were doing a surf competition. We went down there just to check it out, chilling and then obviously we were taking the coast on the way back. So we came back up through PCH and stopped off in Newport Beach. We had some guests with us, so we stopped off at one of the burger joints that was there. Obviously, you know the story of the other place that's there, and yeah, we were just chilling. Basically having some burgers and fellowshipping in the sun, and then obviously, some other things happened and yeah.

TRINA on the Blackie's incident: I just heard rumors. I don't know. It's not something I really want to talk about. I don't like to talk about any of that stuff. It brings back really bad memories for me, and I just don't like - it's nothing I want to talk about. It was a mistake that they all made. It was stupid. Especially because they were friends with people that - it was just dumb. I don't like to get into biker stuff.

GEORGE NATZIC on the Blackie's incident: Well, I was glad I wasn't there, and it was really unfortunate that it occurred. I was just surprised once again that it even took place. I just can't - I don't know what the reasoning was behind it. So all of it is pretty much a question mark for me. I just don't understand why and how it even took place.

MJ on the Blackie's incident: Oh man, that was the day of Blackie's, Newport Beach. I don't know man. It was like a normal day. You know how it is. It always starts out as just a normal day, nice out. We are going to take a ride. We had a crew of us - not a big crew. We kept it local. We just went to watch one of our brothers. We did a lot of stuff as family. It wasn't just biker bars or something. Right before that, we were watching a friend's kid skimboard down the road of Newport. Then, from there, we were like, "Let's go get a bite to eat at TK Burgers." I think it's on the opposite side of where Blackie's is at Newport Beach. So we were grubbing there. That's what we did well as Set Free Soldiers. We ate well, and we had a good time eating with each other and hanging out. And then, some were still eating there, hanging out.

I remember we had some visitors too - some Marines that just loved our crew, and we were showing them around because they were from out of town. We were showing them around. Some of our guys stayed back. One in particular - my younger brother Roc, he was there with them. Close, but over there. Some of the other guys wanted to go to the bar and have a drink, shoot some pool. Probably some of our older guys, and they would go. They went and did that. So there was maybe three guys that walked around and went inside the bar of Blackie's and hung out in there. The rest of us were all outside.

Pastor Phil and Set Free Soldiers

We had so many moments where we felt like, "What the heck are we doing here? We are wearing leather. It's hot. It's summer time on Newport Beach. Where's my board shorts? I want to be on the pier with the ice cream." You can't eat ice cream and wear the leather. It doesn't look so cool. I got some credibility. We'd laugh to each other about that, because so many times we were in those moments, and a lot of times my dad would be the one who put us in those moments. Can we choose? Are we going to go ride today? We would ride to the beach, because we never understood riding towards the desert as bikers. Maybe I'm not a biker, because I don't like the heat so much. But it was just funny.

So we're just out like normal hanging out while they were in there. Naturally, we are always watching out and looking out for anybody, because people are crazy. People are stupid. People are bitter. You never know. Our name was well known and gotten around for a lot of reasons. Whether it's with our club. Whether it's with our church. Whether it's family. Even the ministry was still going off. Club Roc, which was what we part owned, that was kind of our clubhouse in a lot of ways. Had fun there. You are just looking out for everything.

While a few of our guys were in Blackie's, and we were outside, me, my brother Dave - I remember his face pretty much. He was right next to me. We are talking about how hot we are, and they are in there. We see a couple of guys go inside, and we recognize one of them and guys kind of scatter. About a dozen of us maybe and some are still on the other side. These two guys walk in, and we just follow in right behind them, because we know one and you just never know. Is he going to mouth off? Is someone drunk? Does someone have some issues that are deeper than maybe what we even know? So some tension was built. This guy wanted to have a conversation, but it wasn't one of those that really want to talk about. You come in ready to do things. So after we came in, I think a couple more guys followed us.

At that time, you are really locking in, looking at things, observing the situation. So a few guys, some of our club brothers came in behind us, and the talking escalated pretty quick. Then, there was a loud mouth behind, because this was kind of more my dad and this guy. But then there was this other guy that's not even apart of our club who was the loudest mouth of all. It's always that one. It's always that one that you invite and you go, 'Who is this guy? Who brought this dude to the barbecue who is stirring it up?" Being an idiot. This was our guy that day. Not a club member. A lot of people don't know that. It wasn't a club member. It wasn't even a friend. He was like a friend of one of our club brothers. Brought him around, and this guy couldn't shut his mouth.

It wasn't even my dad and this guy with the issue. It was the guy behind my dad and the guy behind the guy that had the issue that were kind of woofing to each other. That's how it happens. They just - the guy let loose, and they went in. After that, it's just look out for your brothers. It happened over that couple of minutes, and things were just going off. Patrons were hiding or leaving. One of those where its slow motion, but it also happened just like that. To be honest, there are so many times where you are trying to forget about it. Obviously, it's something that even though it was years ago, it was pretty serious times for me. I changed a lot. It formed me. I was really protecting - I was thinking of protecting my father, number one. All my brothers, yes, but they can handle themselves. But in a lot of ways, we are built for times like this. This is what we are doing, so I was by him the whole time pretty much. Yeah, the whole time. That was it. There was a guy by him, and I was making sure that guy - because they start to grab whatever is close. There was a pool table, and there is glass. So many things that can be a weapon. So that was it.

I'm protecting him, and I know a lot of guys felt the same way that day when he came to Chief, to Pastor Phil. So of course, being his son, I'm going to be the first one to probably think that way. I was, and that was it. Until it was completely - they were gone. They had left, and everyone was out of there, completely gone out of the place, then I was like, "What just happened?" That's when you really kind of, "What just happened?" At that time, its just protect. You are holding on while looking at everything going on, and that's what I tried to do.

Something I learned from my dad a long time ago is to not just hurt people to hurt people and to beat people up for the sake of beating people up. He was trained in martial arts and a lot of it was discipline. It was restraining people. And in this case, I was in a moment where it's like I don't want to just add to the - there is no need. There is plenty going on right now. So it was really just about restraining a particular person and protecting him, protecting all of us from it going any further. It was like, "Yo," I was telling this person, "You good? Are we done? Put it down. Relax." I don't want it to go that way. I don't believe to be a violent person or start something like that. This was something that unfortunately happened. Just a big miscommunication on both parties, and it just shows.

SANDRA on the Blackie's incident: One of the guy's wife just had surgery, so all of us ladies and kids were over there swimming and hanging out with her. We get the call that something happened there, and we all know that's not good. So we all start making our way home and then find out when they got home the story of it all. The confusion, a lot of confusion. A lot of different stories, because it all just happened. So then we realized that they are worried. My sons are very worried about their families, because they think there is going to be retaliation. Then, before you know it, a couple of days later, a couple of reds pull up. So then everybody is like - that's just not allowed. You don't just pull up to someone's home. So then a couple of guys, a couple of my sons, Dave, they went over to talk to them. Then it went on from there, but nobody really knew. It was all secretive. Nobody knows what was really happening. So in everyone's mind, there was going to be some sort of retaliation - some sort of attack.

Pastor Phil

CHILL on the Blackie's incident: Well again, you got to remember this event happened a lot of years ago. For me, I was definitely angry, depressed and mad at my life. All of the stuff that I'd seen and been through in my younger Set Free days, all had now added up to like I said - I never went to therapy, never got counseling. And me and my little brother are probably time bombs waiting to go off. So I think they are more happy we weren't there, because I'm not a tough guy, and I don't ever claim to be some thug or gangster.

At that time, I would fight for what I believed in. I don't think that we would have - we may not have stopped, me and my brother. A lot of people I guess involved with that - I only hear hearsay - weren't even throwing punches. So most of the guys that were our brothers at that time, we were a little upset they weren't even throwing punches. Because the reality that happened, whatever happened there, I wasn't in there, but we were more mad why weren't other guys - why were you standing against the wall? Like a coward. Why did you hide?

But I'm glad that me and my little brother weren't there, because we probably still would be in prison or in jail. Because like I said, me and Turtle and a few other guys, we just have a short fuse. We were mad at life already. We were in sin. That would have lead to - we could have been beat real bad or killed. I'm not the guy to tell you most of these wannabe gangsters or dudes that think they are hard. They are this tough guy where they are going to hurt everybody, or they are the enforcer.

I was just a guy. I got tired of people talking bad about my family. I got tired about people disrespecting us, because they were Christians and couldn't do nothing about it. I remember my dad would get mad at me, "Hey, don't punch somebody. Don't do this." And I go, "Dad, when you punch one of them, most of them stop running and talking their mouth." That was just a sick way of thinking to justify what we were doing - what I was doing, nobody else but me.

JOHN "QUICKY" JUAREZ on Pastor Phil and the situation: I was happy that he handled his own business. That things happened - he didn't initiate anything ever, but things wound up the way they were supposed to. Sometimes a bully doesn't win, and somebody tried to bully him. The ramifications were severe towards those people. That was it. We don't get involved. If Pastor Phil was next to me, I would definitely - nobody would ever touch him. But he's got his own family, and I'm part of his family, but I can't roll out. He knows that he will take care of his own business and he did.

Let me tell you something. I had complete faith in God that everything was going to be okay. I didn't even give it a second thought. I had faith in the man. I have faith in God. God didn't bring me to him, and everything that happened - it happens in life, but it didn't matter to me. I still loved him. No matter what happened, I was going to love him until the end. And I will. So that I paid not one iota of attention. If somebody came to me and said, "What about Pastor Phil?" I'd say, "Hey, you know what? You need to talk to him about it. Don't talk to me. He's my friend. I will not talk about my friend behind his back."

THE FIGHT, THE RAID, AND THE TRIAL

PASTOR PHIL on the raid of Set Free Soldiers' homes in Anaheim, California: A week later, I heard an explosion at my house in Anaheim. Little did I know, that a flash grenade has been shot at our front door. Little did I know that there were 150 SWAT team members there with M16s pointed at our homes that we had on the block.

We had about five houses on the block where people in our ministry lived. My grandchildren, my daughter-in-laws, my son-in-law. Little did I know, we were being surrounded. There was a tank from the Anaheim police force there, and helicopters were overhead. There was ATF, DEA.

An Orange County Sheriff's Department bomb squad member walks his explosives-sniffing dog after the raid on Set Free Solidiers. (photo by Mark Boster / Los Angeles Times)

All these people were coming to see me. Little did I know that they'd had a search warrant at five in the morning, and they decided to wake us up and take a number of us away. As my grandchildren were traumatized, my wife was put in a paddy wagon with handcuffs on. Little did I really know, I did not know that they were coming especially for me, and the police that came said, "You are going away for life." I honestly did not know why I was being arrested.

Next thing you know, I'm at the Anaheim police station, and they are interrogating me about some alleged fight that had happened and what we had to do with it. I say, "Hey, you know what? I don't know what you are talking about. What are we being charged with?" I find out I'm being charged with attempted murder, street terrorism, and a whole number of things like that. Next thing you know, I'm on a million dollar bail, and I'm going to jail. They arrested I think another eight or nine Set Free Soldiers with me. They tore up our homes and just moved our families out of them - took all of our vehicles, computers and things like that. Made life hell on earth for my wife and kids and grandkids, all traumatized. It was a horrible day, and here I am locked up getting ready to spend the next couple of years fighting a case that the newspapers and the news made go worldwide and appear like I would be locked up for the rest of my life.

Of course, the A&E program was down the drain. Anything else could go down the drain. While I had those three days before I got bailed out in the Orange County jail, I had time to think about that experience kind of like Jonah and the whale. I was in the whale's belly for those three days. I was Jonah, and God pointed out, "I sent all those officers, all this attention just to let you know, Phil, that I love you, but your pride has got out of hand. You think you are legend in your own mind. You guys riding around like you are all this, and you aren't about any of that. You are a servant of mine. You are one of the King's kids, and you need to get back to what you are supposed to be doing." I just took it all from the Lord there, and my third day in jail, I made a commitment to God. I'm done with the life-style that I've been living.

Anaheim police look over the motorcycles that were being impounded after the raid.
(photo by Mark Boster / Los Angeles Times)

ELIZABETH AGUILAR BUCHANAN on hearing about the raid: I was at work, and my friend in the next cubicle said, "Elizabeth, I think this is your brother on TV." I was so scared for my brother and my sister-in-law and my nieces and my nephews and all the children. I'm so disappointed in the city of Anaheim. The city that I love. I went over there pretty quickly when we could. The police were everywhere. It's like the whole of the city of Anaheim police force was there and did not find anything.

They put my sister-in-law in one of those trucks and didn't let them change and had them somewhere for hours. I was very disappointed in the city of Anaheim, the police department and all of authorities, the mayor and everyone that allowed something like that to happen. I couldn't believe it. It was heartbreaking.

BILLY AGUILAR on the Soldiers: I just didn't think at that time Phil was quite centered. He had a lot of guys - some dangerous people with him. They were doing dangerous stuff. They were messing with dangerous people. That's a lifestyle I came out of. Why do I want to go back to it? I was with all of those dangerous people back in the 70's and 80's, early 80's. I don't want to go back to this lifestyle. If I'm going to end up in prison, I'm going to end up doing a rap for somebody saying something to my brother, and I end up shooting the guy. I'm going to end up doing time, just because I couldn't control how God wants me to raise my family and live my life. The Set Free Soldiers - a lot of those guys were born again Christians, and a lot of them weren't. A lot of them just wanted to hang out with Phil. They thought it was cool and fly these colors and think that it's all okay. It got pretty sour there at the end there - fighting with the different clubs. It was sad to see my brother take another beating. It was sad to see RICO knocking on his door. They can come and take anything out of your house, and you have to prove to them where you bought it.

SANDRA on the raid: When the raid happened, obviously everybody that was aware when it first started thought it was a retaliation. So my son-in-law who lived in a different house pulls out his rifle that he had on guard, and then that house was hit first by the raid. Then it went down. Ours was the last house. We lived with Phillip - Chill and his family. They lived in the front of the house, and we lived in the cabana, which is not attached to the house by a door. So we really didn't hear anything, because you are kind of like in a closet. There is no windows or anything. We didn't hear anything, and then all of a sudden, they put off one of those flash bombs.

I woke up, and I told him, "Did you hear that?" I opened up the door of the cabana, and you can look to your right and see the whole backyard. There is a brick wall to the parking lot next to us, and all I saw was red beams and just literally, they were in their gear - their battle gear, whatever that is called. So I shut the door real quick, and I'm like, "Oh, don't go out there, because they are looking for somebody." That's happened before where the police are looking for somebody. He's like, "Really?" I'm like, "'Yeah, you don't want to go out there."

The next thing is his phone rings, and it's the police. They said, "Okay, we know you are in there. You need to send your wife out and anybody else that might be in there with their hands up." That's kind of how it started. In the meantime, he is calling all our boys, and no one is answering their phones. He doesn't know what's happening. We had no idea. I came out with my hands up like they told me. They made me walk backwards all the way from there, all the way across the street backwards with my hands up. As I'm walking, I'm seeing my boys on the curb handcuffed. I didn't know what was happening. It's so surreal. You have no idea what is really happening. Put me in the paddy wagon. I'm waiting now next should be my husband. He doesn't come out. He doesn't come out. I'm wondering, "Oh my God, they probably shot him. He probably didn't want to come out." All these things are going through your mind.

He finally comes out - gets in the paddy wagon with us. So I'm like, "Where is my kids? Where is my grandkids?" My husband is saying, "Don't say nothing. Don't say nothing." So, I'm thinking, "Okay, we are going to jail and I'm not going to know what's happening?" Well no - they took me a couple of blocks away. This is pathetic. Here is my daughter-in-laws, my grandchildren, but not Chill's wife and kids. I still don't know where they were.

Here they are in the middle of the street, and the sun is just finally coming out, because they did it while it was still dark. They tell me, "Okay, we are letting you out, and then we are going to put you guys in another van and take you to a safe place." They took me and the kids to a safe place? No, it was just the bottom part of where the detectives have an upstairs. They took us all there. A couple of my grandbabies were babies that still needed diapers and bottles.

They had these ladies come in and bring some snacks and some diapers. Then, they called me upstairs. That's really why they brought us there. They wanted to interrogate me. When we were done, they said, "Okay, you guys can all go home." And Chill, Phillip - it's hard to call him Chill. He was the only one who they did not end up taking in to the police station. So him and his family were still somewhere. I didn't know where. The next thing you know, they showed up there at the safe house, and he got ahold of a friend who came and picked us all up.

MJ on the raid: The raid happened - I think about within the week. The raid came after the incident at Blackie's. It was crazy, because some people know it and some don't, but we left Blackie's that day. It was just like - how many bar fights are there a year? You know? So something happened, we got into it, everybody walked away. Nobody was left on the floor. No ambulance came. Nothing like that. The cops did come, which a lot of people don't know, to the bar. Again, I'm right in front of the beach. This beautiful Newport Beach. We are all out there in our black leather. They called the cops of course and everything. So they came, and it was just the Set Free Soldiers and maybe a dozen of us at most. By that time the guys on the other side heard about and saw people moving and running scared. The whole beach - it was a pretty big scene at the time. So the cops came, and they searched us, checked us for knuckles and weapons. Did we having anything? Let every single one of us go. So as much as people think we got locked up the day of or raided that night -

no, they were like - it's a bar brawl with some issues. It happens. You guys be good. We all got on our bikes and rode away. Not one ticket. Not one arrest or nothing like that.

So we get in, and we just figure, "You know what? This is some street stuff that we are going to have to address sooner than later," but nothing legal. Nothing with the law. They are not involved in it. They let us go. If there was something, they would have detained us there or held us there. They didn't. So I think, it was within the week - I forget exactly. We had a big group of us meeting and talking about some of the stuff that we had to address, but I think it was probably within the week where just at night - I'm not thinking about - I'm thinking about other people to be honest - and thinking of things that we have to do to protect our family. It was a pretty - it was a scary time. It really was. Because our house isn't unknown. Most people don't know where people live. We've made a reputation for our block and our house. My brothers and our club hang out there all the time. It's kind of an unofficial clubhouse, but I lived there with my wife and children. So for me, it was a different story.

When everyone else went home, I'm still there. When people would ride down my street or be over my wall or make certain threats, that was scary. The way the raid happened, finding out later on, was that they had been - meaning 'they', the feds and the local law enforcement and the sheriff, they'd all been watching us for years, wondering, waiting for us to slip up. Which in that case, that incident at Blackie's was enough for them to have grounds now to get a search warrant. For years, they were trying to get a search warrant, but we had never did nothing - nothing wrong, nothing illegal. We had annoyed some people. Some neighbors didn't like us, because we had people or loud bikes, but nothing illegal. But that day was enough for them to now be like, "Can I get those warrants?", and they did on many homes and many properties of ours all at the same time. That's what they needed. It was because they had surveillance. For I think two to three years, they had some surveillance going on. We didn't know. I guess that's what surveillance is, right?

It happened that day where it was early in the morning, and I don't know, Wednesday or something like that. I sleep pretty hard, and there was a phone going on. I didn't really hear it until the sirens. They had the loudspeaker as part of their truck. They pretty much brought their whole substation. They brought the big guns out for us. They really did from whatever they had in their mind over these years. They were trying to call for me to come out, because they were so scared to go in - thinking that we were going to engage. They had people at the back of our walls, sides, fronts, you name it, they were everywhere. They wouldn't - they kept calling. They called so much that - I had it for a long time, but I think

TRAINED TO SERVE JESUS

I erased it - but they left a voicemail. The sergeant who is outside in the front, "MJ, this is Sergeant Bilko. This is the Anaheim Police Department. I need you to come out now with your hands up." Since when do you leave a voicemail for a raid - for someone to come out? I laugh now, but it was just crazy.

So my wife woke me up. I slept through three phone calls, it's four or five in the morning, because they get you when it's dark - again trying to catch you on your back. She was like, "I think something is going on," because now the lights are flashing on the side of our house. They had this repeat message of, "Come out." They would not come in the house for nothing. They wouldn't. They wanted to make sure that we did. So once I knew that, I told my wife, "Stay in here." I think I just put a t-shirt on. I saw the lights. I'm like this isn't normal. Its an alien attack.

I've never been raided before. They told me to come out. I told her to stay back, and as soon as I did, you just saw a dozen red dots all over your body stepping out of the house. First, they tell you to turn around backwards, hands-up, the whole routine. But right before that, you are just seeing the lights blinding you. The noise is so loud, and it sounds like you are just in another country or another time. Then, you just see the little lights everywhere. I walked backwards at least twenty or thirty yards until they finally ziptied me and put me in paddy wagon. They did that one by one with my family. Every single one of us - any adults they zip tied. Kids had to walk on their own. You couldn't do anything. Then, there was a lot of horrific, sad, scary stuff that happened from that point.

We were expecting to deal with people and things from the incident, but not the raid. It was pretty crazy. Then it was tough. One day, you are here, and then the next day, you are in a paddy wagon with your mom. Seeing her - she's on the curb next to you ziptied. Then at that point we were just - I think it was me and one of my other brothers. We were just yelling at the cops. We didn't want to make it worse, but that's their grandmother. My kids have to see their grandmother on the curb right now? You want us. Do whatever you got to do, and we'll figure that out. They did. They kept us, they took all of them to a safehouse. Which was again just crazy to think that they can't be home, because they were tearing apart our house at that time - tearing apart the inside of our house, the attics. They dug up our lawn thinking, "Where are these guys hiding the drugs?" "Where are they hiding the prostitutes?" "Where are they hiding the boatloads of whatever we feel they are apart of - the guns, the ammunition?" None of that.

THE FIGHT, THE RAID, AND THE TRIAL

At the end of the day, they got me personally in my house for brass knuckles, which are technically illegal, but they weren't there the day of the fight. There is no blood on them. They are a keepsake from anyone that lives around here that goes to Tijuana, Mexico, but that was enough for a felony. Yeah, so don't let nobody tell anybody that brass knuckles are a paperweight. They can use it against you, and they sure did for me. So we are all getting interrogated. Then, we end up going to jail. That was probably the hardest time, because my dad was going through a lot of health issues already. Just a lot of health issues.

Then to be thrown around the way they were, because they still knew this was the man. This was the leader, and we've got you. There is lot of wicked people on that side. Just evil. It's not enough for you to be locked up. It's almost like, "Ha, we've got you." Even though they still never proved anything, they were able during that time to almost put him down and have their way - where they could just muscle him around a little bit while we are all handcuffed of course. We had like nightgowns on for the first part, because they stripped us all. Then we are in a hold together. Because me and him obviously had the same last name, me and him were in a jail cell together for hours figuring out the next step.

Those hours were probably the longest hours of my entire life. Just to see my dad - I don't even think we said one word. I think he said, "Are you okay?" He didn't even have the energy. He was so weak with everything happening to him. Especially because I think he knew - he took ownership years later. "That was my doing. I brought us up and I brought us down." He's always taken that one for all of us. Some of us knew that or not, but still to me, it was seeing my father in this state. I wanted him out of there, and he wanted me out of there. I felt that he's my dad and he's older and he's struggling with his health issues. And of course, he thought, "It's my son. I'm used to time, my son is not." You know what I mean? That's not my thing. It was hard.

CHILL on the raid: Well, the morning of the raid is probably one of the worst days of my life, but the greatest day of my life, because God did something in that raid. I can't speak for my brothers or sister. They have their own opinions. But for me, the first thing I did - we were in the front house. We got it pretty bad. They watched a lot of YouTube. They watched a lot of videos. I don't blame the cops. Some of them were just doing their jobs. I don't blame them. The higher-ups are the ones that put it in their brains that you are going in against an army, which is understandable. We didn't look like choir boys. I get it. I get that part.

TRAINED TO SERVE JESUS

The thing that hurt me the most - firstly, I was prideful. When I woke up, the first thing I did was make sure to have my Soldier gear on and what I represented. I wanted to go out with a bang. I thought this was it. I thought this was the end. I thought end times - Armageddon is here. God is coming home. We are going to fight against the bad people. My mind was out of whack. I tell my wife, "Hey, this ain't right."

All these alarms are going off and hearing sirens. We look out our window which looked directly to the right that looked at my brother MJ's house. I remember telling my wife, "Oh, shit. They are raiding MJ's house. We gotta get out of here." My wife starts throwing stuff in bags thinking that we are going to get out of here. So our baby was one year old at the time, my daughter. We are grabbing stuff. Dogs are barking. I'm just thinking all hell's breaking loose. I'm thinking its end times. They wake you up out of your sleep. That's what they do. They paralyze you. "What do I do? What do I do?" You make some dumb decisions.

So right then, I was like, what do I do? I had a pistol in my drawer, and I already knew my dad - I'm thinking my dad is a felon. He could get in trouble for this, so I put it on my belongings so they knew that it was mine. Then I was thinking, "I got to put it back, because I'm going to get shot." I wasn't that down, because I knew it was the cops by now. So I run down the hallway and had some partners that were in the living room sleeping. I looked down the hallway. It's just filled with flash bang grenade smoke. So I'm like, "Dude!" I didn't want to go nowhere. I wanted to protect my wife and kid.

Chill (third from right) surrounded by friends

250

THE FIGHT, THE RAID, AND THE TRIAL

I had to make some quick decisions. "Lord!" I was so backslidden in sin, but I was like, "Lord, I know you got this dog! We are going out in a blaze of glory!" You are scared, so you start telling yourself - I don't care if any bad dude says or anybody that has been raided, when it wakes you like that and you don't get a bang on the door, you get flash bangs through the window and something is breaking. It's like a wreck. Just wild. It shocks you. I always tell people, you can't be a good gangster if you've got a daughter and a wife. It's just not possible. Because as gangster as I thought I was, my heart broke when I looked at my wife and kid. Just standing there holding my baby. Especially when we started going into the front. We are going slow, and they are going, "Come out with your hands up. This is the Anaheim PD." I thought it was maybe just some small thing at first. I looked to the right. I don't know if you've ever been to the 301 house on the corner, but it's like - not now, but at the time, it had a doorway where you had a long hallway and then it cuts to the right. There is a door.

I look out front and one of my partners Gabriel. He was a tough kid - a boxer, and he rode with us. He was from the Inland Empire area. I seen him lay down on his back in the front yard. I seen a tank on the front yard. I just saw dudes in fatigues. "Dude, what happened?" I didn't know much. I didn't know what happened or transpired. What was crazy is my partner is a tough kid. He ran out there thinking somebody was attacking us, not cops. It was early. He's throwing a front karate kick, and they shot him out of the air with bean bag guns. So he's bleeding, but we thought he'd been shot.

So I run back and tell my wife. This is only a few minutes of time. I'm telling my wife, "They are shooting people. This is serious." Before all the police brutality, all the videos and stuff, we'd been getting picked on by the cops since we were little kids in L.A. So that was nothing new to us. They were always beating up our friends. We weren't shocked that he was shot, but I'm like, "This is real life." They all got masks on. That's what tripped us out. There is all these masks and flash bang grenades are going off and smoke. "Dude, who are they coming for? John Gotti?" I was just thinking - you go back to those innocence of a kid. I love Jesus, I'm a Christian kid. I thought about how far we come - how I at least messed up my life by being angry and prideful.

I get my wife and kid, and I get my wife to the door. My daughter had no shirt on just diaper. I saw over 60 infrared red beams on her body. Right then, I was so angry. I was so mad. I was like, "Fuck you." I was pissed. I don't know if anybody has ever - I hope they never have to experience that. But seeing your baby, one slight move - if I would have went out there with the gun that I was going to go out there with, I would have been shot. She would have been shot. My wife would have been shot. Everybody would have been killed. I understand they are on edge, too, and I would have gave them exactly what they thought they were coming for, which breaks my heart at the time as I think about it. We walked out, and there was - they put us all in zipties.

They threw my kids on their face. I had some teenage boys. They threw them on their face. My teenage son is right next to me, and they smashed their face in the mud. One of my friend's son, he had broke his leg a few weeks before. He was only like 14 at the time. I said, "Hey, his leg is broken." They threw his face in the mud, cussing him out. I was so mad. I couldn't do anything. At that time, that's what I said. I had an experience with God, "I got you covered, son. I love you. But now it's my time to work in your life." I also thought that was Satan. At the time, I wasn't sure. I remember a tear came to my eye, because I was okay. I'm okay. I'm going to be good.

My dad always says, "If Chill or Roc goes to prison, they'll be fine. Don't ever let MJ go. He's too pretty." I wasn't worried about that. I was worried about one slight wrong move and my daughter and my innocent wife who had nothing to do with any of this stuff that I brought in - sin brought into their life, and it affects the family. So they dragged all of us to the main corner. They threw us out there, and I looked - man, it was like dead silence. They took us to where the street Brookhurst is, Brookhurst and Broadway. Usually at that time, this was about 6:30, 7:00 a.m., people were going to work so it's busy. Dude, it was like a movie. It was dead silence. You could hear a pin drop. I look, and there is over 60 - there was a liquor store, you've seen it, that overlooks our house. A little shopping market area. There was over 60 undercover cars, and everybody had masks on.

I know cops in their uniforms, but these were masks, and they were in fatigues. So I was like, this is SWAT team. I looked back, and I see in my backyard where my dad lived, I see SWAT team on the roofs with infrareds pointing at the backs. They are at my brother MJ's house. I was freaking out. "Dude, they are going to shoot somebody." I heard dogs barking. So they took us to the corner, left us zip tied there for 6 hours, and they wouldn't let my wife go. They let other wives go, but they wouldn't let her go. They took her baby, my daughter. Why? They took my wife, because they wanted my wife to give information on me and on us. They took my wife - they had a van off-site, and they took my wife to the van, and they had masks on. They took me to the van, and they kept me there for an hour.

They were like, "Come on, Chill. Be honest with us." "You can't even be real with me. You got a mask on." They were like, "Be a man." I'm like, "You be a man and take your mask off." Remember I was from the streets. I had code. I wasn't going to say nothing. I didn't know nothing. There was really nothing to say other than, we rode. I got in some scuffles, we fought sometimes. If somebody was picking on us or pushed my family, I'm going to fight just like a normal guy anywhere.

They were looking for drugs and guns. Everything they thought that we were. I understand now as I'm older and a lot more years later, they were scared. They thought there was - they thought they were going to find the hidden treasure in our house. They just interrogated us forever. They didn't take me in, because I wasn't there when it happened (Blackie's). They didn't get my ID. The thing that happened at the bar, whatever happened there, they got the IDs of - they gave IDs. Because my dad didn't run afterwards I guess, he stayed right there. So they got the IDs. Whoever gave their ID that day, that's who the cops took.

They wanted to take me. They were so mad. They were like, "I can't believe we are not taking this guy." At the same time, they are yelling at me. They are going nutty. "We can't find Pastor Phil." Dude, I'm watching my house from afar - it's up in smoke. They were like, "We are going to kill your f-ing dad. We are going to kill. Where is that dude?" I was like, "I don't know, he went for a jog?" I was so tired and out of it. This is an hour later. They couldn't find him. Then, they are like, "He's in a car. We found him. He's sleeping in a car. We are going to blow his f-ing head off. You better tell us where your dad is." You can ask my wife. We were like, "Dude, what happened?" They were going nutty. I kept on hearing them - we were sitting there for like 5 hours on the curb.

It was weird. Rewind a little bit. As we were walking out and it was dead silence on that street, the moment that we hit the gas station, I see cops like this, "Bring it in, bring it in." I see Channel 11, Channel 13, news people, friends that used to be apart of Set Free standing across the street with signs. "Guilty, Guilty!." I'm like, "What?" Dudes that I lead to the Lord. There wasn't a friend in sight. Everybody wanted something from us just days before that. Now, nobody wanted nothing to do with us. They were like, "I knew you guys were bad people." Our neighbors who we helped get off drugs, "They are terrible people." Everybody just started joining the party, which I get, I've been there before. We were on the corner and all the news came, the choppers. I started seeing buses, paddy wagons being pulled in. I'm like, "Dude, we don't even have that many people." Basically, they got a lot of kids in the raid, all of our little kids. There was more little kids than there was grownups.

TRAINED TO SERVE JESUS

TRINA on the raid: I was actually in Mexico. I wasn't there. I only found out what happened because my friend called me and told me it was all over the news, so I had to fly back from Mexico. God spared me on that, because I did not want to be there. That's for sure. I was there for all the aftermath. To be honest with you, I was thinking, "Shit just got real." I was like, "Oh, I do not want to be apart of any of this stuff." That's what I was thinking. I didn't see any specific thing coming, but I've seen everybody going down a path that we shouldn't have been going down. Where everybody lost their - nobody was about Jesus anymore. It was all about being cool and being whatever. Even though I wasn't doing that, I was apart of it just as much as anybody else, because I was there and engaging in everything we did. So I knew that something was going to happen. I didn't know what was going to happen. It was pretty scary actually. I was scared.

When I got back from Mexico, Turtle was in jail. My dad was in jail. Matthew was in jail. The guy we lived with was in jail. Because the house that me and Turtle lived at, that's the one that they raided first, so those two were the first people taken. Then, a whole bunch of people from our homes were in jail, too. So basically, I just came home trying to figure out what was going to happen next and if they can get bailed out. Their bail was set pretty high. Then my mother-in-law ended up bailing my husband out and getting him a lawyer. Then, my mom got a lawyer for Matt and my dad.

TURTLE on the raid: Obviously, that was the cops that came to hit the pad. The guy I was living with - he came and woke me up. I think it was four in the morning. He came and woke me up and he said, "Hey, they are here." I didn't know he meant the cops. I thought he was talking about somebody else. So I got ready to protect the house. When I opened up the door, thousands of red lights all over my body. Them saying, "Get on the ground. Put your hands in the air." They hit the pad. That was the day of raid. Actually I think the pad I was at, that was the first pad to get hit, and then obviously from there, they took out the other houses that were on the block.

I was calm. I knew what they were there for. I knew. It wasn't a surprise that they showed up. We knew they were going to come eventually, but I was very calm. I just figured, "Hey, we got to deal with it. It's the day of reckoning right now." So yeah - they put me in the van, and we headed off to the county jail. So yeah.

Thank God at the time Trina wasn't pregnant, but I was happy she was gone to be honest with you. God actually set that up in a beautiful way to where she was obviously in Mexico on a trip, and they came at the time that she wasn't there. Because I definitely think Trina's got a different loyalty to her dad than any of the other kids and that goes without saying. So I don't think that she would have took it real well seeing her dad being hauled off in a paddy wagon or all of that stuff that went down. I just don't know how Trina would have reacted, but it probably wouldn't have been as calm as I was. I figured she would catch word at some point, and we'd figure it out when she gets back.

Newport Beach police sergeant Evan Sailor conducts a news conference to display items taken into custody. In the foreground is a photo of Set Free Soldiers' Glenn Arthur Schoeman, left, and Phil Aguilar. (photo by Eugene Garcia / The Orange County Register)

PASTOR WILLIE DALGITY on how Set Free Yucaipa was impacted by the raid: I believe I heard about it on the news. I wasn't just blown back on it going, "Wow, how could that happen?" Because I know Phil - he always goes right behind the lines like he says. So it didn't surprise me that he'd be at Blackie's, you know? I think what happened there surprised him. It got out of control. What it did, it really - that went national. That was on Fox News and CNN and stuff, so it's like a real big thing.

Here we are up in little ole Yucaipa, people going, "You affiliated with him?"' I always just said, "Yeah, I am." Sometimes, stuff happens. But I always bring it back to this, that me and Phil we got knit hearts when it comes to winning people to Christ. I love him, man. So during that time, I was praying for him, because I knew he was going through it. That was the big one there. He needed people to love him through that. So again, people said, "Let's take the name off. Take the name off." I said, "No man. We can't do that, because we are doing this Set Free work. I'm never going to apologize for it."

SANDRA on the condition of their homes after the raid: Tornado. It was disgusting. They tore up our houses, put holes in the ceilings, dug in the yards, and destroyed everything in the rooms. Just like you see in the movies, but 10 times more. They go through your dirty laundry. Now if that's not humiliating, nothing is. Then you are talking to the same person who just went through your dirty laundry. Everything is completely destroyed, and then they wouldn't let us go back. Once we were at our friend's house, I wanted to go back there. The streets were all detained, and they said, "Oh, no. You can't go in there still." So we didn't even get to go back there until six o'clock at night. And, they towed away all our cars.

Ransacked bedrooms after the raid

MJ on the trial: We finally got released on our bail, which was crazy. Especially for me, I had no history whatsoever. So to have them have the bail that high was crazy, but after a few days, we are out on the streets and only just to see how they tore apart our house. They took everything that we used for our livelihood and property, vehicles, you name it. So at this time, we are just like, "Man, we've got to get a lawyer." We get the best that we can, but despite what they think or the public thinks of the law, there wasn't money like people think. There were some people in our club that had money, but that's their money. Again, even during that time, not everyone that was as close was as close when that happens. People started looking out for their own selves. So for me and my dad and for my brother-in-law, Michael, Turtle as we call him, we were all on trial together, because we were the ones that actually got charged. Me with the felony possession of what they consider only to be used for harm or extortion, brass knuckles.

THE FIGHT, THE RAID, AND THE TRIAL

My dad - he has a history even though it was a long, long time ago for I believe what it came down to having one round, one bullet. It was an old - I know exactly what it was when they talked about it. I'm like, "Are you serious? It's like a trinket." I didn't even think it would fit - maybe from the wild west or something. It was so stupid. And then Turtle for something he had, and I think for something from the day of the incident. The little history that he had. So they brought us all - this was the prosecutor's goal - was to put us all together, because usually you break everybody up, and we have our own trial and our own lawyers and all that. But they wanted - it was their decision, the prosecution, to bring us all together. Me, my dad and my brother-in-law, because they felt if they can get us all in the same room at the same table, same time, they would see just how rough and hardcore and how just incriminating we look from the outside. I think we are pretty cool, sweet guys, but this was their game plan that we found out at that time and later on.

The three lawyers of each of us were like, "Well, alright, let's try to use this to our advantage." We teamed up, and we had our little dream team going. So what they planned to kind of work from did end up backfiring, because everyone was able to help each other and get either the least time or the least probation. For me personally, I had probably for I think it was a year or two. Its sucks. You know what I mean? It definitely sucked. The court part was terrible, because you are not getting paid to go to court. People don't realize. We had to go to court for a year and a half or two years after that. I'm talking about days. It was in Newport Beach, because that's where it happened. You have to drive there. You are not working. During this couple of years, it took about two years, and we still never got all of our stuff back from the Anaheim Police Department or the Newport Beach Police Department. I'm talking about things that we worked in the music business. If someone just came and just took what you worked with, your tools of trade, your hard drives, what do you do? That's what they did for us. They didn't care. They didn't think like that.

During that, we are trying to fight for our life. We are trying to fight for our property. We are trying to raise money. We are trying to get people who still like us, still believe in us. Trying to get the press a little bit to give us a little love, because all they are seeing is this one-sided thing even though they are not telling them that we are out now. They are not telling them that we even won the trial - in our eyes won the trial. Because they were trying to send us away forever. That was their goal. It just became a mockery of Anaheim Police, and it became a mockery of the judicial system. Every single person that was involved. When you are in there, it's you. And after a couple of years, the cameras aren't around like they were. It's just you and your dad and you and your brother-in-law - maybe a couple of supporters and local papers. Then, you see the guy up there saying all this stuff, the detective. You see some people that they are bringing transcripts of people that they say ratted you out or that you guys were doing illegal activities. I'm like, "It's not true. It's not even true."

None of us even took the stand. None of us. I don't think any of us did. Didn't even get to that point. Everything they would do and say made it look more like they had a personal vendetta against us and because the way we took over Anaheim. Because the way people have always thought at one time or another, that Set Free was tied into some organized crime. There is no way that they could just help people to help people. There is no way that they can have that bike because it's a ministry tool or someone blessed them. They just like to ride for the sake of riding. They couldn't. There are so many even after that who still believe we just had these great lawyers and defense and all this money to put into it so we got let off again. You are not going to change the minds of those people, and I definitely don't care to. But it was a long - it wasn't just an incident. It wasn't just a raid. It wasn't just an arrest. It wasn't just jail time. It was a long process that only time can heal. I think for a lot of us, we are looking forward to that, to put it behind us.

Set Free Soldiers

ALEXA TEJEDA on helping Pastor Phil: In fact, he called me, and he says, "I want you to support what I'm going through." He explained it to me. If you have anything to give to the ministry to help out, please do so. So I did. I went to his house, and I took some things and some cash and I wished him well and that he would always be my pastor because he was just - he really influenced my life. He changed my life radically in the fact that I learned how to serve God. That was important. That's a really important base to start from. So I told him I loved him and that he would always be my Pas and that I would always help him no matter what. So that's a great thing. And I didn't judge him. I knew from the beginning he was a trouble maker. He went against the grain, but so am I deep in my heart. So I kind identified with that, and like I say, I'm not here to judge, I'm here to help out. If he needs help, I will. I will help him.

TURTLE on the trial: Oh man, the trial was a trip man. Because basically it was something that they didn't - basically they didn't have anything. They really just wanted to really get at Pastor Phil. That was really what the whole investigation came down to. They didn't care about all the biker stuff. They just wanted Phil. You know, it was pretty sad to see that they would go after a guy that is doing so much good. Obviously, he's controversial and that type of stuff, but they didn't find one thing in any of his houses. They hit him on a little replica bullet. It was pretty pathetic. It was hard, you know what I mean?

We had to show up at court all that time. Obviously, a lot of people got scared. I'm talking about brothers in the club got scared, and they didn't want to show up no more. They didn't want their name attached to this or attached to that. It kind of dismembered a lot of stuff. It was sad to see how certain - there were some people that gelled and pulled together and stayed with him, but there was a lot of people that bounced. It's funny, because we've got a rocker on the side of our cuts that says, "Hasta la muerte," which means "until death". I took that serious man. I took that real serious, and to see people being able to just walk away because there is a little bit of rough patches in the road - I mean it was saddening. But the court case ended up coming out alright. Chief didn't get no time, and MJ didn't get no time, so that was good.

They hit me with some felony gun possession, and I had been a prior felon, but it was for possession of drugs, and I had some other priors. They were looking to give me five years. That was what they started with. They ended up coming down to three, and then basically they found a crack in the case where they knew they didn't have nothing. The warrant wasn't legit, and so they came back with a deal. Basically, they gave me a year in the county, no prison time, which I'm all down with that. And Pastor Phil and MJ, they got some informal probation and things like that, so yeah, let's do it.

TRAINED TO SERVE JESUS

PASTOR PHIL on the trial: Even though it wasn't drugs or violence, it was just the pridefulness. Being around thinking that we were somebody or I was something. Humbled myself, and every day since for the last 8 years, just one step closer to walking with the Lord Jesus. Just loving people more. I got a new patch that I wear that says, "Trained to serve Jesus". I'm a loner rider for the Lord. When I show up, there is 100% perfect attendance. If something goes wrong, I know who the guy is that did it. So I'm loving my life.

They dropped cases on everybody except for my son, MJ and my son-in-law, Turtle. Now, I feel really responsible, because these are my kids here. They just called us back, postponing depositions, postponing this. They just drag it out, drag it out, and drag it out, because we know that most things end up in a plea bargain at the end. That is what happened at the end – just turned into a plea bargain. Turtle got his plea, my son got his plea, and my plea was literally - they came looking for guns, looking for drugs, looking for stuff on the Internet, and they found absolutely nothing. They found one bullet that I had in a jar in a basement full of things. One bullet, no gun.

It was all BS again. All that big story. They spent a million dollars coming there when they could have come knocked on my door, and I would have opened it. What can I say? I believe that we were the picture to the police of the "Sons of Anarchy" show, but "Sons of Anarchy" hadn't happened yet in reality.

In court, they showed that they'd been watching our club for three years, taking pictures, but they didn't see any drugs. They didn't see any violence. They didn't see any of that type of stuff, but it was that little innuendo, that look. Like maybe we are going to get behind their doors, and we'll be able to find this. They found absolutely nothing at my house whatsoever except that one bullet. But being an ex-con, a felon, I shouldn't have even had that one bullet, so I learned a valuable lesson.

It was selling newspapers. Tattooed pastor. Ex-con. Biker. Gang war. All the hype that you could think of - it sold newspapers. It was on the news program all over the place. But, it's like almost everything else that happens in the news, a couple of weeks later it dies down. A month later, it dies down. We went to court. There was no big print of "Pastor Phil not guilty of anything except having one bullet". Didn't have any of that kind of stuff. There was never a retraction. It's a newspaper-selling thing. It's exciting. Is he a pastor, or is he a gangster? Is he a pastor, or is he a crook? Is he a pastor, or is he running a prostitution ring? It all sounds good. It gets it going.

THE FIGHT, THE RAID, AND THE TRIAL

Like I said, sad to say some of the police - they were just looking for some press. I can remember the police officer driving down to the station goes, "Aren't you a little bit old for this?" I go, "Old for what? You guys don't even know what you are talking about." I learned a lot of valuable lessons. I'm sorry to all my Soldiers, and everybody that I led on this trip. People that we had a confrontation with, sorry about all that. It's a new day eight years later now, and I'm feeling really great.

Pastor Phil, MJ, Turtle, and attorney Lloyd Freeberg appearing in court in Newport Beach for arraignment. (photo by Joshua Sudock / The Orange County Register)

While we are going to court, it was difficult, because financially we lost everything. So I have my kids, my grandkids, I'm trying to help out. It was a tough time. I started having church in the backyard. Then we went to a motel down the street and started having church over there. I got in just teaching and preaching the Bible and just getting back to the basics of loving God, loving people. Not being concerned with an image or this or that anymore. But really, just taking it wholeheartedly and seriously how much Jesus loved me and how important it was to get back to my roots - being able to stay every day with Jesus is sweeter than the day before.

So here I am, I'm building that up. We are doing ministry again. We are reaching out again. It was a very, very slow process rebuilding our lives back together. That's when I started something I called becoming a 'professional forgiver'. I started that shortly after my arrests. There were certain people that I knew I'd done wrong in my life - people that I'd hurt, people that I lead in the wrong direction. I started emailing, making phone calls to people, and that started my professional forgiver training. A lot of people want to be professional golfer, baseball player, football player. I decided, God gave me the idea, be a professional forgiver. So I started calling people up that I'd done wrong or offended me for one reason, "Hey, I'm sorry." Most of them said, "Hey, thanks for doing that." Some people said, "No, I'm not going to forgive you." So that has been one of my great things. A lot of people go, "Why do you love so many people?" Well those who are forgiven much, love much.

TRINA on the trial: After the raid, it was like the downfall. It was already the downfall of that time of Set Free, but we lost so many of our core people. We went back to where we had nothing, no money. Selling cars and anything we could. We basically lived like that for awhile. Then, with court, nobody knew what was going to happen. My husband (Turtle) ended up going to jail and having to serve time and one other guy from it. I was pregnant when he went to jail - no, I just had the babies and then he went to jail a month later or something like that.

Because my husband already had prior felonies - so he ended up being charged with - I don't know you can Google his charges or whatever. But he ended up doing half time of what they gave him. He was supposed to do 18 months and he ended up doing 6 or 7 months - something like that. I used to visit him Friday, Saturday, and Sunday. All those were long, and bring a baby each time. That was interesting.

Then when he got out of jail, part of his probation was to be non-affiliation, so that's when we moved out on our own, and we've been out ever since. Not of Set Free - well, we didn't go to church anymore, because we couldn't. He couldn't be around anybody or else. It would violate his probation. I still hung out, but he just didn't come around. It was like so many people were gone anyways. It wasn't like it was before. Then, my brother moved away. Philip moved to Virginia. So, the family just kept getting smaller. At one point, it was just Hebrew and I here with my dad.

TURTLE on being in jail and getting out: You know what, man? It was good. It was good, but it was hard, too. Because the same reason why I came to Set Free, because I didn't want to be a guy who had kids while still living that lifestyle, I found myself in that very same predicament. My kids had just been born, and now I'm behind the glass. I can't touch them. I can wave to them and put my hands there, but they were babies. That was very tough for me mentally. I praise God that I had a date, and I knew I was getting out. I knew eventually I would be reunited with them, which that is great, but there is something gut wrenching inside you.

It hurts your heart to see your family on that side, you on this side, and there ain't nothing you can do about it. One good thing about that is - my kids were so young they didn't really know what was going on at the time, which is good. But yeah, she faithfully used to show up for visits. I had a lot of people show up. I had a lot of support while I was busted. A lot of people showing up just to see how I'm doing and make sure everything is cool. So there was a lot of love at that point, and I felt it from a lot of different people at that time.

I've been there before and got out before so it wasn't - you always get a little bit of excited and obviously wanting to see my kids. But from the stories I hear, I was going to have - Trina was going to come pick me up, and my brother Chill, he said, "Let me jump in the car. I want to go get him." So he showed up, and you walk out and there they are, boom, what's up? A lot of hugs. Chill took me across the street for a Krispy Kreme donut, which I couldn't argue with that one. So yeah, coming home, life went on as normal. It really did. It wasn't a big deal. It wasn't something we bragged about or talked about. It's just what happened, and we made it through so it's good.

SANDRA on the pain of the experience: When we went through the whole cult thing, the greatest thing Paul Crouch said when we were talking about TBN was, "Sue the bastards." That's exactly how I felt, "Sue the bastards," because those people were out of control in the way they handled the whole situation of the raid. For the grandchildren and people like that, not just us but the other people that were raided, they gave the mother a heart attack. The way they went about it was so wrong. I just wanted to sue them - not for any reason, not for money, just sue them so they wouldn't do it to anybody else again. No one would take my case. No one would touch them. In Orange County, forget it. L.A. County said, "Pfft, you know honey you are talking about coming against the whole jurisdiction. Nobody does that." I'm like, "Okay." So I wasn't getting my satisfaction there, so my best way of getting satisfaction was go back to normal. Let's go back to living, ministering, doing all the things that we are supposed to do, and that's what we did.

BILLY AGUILAR on the aftermath: The Soldiers that are left, they are grounded man. They are planted, because Pastor Phil never gave up, because Christ never gave up on him. At his deepest and darkest time in that jail cell again, as a felon, Christ opened the doors and let him out. Amazing. People thought he was gone for 20 years. People were clapping. I was told by a lot of people that they were ready to throw parties on this, and God opens a door and lets him out. Let's them all out, they all got out. It's been about seven or eight years since that's gone down, and I've just been chugging along, doing my thing. Still praying for the red and white, still praying for the black and white, still praying for the green, you know? Vietnam vets, the Haitians, I still have that love for those guys, because I'd hate to see them all go to hell, because I was trained to serve Jesus. Not trained to serve Billy, not trained to serve Harley Davidson, not trained to serve this patch. I was trained to serve Jesus, and I was taught that by Pastor Phil. It's pretty cool. It's pretty cool. I thank God that he's out. I'm sure he's still got a little bit of a mess to clean up.

PASTOR WILEY DRAKE on the charges against Pastor Phil: They were certainly challenges for him, and what I saw was a government out of control. I saw a police department and a government out of control - seeing something that they didn't like. Seeing a hippie movement, seeing a gang kind of movement, but not a gang - not the negative sense. But seeing motorcycles - we had the same problem right here. When I had a hundred motorcycles parked here in the parking lot, the police got upset. They got nervous. Well, they got over it, because there wasn't any dope or any killing and shooting and fighting.

They realized that this 'gang' of tattooed, bearded kind of gang looking people weren't really. We have a senior citizens home just down the street and when they first started coming here, the management there came to me and said, "What's going on down there? Our people are afraid to go by your church anymore. We go walk to the store. We are afraid to go by there." I said, "Don't be afraid. In fact, you are safer on that sidewalk when they are there than you are when they are not there." And so, it was in my opinion a railroad job. They set him up. Phil is not a perfect man by any stretch of the imagination, nor am I. However, he is a good man. He is a good godly man. He serves God. Everything he's done is to tell people that you can be set free.

TRINA on Pastor Phil's feelings of guilt: I think Pastor Phil lives with guilt of feeling responsible of what happened with that whole situation - and getting all his kids involved. But I think mentally - that's what I'm telling you, when people have power and authority, your mind just doesn't think right for men. Something about it, I'm not sure. But I know that I don't think anything was on purpose, it just happened, and it got too big. It just kind of took on a life of its own. I think he lives with guilt about that - feeling like he's the one who messed up that whole situation we had going on. I think that he definitely feels guilty about it.

THE FIGHT, THE RAID, AND THE TRIAL

CHILL on moving to Virginia: It was about less than a year later, and everything died down. My dad was going to court. They were going for whatever they were going for. Me and my brother and Turtle, we had talked. We were just tired of the back and forth. Are you going to be a club? Are you not going to be a club? We were just over it. I just knew that God had a calling on my life, and if I stayed doing the same BS, the same guy who I was - God gave me a clear sign. He said, "If you stay in California, you are going to end up dead or in prison." Because I didn't let it go yet. I was still mad. I was still angry. I wanted vengeance, but that wasn't God's plan. I needed to be humble and to be meek. So I'm going south.

Me and my dad really weren't talking much. Me and my brothers weren't talking. Everything - the raid took a toll on everybody. It knocked us out. Me and my wife were working jobs and just trying to stay afloat and survive. But I knew I had to get - I knew I had to make a move. I didn't know why God was calling me to Virginia, because I couldn't stand Geronimo. I couldn't stand my brother Geronimo, but Geronimo called me and he said, "Bro, God is telling you to come out here. I got a church." I thought, "Okay, this is 10 years later, 11 years later. Geronimo has maybe changed." I didn't know. I hadn't been around him. I haven't even had a conversation with him.

I think we called him to help with bail money. That's why me and him started talking again. He's like, "You got to get away from dad. Dad is trouble." I was like, "I don't think dad is trouble. We created a lot of this drama for him. He was with us, but we were grown men." I always took responsibility. Everybody wanted to blame shift. You've got to take responsibility. I'm a grown man. Nobody makes me do anything. I do what I want to do. So I told Geronimo, "Maybe I'll go check it out." He's like, "Oh, you can come write songs," because I was writing songs and doing worship still. I just didn't believe in what I was singing at the time.

So, that was about 2009, I went out there, and I just need a change. That saved my life. It really did. I went out there, did music, and then did this. Then, after the first two weeks thereafter, Geronimo said he was changed. I realized he was the same guy, and I was stuck out there. My family was mad at me, because I moved. They felt like I betrayed them and left the family. I was born and raised with my dad. I was the guy who would be mad at anybody who left. So I get that dynamics, but I knew how that was going to work. There was no easy way out. I had to do it.

It hurt. I cried many nights out there. But I also cried because now I'm out here with this guy who is a phony, and he's sharing his story. Everything that my dad started and kind of created, Geronimo had took the formula and did it there, but he didn't call it Set Free. He changed the name. He didn't want my dad anywhere around it or tied to it, because he acted like my dad was bad publicity, which at the time we were. He had brought me out, and he told his people, "My brother is crazy. Don't mess with him." So people weren't talking to me there for the first few months. He told them, "I'm here to help him," and the reality was I was going to get some help, but I'm here to help you, because you are nutty. After a few weeks, I realized he was cookoo. So I went there, and I'm glad I went there, because God used me for a reason. After almost three years there, it turned bad. My brother was doing stuff I didn't agree on, and I called him out. He begged me to stay and I said, "I can't stay, because if I stay and cover for you, I'm just as guilty as you."

PASTOR TIM STOREY on how God uses shaky people: When challenges came back into his life around 2008, once again I think you'll always have people that would say, "There he goes again." But really, I think that there we all go again. If we were to do a 24-hour reality show on anybody, I think that everybody's working through things. God uses shaky people to do sturdy projects. If you look at Hebrews 11, everyone of those guys were shaky, but God created a sturdy lifestyle in them if they were willing. Hebrews 11:32 says that weaknesses, plural, were slowly turned to strength. So the journey of Phil Aguilar, of me getting to know him in the mid 80's to knowing him now into 2016, 17, and 18, is one that we are all on. Our weaknesses are slowly turning to strength. Some of us - our weaknesses maybe surfaced in a different way because of fame or people know about someone, like a Phil Aguilar. So they are amplified. But I believe that Phil Aguilar is on life's journey and that he is gaining momentum every day of his life.

God uses shaky people to do sturdy projects, because He knows that if we stay in Him, we will not remain shaky. So the idea is never for God to get a person who is in a shaky place, shaky foundation, shaky character and leave them there. We go through recovery and discovery at the same time. So Phil Aguilar - one of the things about failure that is good, is that it exposes you to, "Wow, this is the weakness that probably a lot of us saw." We all have blind spots. So now you can fail, but you can fail forward back into the mercy of God. And so Phil Aguilar I think was shakier in the early days in certain areas of his life, and for that, it may cost him certain things whether it be friendships or opportunities. But, in the Bible, people that made big mistakes had really big comebacks. And the bigger the setback, the bigger the comeback, and that is what we see in the life of Phil Aguilar.

CHAPTER NINE
A CLEAN START

In the aftermath of the trial, Pastor Phil worked with partners to open Broadway Treatment Center as a state-licensed residential drug treatment center in his own home in Anaheim, California. After several years in operation, the partners went their separate ways, and members of the Aguilar family opened multiple treatment centers including Black Sheep Recovery.

In the meantime, Phil was approached by Pastor Eddie Banales to begin working with the Church of God. With the support of the denomination, Phil helped revitalize a small church in Anaheim, and transformed a COG church in Burbank where his son, Chill, is now pastoring.

With Set Free churches still thriving across the United States, Pastor Phil, Pastor Willie Dalgity, and others are confident on the future of the movement.

PASTOR PHIL on starting a treatment center: There I was - getting my life back together. I'd lost everything, but I'm getting the ministry going back again. A partner of mine was sharing with me how he does treatment centers. It was the same thing I'd always done, helping addicts, but I always called it "beans and rice and Jesus Christ". Just a rough little place - some trailers, some place, some food, some showers and just tell people about Jesus. But, for these treatment centers, I had to go back into school and study some psychological things about relapse prevention.

The place I was living in when they raided me - that turned into a state-licensed treatment center. The next thing you know, I've got Black Sheep Recovery homes, and I'm helping out people like I've been doing almost 40 years. Now, it's a little different flavor, because I'm working with therapists. I'm working with clinical psychologists, and everybody is a certified counselor. I'm all certified now. I'm working with people, but it isn't just being out there at the ranch and raking leaves and doing that stuff. Now, we are having therapeutic groups. We are talking about cognitive behavior. Now, people are having insurance programs, so I'm learning about paperwork and business. I've always run a non-profit. So now I'm turning real Republican, because I'm running a business here. It's just a whole new flavor.

DR. RICHIE COLE on working with Pastor Phil in a treatment home: Well, it was a 17 year journey to get a Bachelors, two Masters, and a Ph.D. in Clinical Psychology. I didn't do it with a specific intention about what population I'd work with. When I was in 11th grade and I took that psychology class, I really dug the subject matter. I was fascinated with the mind. It's crazy how later it ended up becoming a great interest in Theology, because they are linked like everything else. So it wasn't like - if you ask most therapists or psychologists, "Why do you want to help people?" They will say, "I wasn't thinking about helping people, that wasn't my trip. I was just fascinated with the

Pastor Phil and Dr. Richie Cole on the cover of "In Recovery" (Winter 2013)

subject matter." And in a way, my baby's mom clowns me, because she says I took the easy way out. It was kind of laziness. I knew if I went to school through time I would acquire degrees. But if I was still selling drugs and running amuck, I would probably get busted. If I tried to be an actor, I could do it for 20 or 30 years and never make it. So it was kind of like the softer, easier pathway in a sense.

When I first got started with Phil at Broadway Treatment Center, we had already known each other, and we were both kind of unique and unconventional people. But he is a total alpha male leader. I'm more of a number two guy. So he would call it the one-two punch. I had a lot of years of experience. I knew how to do it. He knew how to do it, but more through the church thing. I knew the regulations. The three other owners - they were just businessmen. So it was me and him in the trenches and he - we are all control freaks but in different ways. So he pretty much controlled it, but he would always ask for my feedback on a certain thing. He just always gave me total love, total freedom, but also I wouldn't question him. Like if he's like, "Hey, let's go." I'm not going to say, "Where are we going?" because you roll with him. You just roll. Trust the process, sit in the passenger seat, and it will work out. So we just get along really good together.

I've worked at 30 programs in 30 years. There is the kind that are super hardcore straight - like a Salvation Army. Great program, helps people. But say somebody donates clothes and a guy who is in the program, a ChapStick comes out of a Levi and then he puts it in his pocket. Now he is kicked out. Whereas, dudes would relapse a hundred times, steal, do crazy stuff, and I would be like, "Dude, I would have kicked him out 50 times this week." Chief had that grace and would just give him a chance. So I saw it as someone is trying to allow the self-fulfilling prophecy of, "I'm a loser. They are going to throw me away," but it doesn't happen, because Chief doesn't give up on people. He loves them until they love themselves. I would see this transformation that would blow my mind, because the mental health profession is pretty conservative even though I'm not a really conservative person. That's why I loved working with him. He would do unconventional stuff. He just did it his own way. He had that discernment to be able to help people, because we are of that same fabric. We are the type of people that get judged. We live that life. We've made a million mistakes. So we are not inclined to judge, and we are not in a position to judge. So that helps people feel that they can be open and relate.

TRINA on working with Pastor Phil: Growing up, we had lots of ministry homes, and we had lots of people helping and that were involved in running them. So my dad was more like - he was around, but he didn't run all the day-to-day stuff. But then, when I was a teenager, he was super involved. He ran the day-to-day stuff. He had assistants, but nothing like back then. So then, one time this guy who went through our program, who was actually in the home when I was in the home, he moved up to the mountains him, and his wife and started a treatment center. Him and I went to school together for drug and alcohol counseling. My dad made me go. I didn't want to go. But we went there and got our certificates or whatever. Then a couple of years later - not a couple years, it was like five years or something, he told us that he met this guy who did a treatment center and that him and his wife were going to start one. So they started a treatment center up in Lake Arrowhead, and my mom and dad both worked there. Then him and his wife were telling my dad they should open one. So we were already basically doing the same thing but for free.

We figured it would be just right up our alley, because we needed the income at the time. So we opened one, and it's completely different in so many ways. The ministry homes, everybody is there for free. They are so much more grateful, because they don't have a place to go. People are helping them. Where then you deal with the treatment center, they are all very entitled. Not all, but most of them are entitled and feel like they are doing you a favor by being there. The only difference though on treatment is that you've got to say things different. That's really the only difference. We still pretty much act the same way as we did with the ministry homes. I think that's why people like our place, because we are more like a family and not like a business.

Certain things you can't say to them, because it's a business. You are running a business. You've got to change your language even if it means the same thing in a different way or different wording. I say the same stuff no matter what, because that is my personality. I'm talking about Pastor Phil has to word things differently. Not me, because I say the same stuff.

TURTLE on working with Trina and Pastor Phil: Yeah, so now we are doing the SoCal Treatment Center, which also has the outpatient program with the Black Sheep Recovery house also in correlation with Chief, Pastor Phil. He's helping us out. Obviously, he's the magic man when it comes to that - and really what it is - is ministry. Again, being an addict myself, being somebody that lived that life, I'm now able to help the same kids. Maybe they haven't gone down the paths that I've gone down or been in the institutions that I've been in, but nonetheless, they are down and out. They are hard on their luck, and they are strung out on dope, and we get an opportunity to bring them to our program and help them get back on the road of life. And at the same time, teach them about Jesus.

GEORGE NATZIC on Pastor Phil's role in the drug treatment community: I've recently been introduced and become involved in the detox industry in which has put us again, Phil and me, back together in certain ways. One of the things that I often hear about Phil Aguilar in the space, is that no one works with the youth, the drug addicts, like Phil Aguilar does. He is absolutely iconic in the space. He is one of a kind, and he is able to connect with people on any level, young or old I would say for sure. He really cares about people, and I think that's what really makes the difference.

When you have someone that is completely down and out, Phil has the ability to connect and to really love them where they are. I think that's a game changer, and I think it really breathes new life into people, and that is where Phil is at. Not a lot of people can do what he does at the level he does it. It's very clear when you look at Phil's life. When Phil is on, what I would consider his A game, he is the best at what he does. The Phil that I have most recently come to know is - that's the road he's walking. That is the journey he is on. He's helping people. He's really getting outside of himself in every which way, just for the greatness of - everybody that he comes in contact with, he builds people up. I can't say enough great things about where Phil is at right now.

PASTOR TIM STOREY on the atmosphere of the Black Sheep Recovery home: What I liked about the home that he is overseeing is that there is a lot of peace there. There was a really nice spirit and temperament, because I'm in the recovery world as a comeback coach, and so I'm in a lot of rehabilitation homes and centers. I speak at them. Sometimes they can have a lot of chaos in them. This one felt extremely peaceful. There were a lot of guidelines. There is a lot of leadership, but there was a lot of respect that I saw back to the leader, Phil Aguilar. And you've got to remember that a lot of these young people, they don't know him as Phil Aguilar. Even if you see photos of him in the house, one has to explain those photos of him in the 80's, 90's, and into the 2000's being this leader that was on top, sometimes ridiculed back on top again. But I loved the vibe that he's created, which is that God is not finished with us no matter what life brings us. That's the vibe that I feel at the house.

PASTOR PHIL on the difference of working with a new generation: It's a new generation of young addicts who start off with these pills. These Oxycodone and Xanax and all these different pills that they use. Before you know it, they are shooting heroin - kids from police families, attorneys families, doctors families. 18 to 25 is the average age of these young people. So, I'm really focusing in on that. I still have a "beans and rice and Jesus Christ" ranch that Pastor Willie Dalgity and my partners have, but this whole new version is real discipleship, because we document everything from the minute they come. It's really learning how to love them. A lot of these kids - it's the first time they've ever been homeless. It's a whole new world.

Pastor Phil on the set of "Addicts & Animals", a short-lived reality show on his work with drug addicts.

The Black Sheep Recovery homes are not like a Christian home where our "beans and rice and Jesus Christ" is mandatory. The Bible ten times a day, seven days a week. Here they have an opportunity to go to church. I take them to my partner, life coach Tim Storey. I take them to my son Chill's church, Set Free Church of God in Burbank. I take them to different churches. We go to different power meetings where motivational speakers are at, but it's all their choice on how much they want to receive, how much they want to get involved. The structure is a whole different thing, because most of these kids have come out of enablers that have enabled them in different situations. A whole different breed.

It isn't about gangs and politics from motorcycle clubs. These are just kids, and they've had their hearts broken. They've had trauma drama in their life, PTSD. Young girls that have been raped. All kinds of difficulties like that. So this is a lot more coddling. A lot more sweet, if I may say that word. Just kinder, because they are very sick. The disease of addiction has really got them and ruined their lives. When working with the old crew, the beans and rice crew, it was people getting out of prison. They are a harder group, so they've got to have more rules. This group - I get to coddle them more. Get to love on them more. Get to treat them a sweeter way because it's a different animal. It's a different beast. It's a different situation we are working with.

DR. RICHIE COLE on following Jesus while working with Pastor Phil:
Well, I was an atheist. I wasn't really an atheist when I started working with Phil. At that point, I believed in just a general God, Higher Power that holds all things together - Mother Nature and the positive force of the universe. But I wasn't knowledgeable about scripture. My father who came from Jewish heritage, who is one of the most Christ-like people I've ever met. Integrity, great morality, and he didn't believe in God though. He was such a good father. I just embraced his beliefs. So I didn't get educated about the Bible, and then when I started to learn about it later I looked back. I'm like, "Dad, you raised me with all those principles. Have you ever read the Bible?" "No." "Well, didn't you read the Torah or whatever to get through Hebrew school?" "No, I just learned what I had to memorize, and that's it." But earlier, when I would look at the Bible, it didn't make sense to me. It would piss me off. It seemed stupid. I just didn't really understand the depth. I didn't get the bigger picture. I'm a big picture person. So it took a lot of years.

Pastor Phil (left) baptizes Dr. Richie Cole alongside the Black Sheep Recovery crew.

Phil doesn't proselytize. Say he would tell the story, he would say, "There is this guy named Noah," and he would break down the story - a biblical story in modern vernacular and in terms where you could totally understand it. And later, when you realize that it's in the Bible and it's said in a different way, but you already have a frame of reference for the story. So that was one of the ways - I mean a million ways. When I started getting really interested, I asked him questions. I would just ask him a lot of questions. Sometimes, he would give me his answer. The thing I love about Chief is, he's not going to give you the party line answer. Because being in mental health for so many years and being atheist, I supported gay rights and gay pride and same sex marriage. I was very liberal. Or, someone who has gender dysphoria, well, they feel that they were born in the wrong body. Maybe they were.

So then, when I started to get knowledge about the Word and especially after I accepted the knock on the door of my heart, it was a trip, because I'd try to reconcile those things. Because I'm thinking this is 100% true, but then again, His ways are so much higher than our ways. Different people interpret in different ways. Ten different Ph.D.'s in Theology will all be in debate about doctrine and stuff like that. So one question I asked Chief - I'm like, "Is it possible that when it talks against homosexuality...?," and it almost always connects it to sexual immorality,"that it's talking about a certain type of homosexuality where there is depravity or just lust driven? That maybe people that love each other, a same sex couple that have been together for 50 years, maybe that's not included?" Those type of crazy questions, he'd be like, "I don't know." No other pastor is ever going to answer a question, "I don't know." That's what I love about him. So much stuff we don't know.

SANDRA on her family's work in drug treatment homes: Well, I think they've all had the best training in dealing with people on drugs. So everybody has a profession, so that's their profession obviously. Except for Philip (Chill), as well as he does with people, God has given him an amazing gift of music. So, that's basically his profession. I feel great about how I raised my children. I have no regrets how great of a wife I was, how great of a mother I was. My intentions were always for the best.

Did I make wrong decisions? Could I have handled things differently? Was I an enabler? Of course. I'm a human being I did all those things, but I wouldn't change any of it. I go back to what I said from the beginning with Herb Sokol when he said, "I've never married anybody before, and I'm only marrying you because God told me to. Because I know you two will keep your commitment." We've kept our commitment to each other, and our life now with the drug people - it's just like ministry. It's no different.

It's a little bit of tentmaking, but once again, like I tried to tell you, my husband gives more money away then he receives. So for all the people that think we are wealthy, please come to my house. Look where I live. Look at my bank account. I really don't care what anybody else thinks anymore, because I found out like you said, rumors, people who actually said this happened and that happened. Obviously, they don't really care about me. So I just try and focus on the people that really need help. I try to stay away from Christians actually.

PASTOR EDDIE BANALES on becoming a Church of God pastor and district overseer: I was pastoring this Center of Hope and renting the building month to month. They came to me one day and said they are going to put a sign on the front and they are going to sell the building. They go, "We want a million-two-five." Well, they could have sold it to me for $100,000. I didn't have it. I went to my office and cried on the floor and I prayed and said, "Lord, I don't have this money. What am I going to do?" I had already went to schools. I was already doing storefronts, and my church is already 200 people at this time.

The Lord really spoke to me and said, "You know what? I established you and now I will root you." That following Monday, I read the newspaper and it says, "Church victim of vandals. Pastor at wits end and don't know what to do," on the front page. It was this church right around the corner from where I'm at.

I said to my men's home associate pastor, "I want you to go down there." I drove by there. "I want you to paint all the graffiti. I want you to cut the grass. I want you to clean that building up." It was a little Asian gang next door. I had a lot of ex-convicts here at my mom's home. "I want you to go knock on those doors. You tell them, 'It stops now. It ends now.'" And he goes, "Well, what if they give us problems?" "Well then handle them." "Do two things. Handle them or call the cops. But fix it."

That pastor was, "Oh my God. Oh my God. I've never seen anything like this before." So he called me to meet with me. So this was in January of 1996, 97. I had this vision in December right after Christmas. So when I came and met the pastor, he goes, "You are looking for a building. We are looking for a pastor." I go, "Oh yeah. You are just going to give me the keys?" He goes, "Yeah!" He opens the door and tosses me the keys.

He goes, "I just got to make one phone call." So he calls the state over-seer and goes, "I've got a guy here." He told me about his congregation called the Church of God. Overseer says this, "Okay, you tell him to bring his congregation on Sunday," this was on a Monday. "You tell him to come bring his congregation on Monday. We are going to meet early in the morning. I want to explain to him our doctrine so that he understands," and Church of God and Assembly of God are pretty much the same. He said he wanted to explain to me a few of the rules and everything. "I want to hear him preach. I don't want to say nothing."

So of course, I bring my congregation, and this congregation is full. I preached the message that day called 'David and Goliath - Seize the Moment.' Because David didn't go there intentionally to slay Goliath. He was supposed to get his brother bread and cheese. He was supposed to inquire and come home. He ended up fighting Goliath. So he seized the moment that God gave him.

When I preached that message, the overseer was sitting right there, and he got up and says, "I'm going to seize the moment. I think we found us a pastor." So in February 1997, I was appointed the pastor of this church officially, and I've been here ever since.

I got to know the Church of God, and I was given an exhorter's license on my former credentials. Earned my ordained ministers. I got my bishop license. I served eight years on the evangelism board. On the state council, I would come to a state council meeting one day and I'm sitting looking at the agenda and it says, "District Overseer: Eddie Banales". I'm saying, "Whoa, whoa. What does the district overseer do?" "You'll find out, here is a book." So I was appointed district overseer.

So I've been in the Church of God, and it's good to be apart of something bigger than yourself. And of course, me and Phil have been in contact for all this time. I know that churches are sometimes looking when they have an abandoned church or a struggling church or a church in an area - so my associate pastors have gone. They need a pastor that knows how to work the area, and of course, Phil was always on my list. So I made that connection with the former overseer and Anaheim opened up the door. Then this new one in Burbank, this recent one.

PASTOR PHIL on working with the Church of God: My friend, Pastor Eddie Banales, was one of my leaders in Set Free Worldwide Ministries, and he got involved with the Church of God. They are a worldwide organization, and he was involved with the California, Nevada Church of God. So he spoke to me, "Hey why don't you get involved with this?" There was a man named Steve Darnell who was the bishop of California. He used to watch me on TBN, so we had a connection. He just loved me all the way into his group, and they gave me a little property in Anaheim to start doing ministry. Then, he introduced me to the next bishop who came on and helped me do a place in Burbank, Hollywood area. The cool part of it is they know all the stuff I've been through. They know all the troubles I've been through, but they didn't give up on me. They saw some treasure in this earthen vessel. Now, I'm just representing the Church of God in California. Loving on people, doing outreach ministry. Going to the parks. Helping the addicts. Doing Black Sheep Recovery. Church of God, they've just re-kindled, given me new hope in my life. It's just been a beautiful thing.

PASTOR EDDIE BANALES on Phil's leadership in the Church of God: First of all, he's got the place filled up. One of the things he does great, he does Saturday nights. And the reason why he does Saturday nights is because he wants us to get out of the mentality. Don't be a Sunday Christian. You can be a Saturday night Christian. You can have fun and a good time on a Saturday night. So he definitely does that. Another thing is that with the area that he lives in, I've seen him do so much ministry just walking his dog. Because I only know dog lovers like dog lovers. There is something to connect with right there in that sense. So he's been there.

But one of the good things about this story that I want to tell you about Burbank. Not only did he transition that church, he transitioned that pastor. He helped that pastor move. He helped that pastor fix his house. He helped that pastor get - that's the Phil Aguilar that I know and love. He didn't have to do all of that. That was really my job, because I'm the district overseer. I'm the district overseer now in that church. But he didn't have to help that pastor, that was my job. But he ended up getting the electricians, the plumbers into it. He has a house right over here in Pomona by the way, the pastor. And he helped, and it had been empty for 15-17 years. He helped him clean it. I've seen him on several occasions himself with a little crew. Fixing, painting, and doing everything. So that's the Phil Aguilar I know. A guy that knows how to get people to get things done.

TRINA on Pastor Phil's faith journey: Growing up when Set Free was in the beginning stages, Pastor Phil was a new Christian. He was super gung-ho on God. It's different in the beginning for everybody. And then the people he surrounded himself with were all about Jesus too, and it was like a whole group of great men and women who wanted to see people's life change and stuff. Then, there was point when Set Free got big, and all these other people were there for the wrong reasons, and that's who my dad was surrounding himself with.

A CLEAN START

You are who you hang out with, no matter what anybody says. So they start putting other things in your head, then you are like, "Yeah, that is cool. I can do whatever I want." So that was like the downfall for Pastor Phil in the big Set Free days. The people he surrounded himself with. It wasn't his deacons and elders no more. It was all these young kids, dance posse group. My brother, they were like performers on the road. That's what they did. They lost their way. And then when we moved to Venice Beach, my dad decided that he did not want anything to do with Christians and was angry at God, angry at everybody and called himself the chief of sinners. That's where the whole Chief thing came in.

When we went to Los Angeles to do the Dream Center is when we really started getting back into the Lord and everything. My dad was at a very good place, I think that I had seen him in a long time. And then when we came and did Anaheim Church again, we did it in Buena Park, and it started getting pretty big. Not as big as Set Free was back in the day, but it was big. He always had a biker group, and there was Servants for Christ and they were a great group of men too who wanted to serve the Lord. Their lives were changed.

Well, then something happened where they decided because a whole bunch of younger people wanted to join in the group, so they changed and made a different group. Then that group was supposed to all be for the same reason and then sure enough, little by little, all these young people including my brothers, and everybody started losing the sight of what it was for and acting like they shouldn't have been. Forgetting that they are a Christian club - not even Christian club, Christian motorcycle group. Same as before, he started acting like all the young people, and it turned into a mess. Probably right now is the best I've ever seen my dad in his Christianity and his faith and really living good. This is probably the best time.

TURTLE on changes he's seen in Pastor Phil over the years: You know what, man? I see him now, and he's a lot more gentle in his approach to people. A lot more loving. And he loves people a lot back then too. He just had a different way of doing it, but he took a lot of responsibility for what happened and that whole situation and how things went down. He felt guilty for a lot of things. So I see him now - he's just on that path where if you mess up, he's right there to pick you up. He's the first one to pick you up. He's the first one there to tell you things are going to be okay. He's the first one to tell you that God still loves you and that there is still hope in Christ. And he continues to be that guy who helps those that nobody else wants to touch.

PASTOR EDDIE BANALES on Pastor Phil's season of life: I think it's the season of a father wanting to really hand down something to your children and your grandchildren. Sometimes you don't see that. There is an age where everybody pops, and you start to think about the next generation. I think for a couple of years now, several years now, he is thinking about the next generation and what he could take advantage of to hand out to his children.

Pastor Phil hanging out with one of his grandchildren

Proverb 17 talks about a man hands down an inheritance and tries to set up his children. And I think that's exactly where he is at. I don't think he is looking for any more accolades or 'king of the hill' type of stuff. I don't think he's looking to be the top seeker. He just wants to be relevant. He's there. I'm happy to be here. You used to be the rockstar. I'm happy to be part of the concert.

I think that's really him. I've talked to him intimately, and that's where I really feel where he's at. But you've got to remember to the Anaheim to the Burbank to the now, I'm the one that kind of put myself out. I'm the one that spent the 19 years in the Church of God. Actually it's been 16 when I brought him in. But I'm the one that put the 15, 16 years and turned my reputation in the Church of God and my character and my integrity to put it on the line to say, "Look, I'm willing to - I want you to consider this man." So that speaks volumes in itself.

I just feel like he was a good light bearer - a great light bearer. Remember he did things - and I already told him this by the way. He was doing rap music and oldies converted, and everybody in the world was condemning him. Now, they all do it. I'm going to be specific. You had your Victory Outreach. You had your Calvary Chapels. They were like, "What's this guy doing? This guy came in like Elvis Presley. He came somewhere out of hell. He's supposed to be a Christian." And now, they are all doing it, because they understand the relevance.

Remember, it's always been this old fashioned saying, sometimes we say it, but we need to understand it. The method can change, just not the message. So he was a light bearer when it comes to different methods of just reaching out. We already had a bond, because I had people living with me, and he had people living with him. Pastors just don't do that, but I looked it at it like I was involved with gangs. I was running these streets. I'll be danged if I'm going to let some Chewie, Lewie, and Gooey run my house. They are going live here. They are going to be just like my kids. Do what I say, or pack your stuff.

So you gotta have that kind of edge to you. But that's what I would say. He definitely meant to me being a light bearer. I haven't told him, "You've gone through some doors that I would never go through, but you went through them." There are some doors I did follow him through, but there were some I just said that's just a little too big of door for me. Be your own person.

PASTOR TIM STOREY on the growth of Pastor Phil over the years: I believe that Phil Aguilar has become more of an introspective person walking in more humility. I don't believe it's just age, because he's young for his age. But I do believe that it's allowing Christ to work within him. When Apostle Paul said, "I'm crucified with Christ, but nevertheless I live." That was not instantaneous. That was a process of sanctification. So that's a beautiful thing about spirituality and Christianity - if you are patient with somebody, you might like the results even if it takes you about 28 years to see the person manifest into what you would like them to be.

BILLY AGUILAR on the 'new' Pastor Phil: It's almost like he went from 'look at me mom, no hands' back to training wheels. He just wants to be that grandfather now. He just wants to love his grandkids and give peace to Sandra his wife for all the times that she's stuck through with him. I see it in his face.

I know my brother longer than anybody. Anybody here, anybody over there, I've known him longer than all. I've known him longer than his wife. I can see the peace in his life now, and that is what I tell my friends. The peace that passes all understanding - Pastor Phil has it again. Now, God is going to use him again, and God would use the jawbone of a jackass. That's what the Bible says, and all this time, Phil has been the jackass instead of being the jawbone. Well, he's back to being that jawbone again, and it's amazing. I'm excited, because not that he's going to start some big movement again, or he's going to move mountains. I'm excited that he's focused on his grandchildren and his wife and his boys and his daughter Trina. Just saying, "Hi" and people say something to him, and he's just whatever. The old Pastor Phil wouldn't have been that way, but you just see a peace in him now.

I don't have to cruise on through his house. He didn't know I used to cruise his house at night packing a gun, because I don't know who was out there to hurt him. Because it came down pretty heavy, dangerous. There is a lot of people that don't like him, and there's a lot of people that hate him, but they don't know that he still prays for those people, and he still loves them. Truly does. It's amazing.

I go, "What's that guy doing here in church? I thought he just bad mouthed you bro?" "Oh, I forgave him bro." "My gosh. I'm outta here man. I can't take it. I'm just a regular guy. I can't take it. I can't take that guy knocking you down and talking about Geronimo, and then you just let him walk right back in like it was nothing. Bro, at least let's give him a beat down. You know?" He goes, "Nah bro. let him go. Let him go."

PASTOR TIM STOREY on people who have been hurt by Pastor Phil or Set Free: I think for people that feel like they've been hurt through the weaknesses of Phil Aguilar, some of the people that have been hurt, rightfully so. I think they have their own unique stories of what they may have felt happen or did happen through Set Free Ministries or the leadership that sometimes went awry. But the reality of this, if we put everything into perspective, His grace is sufficient for us, and then grace fills in the gaps. See a lot of people say that time heals all things, but time doesn't really heal all things. Because if you don't choose to change in that allotted time, then it can be the same. So for people that have hurt me in my life, I choose to get better within that allotted time - and to learn to forgive, forget, and move forward.

It doesn't mean that they'll be as close to Phil Aguilar as they used to be, but sometimes it's just letting something go in your heart. But I think as leaders, if we are going to get blessed and we are going to get applauded, we need to take the shot too. And so even in my own life, for shortcomings in my life, I'll take the shot. Because I've been applauded in 75 countries of the world, so people feel like I've let them down. So if you've got to take the shot, then you've got to take the shot as part of leadership.

TRINA on going back in time: If I could go back to any part of my life, it would be when I was younger, and we had our Set Free on Anaheim Boulevard. Because there was so many great things about it, and I wish my kids could grow up like that. Because now like my husband and I, we don't even go to church or anything. So my kids are growing up. We talk about Jesus and listen to worship music. But they don't have what we had growing up, and it was really a great foundation to have. I guess I just wish my dad would have not been selfish and thought of all of us and not just himself during that time.

KELLI MORENO on how Set Free changed the course of her life:
When I was 15, I wanted a car. So I told my mom, "Mom, I want a car." She goes, "Okay, you pay for the insurance you can get a car." We were sitting at Del Taco eating. I'm like, "Okay." I went and got an application, and I filled it out. That's how I am. So I worked, and then I became a very good drug addict. I made good money. I became a manager at Del Taco, and I partied. So my life just kept getting worse and worse into the drugs though. But thank God, I did have my mom who did give me a very strong work ethic, and I was raised in Christian schools. So by the grace of God, Jesus has always had his hand on my life.

The issue I had with the Christian schools is that they were constantly very judgmental of the way I looked. So by the end of 11th grade, I was even president of the junior class, but the teachers looked down on me. The administration looked down on me, because I wanted to be punk rock. I liked the way I looked. I like tattoos. I like the colored hair and all that stuff.

So coming from that - I think that's what really turned me off from Jesus. It wasn't Jesus. It was just the Christian faith in general. I would look at them and think, "That's not what I want to be." So I ended up doing drugs very heavily. And then when I went to Set Free, instantly delivered overnight. It was amazing. I am truly a walking miracle by the grace of God. Nobody can say against my testimony, because I literally was delivered overnight from all desire to do drugs. Even though people today say you have a disease which there is no cure for. So yeah, there is a cure for it. It's Jesus.

So I was at Set Free for 4 years. What I learned at Set Free was being trained to serve Jesus and who Jesus loved. Jesus loved the common everyday people. But not only that, not just sitting in the pew and getting spiritually fed, getting out and doing something about it. Being busy in the ministry. The one thing I did very well was at all the outreaches - I picked up the trash. Who is going to pick up trash, right? But wherever we left, we left that place clean. So for me, it was important, and I would walk around and pick up the trash everywhere. Because I just thought, "You know what? I want to show a good example of Jesus and leave this place clean." So anyways, that's just a little offbeat story.

So now, I am actually a realtor. I do own a real estate company. I did sell the incense on Venice Beach. We had a booth, we ended up getting three booths then Pastor Phil said, "Alright, I want you to run the booths." So

I became kind of the manager of the booths, and that was a huge blessing because he just trusted me. I knew how to do it. I was a manager of a Del Taco, so that was a blessing. So now, I have a real estate company. I'm very successful. Very blessed. God has totally blessed me. There are four realtors that work with my company. We all work from our home. I homeschool my children with the Christian curriculum, because I don't want them to be at home without me where they are not supervised. Just had a blessed life.

―――――――――――――――――――――――――

PASTOR PHIL on the apology from Jackie Alnor: I'd been through all these different challenges in my life, and lo and behold on November 24, 2010, I got an e-mail that just blew my mind. It goes like this…

> "I want to thank you for writing your book. I've written a book. Of all the critics that have opposed you, your ministry seems to have born the most fruit in helping hurting souls. I wrote very negative things about you and your ministry back in the days when Set Free ministries and Trinity Broadcasting Network were having trouble with the FCC. I want to go down the list of ministries who opposed you and how they failed.
>
> Pastor Oden Fong, the right hand man to pastor Chuck Smith, founder of Calvary Chapel Churches worldwide committed adultery. Divorced and lost his ministry. Calvary Chapel pastor Bob Grenier of Visalia had a church split and his two adult sons are suing him for abuse. Pastor John Duncan, Calvary Chapel of Lake Elsinore lost his position as a pastor. Ron Enroth who wrote Churches that Abuse, lost his career in apologetics. In hindsight, it looks like the Lord put a lot of people on the shelf. I don't think this was all coincidence. It hit me between the eyes when I was reading your book, Phil. I scattered thousands of people who used to go to Set Free people by my public efforts that should have never been a public matter. What I did was not honoring to Christ and I hurt so many people. For my role, please forgive me.
>
> Love,
> Jackie Alnor
> Author, Speaker, Apologist, Woman of God."

Wow, when I read that I thought, "Man, what? God really touched her heart." It isn't going to change anything in my life, but I thought it was so wonderful that this woman of God knew it was time to share it. Just for me, her and the Lord, it was a wonderful thing. I knew all that time things that weren't happening, but I knew that I had things in my life that weren't right. I thank Jackie for just letting Jesus work through her.

I said, "I want to thank you from the bottom of my heart. It doesn't matter if nobody else reads this or hears about it. It's just really cool to know that that's how you feel. At that time, you wrote things because you heard things like that. Some things were true, but some things were definitely not true. I loved the people I was with. So Jackie, I just want to say 'thank you' again."

PASTOR PHIL on people declining to be interviewed for the documentary: There are a lot of people that I wanted to be able to respond and be on camera like Jackie Alnor, Lois Trader, but I understand. For whatever reason they might have not wanting to be filmed, not wanting to be talked about or maybe they don't want anybody to know what their part was with Set Free. I got total respect for anybody like that. Don't judge them, don't look down upon them. But this is my story, and I'm telling it my way. There are going to be other people that have their thoughts and their input that they'd like to give, but maybe don't want to give it on camera. So, I'm cool with it.

Chill preaching at Set Free Burbank

CHILL on what he would say to a room full of haters: I've been in a room full of haters of my dad during times. What I would tell them is that, "What about your life? What about your kids have done? Or you family members? Isn't God a god of mercy and love?" Like I said, Phil knows what he's done. I don't need a speech from my dad. I don't want to hear about the ugliness. I lived it. Some of these people, they want a speech. They want to see him get on a stand like they are the judge and jury. I don't need that. Because I look at Phil, my dad, with the eyes that Jesus would. He's never going to meet the mark or be the guy that I think he should be, and I'm never going to be the guy he would, but we love each other where we are at. I know a lot of these haters. They were my friends at one time. I know them.

I don't even like to call them haters. I just call them people that are confused. This is their passion and burden. This is what they dedicated 25, 30 years to. You've dedicated your life to being mad at somebody? I don't like somebody for a day, and it burns me out. I would basically tell them, "You have to forgive and be free. You don't have to hang with the guy. You don't have to like him." My dad is the Dennis Rodman of Christianity. Not everybody is going to like him, but he's key and he's valuable in the kingdom of God.

Pastor Phil and Dennis Rodman

You need Dennis Rodman on teams. He's one of the greatest rebounders that ever lived.

Pops is definitely crazy, definitely gangster, but that's what those people fell in love with most of the people that don't like him. They fell in love with that guy. He told people from the stage, "I'm bipolar. I'm unsteady. I'm crazy." "We love ya, Pas. I'm here!" The reality is a lot of people are mad. There is not even a lot. I don't even want to say there is a lot no more. There is a small group. Most people just love him. They forgive him. They move forward. Their family has issues or their kids are on drugs so they move forward. They realize, "I judged back then, but I shouldn't be judging now."

The thing about it - for most people, I always tell my dad, a lot of them lost their identity when you left Set Free all the way back in '93 or '94. Their identity never was in Christ. It was in the church. They lost their chair. I hear more complaints not about my dad being this angry, mean guy, and he ruled over us. He's a dictatorship. We only got beans and rice. I don't hear that ever much these days. This is a long time ago maybe. But 25, 30 years later, I would hear, "I didn't get to sing on stage no more." "I didn't get to do this." "I didn't get my chair. I was somebody when I was at Set Free."

Those were some of the greatest times in people's lives. Because then, they went back to their boring non-helping people, not being anybody, no community life. Not all of them, but some of them. So I think that's where it happens. Are you really mad at him or are you mad because the identity, the nickname he gave you is no longer? Nobody really knows you and you don't get to come with 7000 people and, "Hey there's Chip, or there's Bobby. There's Ranch." All the nicknames. Are you mad because the high school reunion is over? I didn't want to wear the letterman's jacket back then. Some of those times sucked. They aren't me. They don't make me who I am. The past doesn't make me who I am - it's the future. So a lot of these people and a couple, we'll say about 10 now that I know - they have to check their own lives. They have to realize God is love. They hate that God forgives.

Believe me, I get the ones who have been hurt, and I feel for them. I stand up for them. I stood up for those girls in Virginia and Texas that were hurt. I was the first to stand up. I was one of the first ones to stand up, as an Aguilar. So, I do stand up, but I still was ridiculed. I wasn't even talking to my dad at the time, but I still was told I was an Aguilar, and you can't trust me. So the reality is the Aguilars back in my dad's days as kids were known as the wild bunch. They always liked to fight and cause problems. And it didn't end. They still think we are crazy, but God has given me favor in places, in spaces that I never imaged I would go.

I'm Phil Aguilar's son playing at Calvary Chapel in front of 4000 or 5000 people. I'm at Victory Outreach doing 'Sonny Jr'. I'm blessed. I had one guy tell me, "How does Phil Aguilar's son work his way into every church in Southern California and even America? All these different denominations." That was one of the greatest things that guy told me was that you get to play and be apart of every different denomination in church. That's unheard of. I said, "It's Jesus."

I get up there, and I give honor to my father, and I tell people the story how, "Hey man, I love my father where he is at. This man is a great man." Instead of putting him down or pointing out his failures - he don't do that to me, so I'm not going to do that to him. That's how life is. If we didn't do that to each other, we'd live in a better world, but unfortunately some people are the best at being the worst. They just got issues with everything.

TURTLE on people who call Pastor Phil a cult leader: Frank words - I would tell them to go fuck themselves, but to be honest with you, I don't see him as that in any type of way, dude. Those are a lot of haters out there and put yourself in my shoes. Like I told you, losing my dad was a major issue in my life. For God to put that man as my dad figuratively and also now being my father-in-law, the guy has nothing but love for people. He loves Jesus. He does have kind of a funny way of making you want to, at least for me, be loyal, but he never demanded that from me. He never demanded me to do what I did for him. It was because I was so grateful for what he did for me when no one else wanted to touch me. Yes, of course, was it kind of cultish? Maybe, but for me it was always a church. It was always family.

My loyalty to him wasn't anything that he demanded from me. It was something that I wanted to give to him in gratitude for what he had done for me. So the people that say, "Cult leader this, cult leader that," I really don't think they've gotten to know the real Pastor Phil and actually sat down and broke bread with the man. Actually, a lot of pastors have sat down with him, but when they do, they put on their costume. They don't want to talk about the real deals that happened in their life. They want to keep that in the backdrop, in the greenroom. When they see Pastor Phil out there living amongst those that he's helping - not putting himself on any pedestal - and they see the love that people have for him, they always think something weird has got to be going on, but really it's not. It's the love of Christ being exchanged between two people.

And let me tell you something. The funny thing about that is like they say, when Christ was in the garden with the disciples, the Bible says they had to have Judas come and give them a kiss, because they couldn't recognize him, because he looked like all of his other people. I've seen that in Pastor Phil where he looks just like us. I've seen people come up to him and say, "Hey man, didn't you used to go to Set Free?" "Yeah," "Well I know Pastor Phil," and they are talking to Pastor Phil. So a lot of these people that say a lot of these things, they really don't know him. I just let them be haters and don't really worry about it.

One thing I never did was tell Pas anybody was talking bad about him. I just handled it. I'm the type of person and not in a prideful way or anything, but you've got to understand who that man is in my life, so I address the issue. If you've got a problem, say it. If you've got a problem, say it. A lot of times, they didn't want to say it. Or like I said, nowadays they hide behind the computers and type it up on Facebook and put blogs out and all that type of stuff. It was really nothing more than just, "Hey man, if you can't stand the heat, then get the hell out the kitchen," type of thing.

The same person that could be talking bad about him on Sunday, he's loving them on Monday. You know? So a guy like me who's like, "Hey man. You can't be talking about my Pas like that. Don't talk about my dad like that." I'm very protective of the man. I tell them they've got to go. I'd see them there on Monday and wonder what the hell is going on. But again, it was Chief trying to teach me the love of Christ and forgiveness and that you are going to have haters in life. So after awhile, I just let it go in one ear and out the other.

JOHN "QUICKY" JUAREZ on people calling Pastor Phil a cult leader: They are nuts. You know what? He has a strict way of teaching. You don't have to be there. Beans and rice and Jesus Christ. You don't have to be there, but if you have nothing and you want help, you'd go there and learn structure.

So the things he did, the way he ran everything was the way those - there is hundreds, I want to say thousands of people that have gone through, that he's helped. I'm one of them that are still clean today - carrying the message and carrying God's Word on a daily basis. Had I not met that man, had God not put him in my life, I wouldn't be right here right now. See that's the problem with people. People say anything they want to say without any - what kind of cult? I guess I'd be a member of the cult and proudly be a member of Set Free.

He's always been a tough guy. There is a right way, a wrong way, and Phil's way. Phil has always been very strict about the way he expects people to do things, and it works. Don't break something that works. It works, and that's all I can say about that. I've seen him change. I've seen him soften. I see the man he is today, and it's like me. I'm not the same guy I was 40 years ago, 30 years ago. I'm not. The person I am - people meet me, and they go, "Man, you've changed." I say, "Thank you," because that's what happens. We mature. I think that's what happened to him. He still carries the same message. Maybe he's just a little softer.

TRINA on broken relationships: We were so close to a lot of people including family members and everything. We just don't see them anymore. I still don't understand how, because of issues that people have with each other, how they cut everybody in their family off. It just doesn't make sense. That part doesn't make sense to me at all. I don't know how - I don't know what I'm trying to say. I know what I'm trying to say, but I just can't say it. Like you know, these people that were like aunts and uncles and like seriously blood aunt and uncles that we don't even talk to no more, because I'm not even sure why. Because they hate my dad I guess so they don't talk to us either. I don't know. It's just so weird. I don't get it.

TURTLE on choosing to be interviewed for the documentary: To be honest, I told you before when we started off, I wasn't even going to do the interview, just because I don't like to get on camera, and I definitely don't like to talk about family business. Our family, we are very guarded. All of our family is very guarded and for good reason. Pastor Phil is like a celebrity in a sense that a lot of people always want to talk to him about a lot of different things. We keep the family as close knit as possible, but I decided to do the interview obviously because this man has a story to tell. They talk about the Jesus movement that happened way back when and Chuck Smith and Lonnie Frisbee and all these type of cats, and it was great. It was great. It was awesome. People got saved. But there was a select few of rugged or half that didn't necessarily make it into those churches, and Pastor Phil reached out to them. He was on Skid Row, not only that he was bringing people in from Skid Row into the same house that his kids were living in, and you don't see that these days. You don't see that anywhere.

The way this guy was ahead of his time back then, and he's still ahead of his time now. I think it's very important. I think the man needs to get some recognition, not just from people that have been helped through his program but other churches. If you just take a minute to sit with the dude and understand where he's coming from and pick his brain as to why he does certain things certain ways, there is a lot of wisdom in that head. My thing was, I just wanted to express my love, my gratitude, because you know, he doesn't have a lot more years left. He's getting up in age.

I thought what better way than to leave a testimonial somewhere that lets somebody know that I come from and studied at the feet of Pastor Phil Aguilar. I'm proud to say that. I'm proud to say that I come from Set Free. I know there is a lot of controversy that goes with saying that name, but I'm proud to say it, and I say it to anybody. I come from Set Free. I'm one of them Set Free boys. The name and the testimony will continue to live on years after he's gone. What a blessing. What a blessing it's been to be able to spend time with that cat and for him to show me, not just teach me about Christ, but show me how Christ lived and how Christ expressed himself to other people with regards for forgiveness, prayer, love, and unending mercy.

I don't go to church now, because obviously Chief ain't doing the church. He was starting one up in Burbank, doing that, but I've got to get four kids ready and all that. It's just a headache to try and do that, so there ain't nothing like Set Free. Once you've been to Set Free, there ain't nothing like it. I don't care. You can't go anywhere else and get that. So because he's not doing it, I just I'm a loyal guy. I don't go nowhere else.

PASTOR TIM STOREY on his role as a mentor in Pastor Phil's life: The way I looked at Phil Aguilar - it's almost like looking at Muhammad Ali who won so many great fights and then he began to struggle for times of his life. Even after Ali had been the Heavyweight Champion of the World, he went through some things. He had a comeback and regained the title again. So I didn't see Phil Aguilar as one who is near retirement. I saw him as somebody that had setbacks that could win the title again. And when you are dealing with an Ali or a Phil Aguilar, you better be careful, because they were champions for a reason. So my leadership to him was never one-on-one talks, "Hey let's talk about what you went through in the 80's or what people say about you." It was more about, "Phil, what is in your spirit? What do you see happening next? How does that look to you?" And coming at him with purity and not coming out at him with some type of angle or prejudice, wondering where he is coming from now. So I feel like that is one reason that he began to pay to attention to me is the way I approached him.

I think that is amazing about a leader of any sort is when they are willing to share what they have. Pastor Phil Aguilar, he shares many things now with the Hollywood Bible Study and a church that I pastor that is called The Congregation. I have a church. It's a new church even though I've been in ministry for years. I've never birthed a church. When we first started the church, Phil Aguilar got in there, even financially. He sowed into the church. He sowed leadership into the church. He sowed different people into the church that said, "Hey we want to be a part." And Pastor Phil said, "Yes, I would like you to be." Wow, that says a lot. In fact, that's very unusual for large leaders to do that. Usually there is a lot of ethnocentrism. Where everybody is in their own lane, doing their own thing, feeling their own vibe. This level of Phil Aguilar is what he shares. He is the kid in kindergarten you want to sit next to.

ELIZABETH AGUILAR BUCHANAN on her love for Pastor Phil: I think what they don't get about my brother is his love for people - absolute love for people. That the number of people whose lives have changed through Set Free and the people that he'll take in over and over and second and third. You know my own son is an example of that. And people like to criticize from afar, but the people that criticize would not do what my brother has done over the years. And yeah, he's made a lot of mistakes, but then once he gets back up his focus is still on people, and it is to this day, and it will always be.

I'm not sure if it's because we are getting older, but I do believe he is a more humble man and is more humble all the time. For me personally, I feel like our relationship is stronger. He jokes around with me, and I can joke around. I'm comfortable with him. I always look to him, because we didn't have the dad. So, I look to him like a father figure, but now I'm more comfortable with him. What I love about him is his love for others. The kids at the Black Sheep - they know that he cares about him. They absolutely know that it's not about the money. It's about keeping them alive for another day and another day and another day and hopefully lose the addiction and become stronger every day. He's one of the most generous men I've ever known and most forgiving I've ever met in my life.

Elizabeth and Pastor Phil

JIM BUCHANAN on his admiration of Pastor Phil: What I love about Phil is his demonstration of the power of Christ. What I love about him is that he is demonstrated by his life and his walk and what we've done through so many years that the Bible is true and it says that, "No weapon formed will prevail against you." And to this day, none has. 90% of them come back and say, "I was so wrong," and I say, "No problem bro. We knew that years ago." But just the demonstration of the power of God. And what I love about him is he is knowing what a dog that I truly am, he's allowed me to teach and to preach on a daily basis. I mean every day for so many years - I will always love him. I will always be so grateful for all of the souls that I was personally able to touch. And I will always be thankful. I've never seen the power of God the way me and him were able to experience it together.

DR. RICHIE COLE on his respect for Pastor Phil: In the alpha male world, which I don't even know if I really qualify, but there is a thing where someone is just ballsy and crazy. Like Chief is that type of dude. Throughout his life, he wouldn't back down from anything. So there is a respect about someone who is that fearless and courageous. You know what I'm saying? So that's - he's just a maniac, but a maniac in a good way. And thank God he got saved, because he'd probably be a very destructive force in society if he wasn't saved. He's been a very constructive source. He's brought thousands upon thousands - if we had the exact number of people that he's lead to the Lord, it would just blow our minds.

PASTOR WILLIE DALGITY on what he's learned from Pastor Phil:
Well, one would be how faithful God is. I've seen Phil's life, man. He says
it himself. When he backslides, he does it all the way, and he don't bump
his head. He just smashes it, but I've seen God be faithful in his life over
and over and over. And Phil will say it. It ain't about him being faithful.
God has been faithful to him. The second thing about Phil is this, and I
mentioned it earlier. That guy is a soul winner. He is a wise guy. Because
he who wins souls is wise. And everywhere he goes, he wins souls.

We were down in L.A. years ago, when he had that Hollywood thing going on. He had won a club owner, a dance club, a Latino dance club
downtown L.A. He won that guy to Christ a week before, and he goes,
"Hey, jump in the truck with me." We went downtown, and we rolled up.
All these people getting ready to go into this club, he calls the guy. I can't
remember the guy's name, the owner of that. And in front of everybody,
he fronts him off and just says, "Hey man, you following Jesus? Are you
loving Jesus?" He made that guy make a public confession there. But
that's Phil. He will reach anything. So those two things, God has been
faithful in his life. Many of the afflictions of the righteous, but God deliv-
ers him through him all. He's said that. I've seen it. I've learned that from
him. That God is faithful, and we are not. And that he is a soul winner. And
that's what I want to be. Amen.

GEORGE NATZIC on Pastor Phil's life: There is certainly a lot as I reflect
back on this life, but just to sort of summarize it, I see an individual who
has been through an awful lot. He's made a lot of bad mistakes, and he's
also done a lot of great things. I think in looking at his life, he continues
to follow the Lord and to help people. So, when I summarize all of that,
I see somebody that has just lived a life in helping people. Made a lot of
mistakes along the way, but also has made much more progress in the
mission of helping people on a daily basis.

There are a lot of takeaways from that standpoint. I think Phil in a lot of
ways is just a great mentor. That's what shines brightly far beyond some of
the mistakes he's made in his life. I really think it would be a high calling
for somebody to really help as many people as he's helped in his life. If I
could help half as many people in my life as he's helped in his, that would
be a great thing.

PASTOR TIM STOREY on what he admires about Pastor Phil: I think
the thing I admire most about Phil Aguilar is not the things that he's done
even in the ministry. It's a strange thing about doing what we do. Billy
Graham can pass and a lot of people will remember Joel Osteen and for-

get Billy Graham. And then down the line, Joel Osteen will pass someday hopefully when he's about 120, and then people will forget Joel Osteen, and they will have a new guy. So all of us as leaders, we have to understand that there is a season for us.

The Phil Aguilar season continues. There is a strength to him. But I'm most impressed with is the fact that he is a good grandfather, and that he is really great to his grandkids. I see the way he is with his grandkids and his kids. He still has date nights with his wife. So to me, that's what I like. I see balance, and out of living life, he continues to give life. My belief in what Phil Aguilar will do next is reproduce himself in the rehabilitation world. And that is whether it be in a church atmosphere, whether it be in a home, whether it be in seminars, whether it be in a documentary - reproducing how God still uses shaky people to do study projects. And then if one is willing to cooperate with God, He can take them beyond. See God forgives beyond, He restores beyond, He calls beyond. So Phil Aguilar, from what he came from, he was in prison - the God of beyond got a hold of Phil Aguilar. That's what I want for Phil Aguilar - that he will continue to share the message of the God of beyond.

Pastor Tim Storey and Pastor Phil at The Congregation in Yorba Linda, CA

ALEXA TEJEDA on regrets: . I was talking to Pastor Phil the other day, which is really interesting - I call him Pas. And I asked him, "What is one of the things that you regret, that you think you would do again?" And he said, "You know, I think that possibly I didn't treat the church with the respect that I should have, and I should have treated it like a business and I never did. I thought that it would never end. I thought that I would have a ministry until the day I died, until forever." And so he said, "I think I took it for granted." So that was an interesting answer to me, and I could see now the difference between the pastor I used to look at, the strong, powerful, charismatic - he knew what it was doing up on that stage. He knew exactly how to get everybody going. What are the key words to say to get everybody excited and pumped up about the Lord? And now I see more of a calm demeanor of, "Learned through my mistakes, and I understand the past that I can't redo."

FIELDY on the faith of Pastor Phil: It's always been the same, because when your faith is tested and it shows up as real or not, it didn't test anything. It didn't make him turn his back. It's just part of living in a fallen world, anything can happen. Anyone can get caught up in the wrong place at the wrong time. It's the way that he handles it. He's just the same way. The same way as if it happened or if it didn't happen. He's still the same guy. That's what I like. It doesn't change him. It's been I don't know - correct me if I'm wrong - he said, 1977, that he accepted Jesus,

Pastor Phil and Fieldy

and he's been walking the same way with mini struggles and from getting raided and getting pulled into jail for 3 days and all of these things, and he still shows you. It's like even me, going through storms in my life. It's like it doesn't change anything, because you can't just get rid of something that is real.

People want to say one-in-a-million type of guy he is, but I told you I've only maybe met very few people that are that style of a person. Someone that is an encourager, a positive dude, lifting people up, and not giving up on people. The impacts that he's left that are so important in life, that everybody tends to just - especially for someone like myself. I'm not naturally an encourager or a positive dude, but I just try to always grab onto a few things that he said. They are just little nuggets here and there that help me through life. It's amazing that you can give somebody a few words that can really get them through 10 years of storms. Just hearing a few words from someone. So his words are important.

KELLI MORENO on her thankfulness for Pastor Phil: I am who I am today because of him. What crazy person opens their house to 300 people and lets them live with them? Sorry, I'm going to compose myself. You know? I just love Pastor Phil and his family so much. I'm so thankful, and it's not just him, but Sandra. Because what wife just goes along with it, right? So I would never be where I am today if it wasn't for him and for what he did. He's taught me so much just by what he does in his life, in the daily bump and grind. But bottom line, at the end of the day, who opens their house up to people like that? And I'm one of them. My life has completely changed because of what he did. I'm just so very thankful for him and for his family. They've been really good to me.

ALEXA TEJEDA on the legacy of Set Free and Pastor Phil: You know I called Set Free, the Set Free movement, and I don't think any one of us realized what we had at that time including Pastor Phil, because it could have been bigger than life. It was something so incredibly different and so aggressive in getting all these people to get involved. I remember at one point in time, I think my trip to Jerusalem, when we went there - it was also a life changing moment.

It was an opportunity to see Phil outside of his element. Away from the hustle and bustle, from the thousands of people tugging at his shirt, "Pastor Phil, Pastor Phil." And here was this calm demeanor, relaxed, out of his element, vulnerable perhaps. And just a wonderful, kind soul, you know? Deeper than what he led to believe, so I got to converse with him and ask him about his life and how he grew up and how he ended up at Set Free and starting Set Free. It was quite a story that he has to tell. So we all have a story, and he has a wonderful one. And he admits he had the opportunity to continue to change people's lives and perhaps our community and beyond that, but what can you do?

Set Free Church of Needles, CA

I hope and pray that his legacy continues and grows the right way - the way God meant it to be, and that is all inclusive, loving, controlling the power and all the negative things that might come your way, being grounded in the Word. Loving people. I pray that they realize what an opportunity they all have individually to make a difference wherever they are at, and that they might understand the responsibility that they have on that calling. Because we'll all have to answer to God in the end. I would want to share that beyond Set Free, there is God. Above all things, there is God. And when we lose sight of that and we think that we're the ones making things happen, then we lose sight of what our purpose is. So all this to say that even today every year 4000 churches are closing, as opposed to

1000 opening every year, okay? And it's due to misappropriation of funds or moral issues. So we just have to keep ourselves in check as individuals, and we are all part of each other and just no judgment. No judgment.

Set Free Church of the Lake in El Mirage, CA

BILLY AGUILAR on current Set Free Churches: They are reaching people. They are reaching the homeless. They are reaching the needy. They are taking in people that nobody wants to take in. They are still doing the same thing that happened at 320 North Anaheim Boulevard. Amazing that they got it like I got it. They've got calendars for the events. They've got free bread night. They've got Thursday night Bible study, jail visits on certain days. They take everybody, and they go visit people in jail. Hospital visits, you know? Very little money, but they are still doing it. To see the Set Free churches still back to basics, still reaching the lost for Christ, it's unbelievable. But Set Free, either you need help or you are in leadership. There is nothing in the middle for you. I'm the middle guy. So I need to take what Pastor Phil and Set Free has taught me and find a church and get structured and be a man of God and move on with my life. Stay sober, stay clean, stay true to my wife, stay true to my kids and my family. Be a good employee. Christ's Son's motorcycle club, it's Christ first, family second, job third, club fourth. That's what we learned at Set Free Christian Fellowship, and it works. Believe me, it works.

CHILL on the future of Set Free: The Set Free name and the Set Free movement - it was so big. It could be Set Free, but there is tons of different ministries and tons of different names. It's not about the name. It's about the lifestyle. It's what you live for. It's what you believe. Everybody has been set free from something. I love seeing Set Frees starting all over the place. I love people that, "Hey man, I was touched through Set Free so many years ago." There is so much more good stories than there are bad, because I've done my research.

When I wasn't around my dad for years, I heard some of the bad stories, and there are some people that definitely have a reason to be hurt. I respect that, and I'm not mad at them. I've talked with them. I've prayed with them, but instead of throwing gas on their fire to make them more angry, I spent time with them and prayed. You've been hurt. You've been used. You've been abused. Now what can we do about it? Because I've been there, too. I've been hurt. I've been used, but what are we going to do about it? I met so many more people that have good stories

Pastor Tim Shaner (left) at Set Free Church of Nashville, TN

about Set Free that are happy and that have been through it. Then, you got a couple they were hurt. They were burned. We didn't meet the mark. My dad didn't meet the mark, and we failed as leaders.

I always tell people that I've spent many years on the sidelines. I took a Gatorade break. I was angry on the sidelines, mad, telling everybody what to do. Telling them, "If I was in there, I would do it this way." Once I got back in the game, shook off the hamstring injuries spiritually speaking, shook off the cramps - those are the bitterness and the pride. I got back in the game, and I realized that I can help so many more people now for what I've been through with my family. People say, "When you sing up there, we believe you. We know you are broken." I'm like, "Yeah, I am broken. I've got a brother who is serving 40 years in prison. I've got family members, relatives, cousins who are still high on methamphetamine. I've got uncles who don't talk to me." I get it. I get brokenness so that relates. Because one thing we all have in common is pain. So they understand me, and I understand them.

I've tried everything else to be honest. I've tried every other job - 9 to 5. A gardener, I've tried everything, security. Nothing has worked. Every door has closed, and God has put me back in the game. That's why I do what I do, because I know somebody with my life and what I've been through can help somebody else. My vision for Set Free or for the ministry is just to serve and to help people - to learn from our mistakes and do better this time. That's my heart. I'm going to do better this time than I did before.

SANDRA on the future of Set Free: My hope is that they continue on the way they are, because there are so many of them now. The whole concept of Set Free caught on fire. There is so many wonderful pastors. I couldn't even name them all, but just carrying on the tradition of loving you where you are at. Not expecting anything of you. How you dress or anything. People keep forgetting and even in this documentary that you are doing about my husband, I tell people all the time, "It's not just about my husband. It's about Set Free. Its giving praise and honor to all the Set Frees and all the pastors that have started Set Frees and how wonderful it is that they've carried on the legacy of Set Free." I think its just great, and I know that there is going to be a lot more.

PASTOR PHIL on his legacy: When I started Set Free Baptist Church, my whole mission - I can remember on my wall there in the church warehouse it said, "Daily in the temple and from house to house, cease not to teach and preach about Jesus Christ." That's all I can remember starting out a ministry. Set Free Church was all about teaching and preaching about Jesus Christ. I didn't know about Christian TV. I didn't know about this. I didn't know about that. I was just in love with Jesus. Started taking people into my home - started feeding them, because I read it in

Pastor JT Coughlan (left) at Set Free Church of Great Falls, Montana

the good book. I read it in the Bible. It says to take care of the orphans, feed the hungry, help those that are homeless, help those that are in prison, and go see those that are in the hospital. I literally just started doing all that stuff. So as I look back on my life, I'm so happy I started doing that stuff. It just became part of my life. Next thing you know, I learn about what you sow, you are going to reap. So then, Paul and Jan coming to my place, and now they want to bless me. All of a sudden, I got people wanting to bless me.

I'm reading these parts in the Bible where great men of God, greater than myself and others, where they took their eyes off of Jesus and put it on a woman, put it on power, put it on possessions, and money. I never thought that could happen to me, but I caught myself looking for love in the wrong places. I took my eyes off of Jesus just for a little bit it seemed like, before you know it – a wreck. I've heard it called being backslidden, falling out of the grace of God. Whatever people call it, all I knew is I wasn't happy anymore. I wasn't full of joy anymore, because I had this thing called sin in my life. I was trying to hide it, trying to cover it up, but it just kept coming out. It came out, because I didn't have peace of mind. I didn't have the joy unspeakable anymore, but I'd get back on track.

I'd start rolling again, start doing again, and start getting things back. Then, I learned about how pride goes before the fall. I realized that I'd be prideful that I got it all back, and I'm doing well again. Big church, being on TV, success is much harder to handle than failure. Being a loser is easy. Everyone says that you are a mess up, "Yeah, I am." You are a screw up, "Yeah, I am." You are the black sheep. You are no good. "Yeah, you are absolutely right." That is so easy to be, but to be successful where people start looking at you as a role model. People start saying, "Pastor Phil, I want to be like you." Or, "Man, I want to be a husband like you are or a dad like you are." That responsibility is heavy.

Pastor Mike Salazar (center) leading worship at Set Free Church of Bakersfield, CA

Through my journey, I tried to share with the whole wide world. Through my journey, I've had many toils and terrors. I've had many pitfalls. I've had many times where I've said, "God, I'm sick and tired of following you. God, I'm mad at everybody. God, I'm mad at Christians. Christians suck. The Christian mafia is heavy." I went through all these little things, but I realized now at this part of life I can see the finish line. I can see that it's all just a part of the journey. People that I did wrong - I didn't realize when I was abandoning people that I was really abandoning people. So I've tried to make up, but I've realized that I can't make up everything. People that I've done wrong - I feel terrible about it, but I've got to move on with my life. So I've asked for forgiveness of anybody and everybody. To let them know, "Hey, I'm sorry about that stuff, but I'm a new man today. I'm a new person today. Sorry about what happened, but God is into forgiveness. The darker it gets, the brighter His light shines. To those that have been forgiven, much they love." So I got a whole lot of love. I realize I got no doubts I'm the chief of sinners in the world that I hang out in. No doubts about it.

A lot of times the haters club doesn't like that. I understand. They like you to suffer and have some disease and burn to death or something like that. But let me just tell anybody this, God is a for-giver, and He will give you a brand new life better than it's ever been before. It's a free gift. I just love that. It's a free gift. I can't be good enough. I can't do well enough. I used to read, "Happy is the man that has his quiver full." I've got my quiver more than full. My cup does runneth over. God is doing things in my life even today that are just beyond my wildest dreams. Little did I know that at 69, I would be thinking about proj-ects, opening new treatment centers, and helping open up churches. Right now, I'm mentoring and investing in people's lives and it is the most fruitful

Pastor Tracy Elder at Set Free Church in Tiffin, Ohio

time in my life. At the same time, I'm getting to go on date nights with my wife - taking her to Vegas - taking my grandkids to the beach. It's fantastic. The thing that I'm focusing on right now is to be a better man, a better father, a better pastor, better friend, and better everything that I can be.

As I look over my life and I think about my legacy, I'm trying to walk the line. I'm trying to have a good time. I can see the finish line not too far down the road. As a young person coming in this world, I had that beau-tiful family, but I got my heart broken. As a teenager, I found love with my little girl Annie but got my heart broken. So I started realizing that life is full of a lot of heartbreaks. There is a lot of setbacks, but every time we can make that comeback.

If I were going to change anything over the last 40 years, it would be like what I've heard people say before on their deathbed "I wish I would have given Jesus more". I wish I would have got more serious about my mis-sion that Jesus had me on. I wish I would have been more loving to my wife and kids. It's just all about – I've been running a race with the Lord, and I've had times where I'm just on fire and times where I let up, a little casual. I just wish I would have given Him more.

The Set Free movement is not stopping. It's going to keep on going as long as there is somebody alive that has the name Set Free. Pastor Willie has been so instrumental in reaching out to so many people. Pastor JT up there in Montana has just been reaching out. Pastors up in Washington and across the United States. I'm telling you - the fire I believe has just begun. It's a whole new wave. That's why I'm spending most of my time now mentoring people.

Pastor Willie Dalgity (right) preaches at Set Free Church of Yucaipa, CA

PASTOR WILLIE DALGITY on the future of Set Free: I believe that where the scriptures say that the latter glory will be greater than the former. I believe that's where we are at with our movement. We are raising up guys. We are training pastors right out of our discipleship, and we are starting churches. We never stopped doing that. So I think we've just seen the tip of the iceberg of Set Free in the future. Because it's not about addition anymore, it's like multiplication.

So our next thing is L.A. We've got a building down there we got our eyes on. I've got some business partners, and we are trying to raise the funds. And I've got a pastor that we brought up back out of Nashville that went back there and started a church. He and his wife - they've come up so they are going to do this thing. The L.A. thing is a big thing, because it's going to be a hub right there, and we can reach into all the areas of L.A. But my man back in Maine - he is doing the same thing up in New England. He'll be reaching into Boston and all that.

We ain't seen nothing yet. I really believe that. So I'm older now, but I've got some young guys man. They are taking the ball, and they are running with it.

PASTOR PHIL on looking ahead: So even if it isn't called Set Free, it's that Set Free style. It's that way of reaching out, that style. Going where pizza man don't deliver. Going to the highways and the byways. Using the gift of inconvenience. Loving people right where they are at. Not having room, making room. All the things that are part of the Set Free lifestyle. Because it's not just a name, but it's a way of life.

I believe the best years of Set Free are still ahead. Every day I don't know how long I got left, but I know that every day, I'm just going to keep on keeping on for Jesus. I'm going to keep remembering those things that I've said. I don't have room, I make room. I've got to remember, don't get left, get

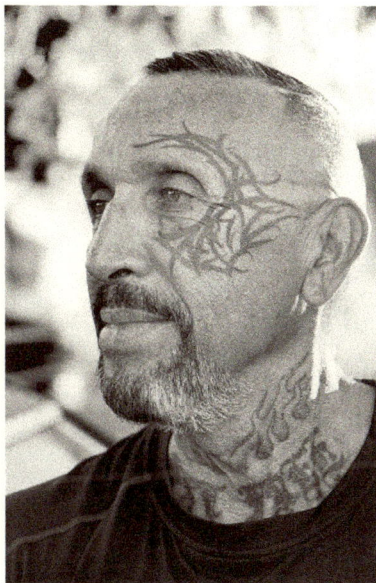

Pastor Phil

right. All those little things I've got in my brain. Don't call in sick, just keep moving forward. Keep the momentum. Your attitude determines your altitude. All those things are a part of my mind, programmed into it. I want to do like the Apostle Paul says, I want to finish the good fight and I want to finish it strong. I want to go out swinging, knocking the devil on his butt and just giving the finger and telling everybody to go to heaven.

CHAPTER TEN
AGUILAR LOVE

Although the story of Set Free is much bigger than Pastor Phil Aguilar and his family, there is something unique about how they have shaped the movement over the years. Their relationships, for better or worse, have deeply impacted the ministry, and their words toward one another are powerful in light of all they've experienced.

TRINA AGUILAR

PASTOR PHIL: Trina is just the best daughter ever. It seemed like she always had an attitude. In her teenage years, she got a bigger attitude. I can remember her telling me as a teenager, "I can't wait until I'm 18 so I can move out of here." But she always had a wonderful heart. People always loved her. So I knew there was something special there. Once I realized that my daughter had a drug problem, but she was ready to receive help and go to one of our "beans and rice and Jesus Christ" ranches that had changed her whole life around. She has never been

Trina and Pastor Phil

the same. She's got a heart of gold. She loves people - cares about people. She might have too big of heart. She cares maybe too much, but she is a storehouse of wisdom. We are like a team. We are really, really close. It's awesome. I would have never thought that would happen, but it's a wonderful relationship.

SANDRA: TrinaJoy, my only daughter. My best friend next to Jesus. We are very, very close, and she is a whole lot like her dad but, she knows when to pull the brakes better. She's got a little side of me where is good. She's a great person. She's got great work ethics. Being a full-time mom is not her first desire at all. God blessed her with four children, two sets of twins. So I told her, "I think you need to shift gears." But she is a wonderful person. She will help anyone, just like her dad. She'll give them her rent money. She's amazing.

TRAINED TO SERVE JESUS

MJ: My one and only favorite sister TrinaJoy. She was a good friend of mine growing up. She was probably my wingman more than my brothers. She was cool like that. If you could have one sister, she would definitely be the one. And I mean back in the days, all the way until now, she is really selfless in a lot of ways and always was that way. She wanted to see other people happy. She wanted to hook other people up. I think she did. I don't know how or what, but she had money at the time that we were in high school or a little younger even. I don't know. She was what we called ATM - All of Trina's Money. Because I don't know what she was doing, but I'm sure it was something like raffle tickets for a youth camp - something holy. She would just hook us up, and do something with us. Like yo, she'd be like that person. Just very giving, and she is still that way. She's later in the years probably we don't get to hang out as much. We both have our families and married and all that good stuff, but she's still right there. Man, she is one of those, if you call, doesn't even matter what it is, she is there. So it's pretty cool.

CHILL: Trina being the only sister out of a few brothers, I think Trina had it the worst. I think her role - she was always - she'd defend her brothers even if they were wrong to everybody. She was kind of trying to just find her place. Me and MJ were more of the stars as kids of the church. My dad would put us on stage, because we rapped. My dad liked anybody who can do a circus act I call it. If you can light yourself on fire, if it was in the circus, it worked for the program, the church. He liked that. Trina wasn't really like that. She would dance, and she can dance, but she didn't really want to sing. Trina was at times - she was vocal, but she played the role of just kind of the backseat, her and my little brother Hebrew, Roc.

Trina over the years - to me, Trina went through a lot. Unfortunately because she stuffed a lot of whatever she was going through and none of us really stopped to ask her if she was okay, because life was moving so fast. We had so many other people with issues. Trina from then until this day, to me I think of her, she's just solid. She loves all her brothers and that's a tough place to be sometimes. But she is always the one who love her brothers, and we were real tight because we were both overweight and fat. We had a tight connection. We'd sneak off and eat because my dad was really into fitness. We were the chubbier ones. He had us running laps at nine and ten. I'm like, "Damn, I don't want to run." He had us on Jenny Craig. So me and her had a connection, right? It was weird, but we kind of always looked out for each other, and we looked just like each other when we were growing up. So people always thought we were twins. So we kind of had a special bond. We are not that tight these days, but we had a special bond growing up, because we understood each other's pain.

HEBREW "ROC" AGUILAR

PASTOR PHIL: With my youngest son Roc, it's always been a little tough time. My other kids were part of the ministry, rapping, doing this. Roc wanted to skateboard, roller-skate, wrestle. He was always doing something a little bit different. He always listened to the beat of a different drummer, but I could see my craziness in Roc all the way all over the place. He's really a good talker - talk people into things, doing stuff like that. He's the first one in the family who went out to start a business on his own and go for it. He's a shaker and a mover.

Pastor Phil and Roc

SANDRA: Roc, the baby of the family. Roc Hebrew Timothy Aguilar is my baby - always will be my baby. He wants to be a grown up like everybody else, and he's always been the baby of the family, and he's always been the joker. So now, he's got a family of his own, a business of his own. He's learning a lot about it. He's a lot like his dad, so they butt heads all the time. It's frustrating for a mom, but he's a great kid.

MJ: Roc is my baby brother, and in a lot of ways, I feel like he's my son. We are a few years apart, you know? Which at this age, it's not too much of a big deal, but there was a long time when he was - man, a lot of people, maybe some of the people that are on the same film know him as a crazy, long-haired. I think he invented dreads, like I don't know how much he washed his hair. He was a little punk rocker from the beginning. He was very passionate about a lot of things. So much energy. Man this guy was full of energy. So he would skate and snowboard, play hockey and try to breakdance and do some of the music that we were doing. He was always there - a lot of times like any little brother, very annoying and all that stuff, but we learned. We all shared rooms back then. We didn't have a choice. We all shared a room. So he was the Tasmanian devil as I called him. He was just a whirlwind. Wherever he would go, he would get going. Not a whole lot has changed. There is still in a lot of ways - he's my baby brother, and he's still crazy in a good way. Very passionate about things. He's a good brother, he really is. He is the same way in a lot of ways like Trina where he will do anything for you. The kind of anything where you're like, "Hey, no I'm good. We are okay." But he's really like that. He'll take one for you for sure. You almost have to tell him to stand down, because he's just wired that way.

CHILL: Roc, these days people think that it's me, but I just lost a lot of weight. So they always say, "Hey, what's up Chill?" And he'll be somewhere, "I'm Hebrew. I'm Roc." Roc was the baby. He's another one that didn't rap or do that, so he was always trying to find his way or trying to make his place in life. Trying to make a name. He was the one always starting fights, and then he'd call me and Turtle up. We'd go over there and back him up. I felt like I was his protector, and I felt like I taught him a lot of bad things unfortunately rather than good things that were about Jesus. He followed our leads, and he made his own life and own career, and he's doing great. I'm proud of him. I have nothing bad to say about him other than he was raised a little - he was one of those kids that was before ADD was big. He was ADD. He'd run around naked in boots until 5 years old, beating people up and hitting dudes in the nuts. He was intense, but that was his personality. You got to imagine being raised around all these crazy people. You are going to get a little nutty, because you had to defend yourself. So Hebrew is a tough kid, but I believe that he's very compassionate too and loves to help people in his own way.

TRINA: Hebrew has always been the baby and always has come across like that. He's never been sure of what he really wants to do or be. Me and him were super close growing up, because we were with each other all the time. Then, as we got older, I kind of became a second mom to him for sure, because nobody really understands what you go through except your brothers that are going through it with you. So, we became really close, but him and my dad always butted heads. They never got along ever since I can remember, and they still don't.

MATTHEW "MJ" AGUILAR

PASTOR PHIL: Others in the family would say MJ is the golden child. MJ is the one I just never caught doing anything wrong. I've learned now he was the ringleader. He was totally involved in ministry. He was on the streets. He went to Afghanistan, to Baghdad, to Bosnia, all over to entertain the troops all around the world. They've been ministry guys. But maybe he took the

Pastor Phil and MJ

light away at times from Chill, so MJ was always steadfast. Always loving, always learning, always growing, always on fire. The first one to have a kid out of wedlock, but it was a beautiful thing. We got to help raise a kid with him, so it was a cool thing.

AGUILAR LOVE

SANDRA: What I love about Matthew, MJ as they call him, is he acts quiet. I think he's a lot more like me in a lot of ways. He's humble in a lot of ways. He had really long hair when he was younger, and they wanted him to model. He didn't want to get into modeling, because he wanted to be a hardcore rapper. He ended up being a rapper for Jesus, and his skills of rapping is good. Him and Chill used to rap together, and then Chill just took off in his world of music. They stopped rapping together, but Matthew went through a lot.

Matthew had to grow up fast all of a sudden. He's not as adventurous as his brothers and his dad. He's a little bit more mellow. He's definitely more mellow, but he wanted to be apart of the bike club. The kid had never done anything wrong in his whole life. Then he ends up being one of the ones that gets arrested and has a million dollar bail on his head. At the time, his wife had just told me she's pregnant again. So now, he's thinking about that. Things that he had to go through. He had to grow up really fast, along with Phillip. Phillip had to grow up really fast too, but Matthew. Now Matthew just wants to be a dad and raise his kids. He could care less about rapping or anything.

CHILL: My brother MJ as a youngster, he was very quiet, mellow. I call him passive-aggressive type personality, but he was great. We did everything together. Even if he didn't want me around him necessarily as a young kid, I would always borrow his clothes or do stuff. I was the louder guy, and he was the quiet and calm. But he had great gifts. He's a great writer, a great rapper. That was his thing. Basically I followed him. My job in life as the middle child was to do whatever my brother MJ wanted. So if MJ wanted to go to the movies, I had to go to the movies. If MJ wanted to eat pizza, we are eating pizza. I didn't really have a vote which is the middle child syndrome. That's just how it is. But MJ was always really heavily into music. That was his gift - rapping and writing good, making rhymes. My other brothers and them in the early '90's were doing MC Hammer covers and Vanilla Ice. MJ would always be doing Cypress Hill and NWA covers and being a little more radical. He had something in him that was a little more radical and a little more gangster. He would always dress more like the guys from NWA or whatever we seen. I'd be dancing, and he'd just be rapping. As we got older, he was always the leader. I always just followed. He just became a great rapper and writer and all around guy.

TRINA: Matthew always was the good kid who never got caught doing anything. He was like the one. He's always an instigator behind the scenes, but a funny one. He just did funny stuff, but I think because he's their first born together, he was always different. He was Matthew. He was the golden child, since I could remember for sure. For sure.

PHILIP "CHILL" AGUILAR

PASTOR PHIL: Chill was the one who it seemed like he'd need a little bit more of my attention, a little bit more of my love. He was the middle child, so he was in the shadow of his older brothers MJ and Geronimo. He and I bumped heads for years for whatever reason, but we came back together in recent times, and now I'm mentoring him and helping him as he helps me. He's just a man of God. I licensed him up as a pastor now. So he's not just a singer worship leader, but he's a pastor. He does his own church in the Hollywood area. It's just a beautiful thing to see what's happening with us.

Chill and Pastor Phil

SANDRA: Chill Philip Anthony Aguilar Jr. My husband said he'd never name a kid after him. He didn't want to ever name a child after him. Accidentally, he happened to be in the delivery room, because he never liked to go in the delivery room when the children were born. He actually had to hold him right away because of an emergency situation. When he looked at him he said, "Oh, he looks just like me. I've got to name him Phillip." So we named him Philip Anthony after a city councilman he liked. Philip Anthony, that's where his name came from.

A wonderful kid. Oh my gosh, he was the funniest kid all the time. I watch videos of him from back then, and he's just hilarious and fun, and he had this squeaky little voice. He'd always be talking, always be singing, always be acting. Now listen to him, he's an amazing artist and a great, dad too. Great dad and husband.

MJ: Oh man, me and Chill - we're close in age. We're a year apart me and Chill. So, we were the closest in some ways, especially before my older brother came around, Geronimo. Because it was just me and Chill, Trina is a girl and Hebrew aka Roc is so much younger. So me and Chill did a lot of stuff together. A lot of fun stuff and then once music again got introduced when we were about eight, nine, ten, me and him we were B-Real and Sen Dog. We were Chuck D and Flavor Flav. We were just homies, partners, bandmates, everything. So we both had a love for it and have for years to come. Still do, both of us. Where we started getting into the music thing a lot, so we shared a lot of studio time, a lot of writing time. At the time at least, he'd be a little more impatient, and I'd be more the opposite in some ways where I'm just like, "Let's write this, we gotta get this right." Even at a young age when I'm writing about school lunch and things like that, I wanted to make sure I had the right rhyme for it and the right delivery, and he was just like, "Tell me when we're going on stage." I'd give him his lyrics maybe or something like that. He was a great entertainer.

He was a good dancer at a young age, like MC Hammer. He could dance anything, and he was already kind of at a younger age a little heavier, a little bigger. But he was like Heavy D who is an old school rapper, real light on his feet and really just got down. The crowd always loved him. He was just a great entertainer. A lot of fun. He used to always steal my clothes, and I would hate that, because I didn't want to match him or him dress like me again. That was the big-little brother thing, but he really - man, if even some of the videos and stuff, if you see him, he really commands the stage.

They called him Preacher. That was his nickname. He went from The Fridge, because of the famous football player when we played football me and him. And he was already like a big boy, but he went to The Preacher because he would just kind of - that was almost like show and tell for us at a young age. My dad, some kids would be like, "Oh yeah, look at my son throw that pitch." My dad would be like, "Yo, Preacher," and he would just run off five minutes of his best evangelism, Billy Graham style. So Chill was pretty good at that.

TRINA: Oh, Phillip was so fun growing up. He was like the entertainer dancing around - always happy, smiling. He was fun growing up. Him and I were close, because we were like the two fat kids who were always on a diet or at the gym or something. Seriously, we were at the gym young. So we bonded in that way. Then as they all got older their personalities started changing. Him and Matthew were really close for a long time, because they were kind of forced to be close, because they did rap together and stuff. But they never really were like friends-friends if that makes any sense. Matthew is very quiet and to himself. He doesn't like openly share stuff. It's hard to get anything out of him. We always make a joke that because you just never know what's going on with him. Then Philip is the complete opposite. He'll tell you everything. They had different friends, but people always figured they were really close because they were together all the time.

GERONIMO "PASTOR G" AGUILAR

PASTOR PHIL: Around 1993 or '94 as things were going tough and I was in Venice Beach, we were down to seeds and stems. We were down to our last dollars. Even my son Geronimo - it was time for him to go. He'd fallen in love with another girl, and he took off. So the two of them, from what I heard, hooked up together. They got married, moved to Texas. He had a lot of friends that were in Texas, so they were in Texas for a while.

Pastor Phil and Geronimo

Then, the next thing I heard, he was in Richmond, Virginia, of all places, where he opened Richmond Outreach Center. My next youngest brother Burt introduced him to some people in Virginia. Well, he took the Set Free recipe that I did – I tell people he is taller than me, he's better looking than me, and he does a little more BS than me at times. Anyway, he's got a bunch of remnants of old Set Free, Ranch Richard, dancers, got his wife as a singer. So he's got a little Set Free Posse together in Richmond. They start off getting songs saved and all the same stuff that I did - reaching out, soul winning. Next thing you know the church is growing. I'm really happy for him. He's got a place, got a new wife. I didn't like how everything went down, but that's just how life is.

I'd heard in the wind that he was giving a little different version of his testimony story of when he came to the Lord of how I remember him coming to the Lord, but it's his story. Next thing you know, there is an Outreach magazine that talks about the fastest growing churches in America. Next thing you know, his church is on the top 20 list of the fastest growing churches in America. So, he is going to have a grand opening now, and he invites me to come there. Then the magazine comes out, he's the third fastest growing church in America. I get there, and he's got a fantastic place. But, because I had a megachurch before, because some red flags went up for me, and I didn't pay attention, I talked to my son in love and I said, "Hey son, I see some things here that don't look too cool. They don't look too right. I think maybe you ought to mellow out. Take a little time off. Let's talk about it." He was intoxicated with the success and just doing great, loving on people.

He had another life going on of some sorts, because I could tell he was troubled. The next thing you know, he's got some accusations coming about him. He's got some people saying some stuff. Once again my consultation was, take some time off. He'd asked me, "Dad, don't you wish you would have just stuck in there? What would you have done different?" I go, "I would have had a better retirement plan." But I said, "No son, when we start having things come up, we've got to take care of those personal issues. Because if we don't, the machine gets you going. Everybody is saying, 'I love you pastor,' 'You are the greatest pastor,' and everybody is telling you how wonderful you are. If you don't watch it, you become a legend in your own mind, and you start believing it."

I'm talking to him and our relationship is getting closer, because I'm loving on him, because I see him hurting, going through a tough time. Then, he is being accused of stuff that happened back in Texas, 14, 15 years ago or something like that. The next thing you know, it gets all bad. I'm there at his church, and it's a megachurch, there are thousands of people. It's doing wonderful. He is helping so many people, but now he's got a court case back in Fort Worth, Texas.

I don't know all the details of it. I didn't read all the transcripts or manuscripts or anything like that. All I know is I went out there when it was coming to a closing at his sentencing hearing, and I know they sentenced him to a long time in jail. I have no idea on the details. I didn't read all the smut. I didn't go through all that stuff. That is my son. I love him, and I pray for him every day. I care about him, and I'm doing everything I can. I know he made some bad choices. He did some heavy stuff, because it doesn't look good.

We received a letter from him from prison, and he's writing how he's getting his life back with God, back together. That's what I'm happy about. I don't know all the little details about his life, but I know God is into comebacks. God doesn't give up on us. As long as there is breath in us, He is going to keep pumping on him. Geronimo might be in the prison ministry for the rest of his life, or God might release him tomorrow. I don't know. That is all God's plan. All I know is, I just encourage my son, "Hey, just one day at a time. Giving it all the Jesus. Accepting full responsibility. I don't know if you are guilty or not guilty. Whatever it is, but you go to God. Talk to Him and make peace with Him." So it's a rough time for him now. It's an adjustment.

He's got three beautiful daughters that he was with all the time, and now he doesn't get to see them. They come to visit him. Life has completely changed, but Jesus hasn't changed. I know my son is going to come out a winner in Jesus, because he doesn't give up. He is going to fight the good fight. So I love him right where he is at, and I look forward to when the day comes that I get to visit him and see him.

He can write a book. He can do all kinds of stuff and talk about things. There will be some people that don't want to forgive him. I understand that. He could write a letter of love and sorry to everybody. There will be some people that want to get that letter of love and light him on fire with it. Then call in the forensic expert to check and see that was his body that was burnt. There are always going to be people like that. But we got a God that I know and my son knows personally that loves him and will always love him forever and ever.

SANDRA: You know Geronimo really never got a break. That's the sad part. The whole situation that happened with his mother, his step-father, his real father, the grandparents. He's a confused boy. He patterned after his father's ministry, which was wonderful. But then once again, he patterned after the pride that comes with it that his father went through also. Even with all the warnings just like my husband had warnings, you just think, "No, I can do this." The power got to him. I'm angry and frustrated with him, because he did not take the deal they offered him. They offered him, "Plead guilty, we'll give you 5 years," which means he would be out soon. But insisting on going to trial against a lot of counsel just made me more upset because the chance he took was wrong. And now, as he sits there in prison, never even going to jail or juvenile hall his whole life, and he's sitting in prison for all these years. I know God is going to do something. I just know He is without a doubt. I feel bad for his girls definitely.

MJ: Geronimo, man well back in the day he was - to me, he was kind of larger than life in some ways, because I kind of adopted him from the very beginning as just a big brother. Again I didn't know how much I was kind of a yearning for that. I could claim him, because I was surrounded by so many. Because my dad wasn't as active, in some ways, my brother was a little closer to that. Whether it was sports or music, we could have the conversation even though he was a teenager and already kind of too busy for me in some ways. You know how it is. But a lot of ways, he was. At the time, I was like, "Man, I want to be like that dude." Like, "Yo, teach me how to DJ. I want to go into the studio with you," and now I knew where my younger brother got it. Because I wanted to, "How do you dress? I want that jacket, I don't care if it's three sizes too big, I'm going to wear that jacket," and I did. So in a lot of ways, he meant a whole lot to me during that time.

Over the years, he had to do his things and things happened where he was no longer living with us. So that was hard. That was real hard. But then over time, I've always had that kind of almost the same thing. I felt like me and him have always had a special relationship through it all. I think we - at least in my opinion, I feel like we were the closest. That could have just been because we were guys, the age, music, I don't know. We stayed in touch sometime over the years, but there is always going to be something special there with me and him. For whatever reason, whether it's sports or the first time he took me to the record store to buy my first LP, my first vinyl that I still have to this day. Anything that he kind of gave to me and shared with me, whether it was words or a talent or an actual record, I really hold those things very close to me. He's a pretty cool, special dude.

TRINA: I remember when he first came around, I wasn't happy when Geronimo first came around. I think I was like seven when Geronimo first came around. He was like 18, 17 or 18. When he first came around, I was not happy, because he just was this guy who randomly showed up, and I was a kid. I didn't really know what was going on. But then, I grew to become pretty close with him. I remember him becoming the number one child fast. He became basically a star there at our church. I hung out with him quite a bit. He lived with us all the time. But the relationship him and I had was fine.

CHILL: Oh, Geronimo. Well, you got to understand the dynamics. Geronimo wasn't ever raised with us. He came into our lives years down the road. He's a step-brother, but we loved him when he first came around. We couldn't listen to any secular music - he brought NWA in the house. He brought in Prince. He was a DJ at the time, so he was 16 or 17, a lot older than us. He's ten years older than me. So we were kids, so I don't know if that corrupted us a little bit.

He was cool for us, because we were coming out of more Baptist. Set Free was kind of cheesy at the time. He brought the hip-hop into the house. We saw him making out with his girlfriend. We were like, "Wow, this guy is cool." We didn't never see that. He was just a cool guy at that time. As time went on, you know the story a little bit. He got more famous in the church, and my dad gave him everything. He was number one son, and we were all just his background singers basically. I didn't even have a problem with that, but I have a problem with people who abuse their power.

We were kids at the time, and he was a lot older. So when lot of stuff had happened and transpired, he left. We hated him for years. I don't think we talked to him for eight or nine years, because he left his wife for another lady, and that hurt us all. I was hurt too by it, because my brother MJ was very close to Geronimo, and I kind of got put to the side. As a young kid I would see my brother Geronimo talking to other girls and his wife would be at home. I was at 12 or 13, I would be like, "Hey dude, why you doing that? You are married." I had some simple - I'd be like, "Bro, that hurts. What about your wife?" God gave me a voice at that time. I'd be like,

"That's wrong, that's wrong." And then I was the bad guy, because he was the cool guy, the leader. So MJ would follow his lead. So they had a bond. Then I wasn't involved with that. They rapped together and did all that. So I think that when Geronimo left, it was a big shock to my dad. It hurt the family tremendously.

We didn't see Geronimo in a lot of years, and when he did that CBN testimony it came out on the news and TV or whatever, on Christian TV. We were shocked. We had heard the story before, and we had told him, "Please don't tell that story. That's just not true." He was making money and creating a big church, so people love hype. People love the circus act. They love the lion tamer. So Geronimo just added more to it. I remember asking him one time in private I said, "Bro, why are you saying this story? It's not true." He goes, "Well, all pastors lie a little bit." I'm like, "Damn, that's a big lie though," I asked him not to say it. And out of respect, he wouldn't say it when I was around, but when it went live and went all over the world, you can't take back what you said. It's there.

So Geronimo, he was never a gang member. I made that clear before. Maybe the Mickey Mouse club or gang-banging with Donald Duck. He maybe smoked a little pot and did some drugs, but he wasn't a gang member guy. So to go on there and act tough, he was just trying to sell. He was trying to make a career for himself and feed his family and feed his ego. And unfortunately, it ended up turning out to be bad. Because he sold a whole city a lie, and it turned on him. It catches up to you. So I don't know why he did that. It was the stupidest thing that he could have ever done.

Well, this is old news. This is all stuff that we've already been though, but so you can hear it. Basically, he had hooked up with a younger girl, a minor. Then he told me and the family about it, because we caught him. I was like the interventionist, but I didn't know he was going to admit to it. I was so mad. I was like, "Dude, I can't believe you'd do this." Then he cried and begged for forgiveness. We forgave him, and we gave him another chance, but he just ended up being more crazy. When you get away with something, you think you can get away with it again. I didn't know nothing about these girls from Texas. I didn't know that he had done something there a long time ago.

Be sure your sin will find you out. It finds us all out. So it was nothing deep or anything crazy - I just warned him. "Get help. Stop now while you are ahead. Bow out gracefully and just admit you are wrong." He just couldn't do it. I left there and me and him became I guess rivals or enemies, and I was the guy who stood up for what I believed was right at the time. But with that, I took a lot of flack from my own family, and a lot of people are mad because it's supposed to be my brother, and I'm supposed to defend him. But the thing about it, I'll defend you if you are right, but I can't defend you for something like that. I left and about a year and a half later after I left, he was arrested.

People went to the police for the stuff that happened in Richmond, Virginia, when I was living there, but the cops didn't do anything about it. "Well, we don't have enough evidence." Which okay, that happens. So we thought it was over. He didn't get caught again. It's over. I'm going back to California. I'm getting out of here. I love Virginia, but I can't stay here with this guy. He has people sold on some lies. I'm just out of here. I don't want to be apart of it when the ship goes down, because I knew the ship was going down. I already watched it in our own lives what sin does.

We just raided a few years before that. So I was like, if we got in trouble, there is no doubt you are not going to get in trouble. The deck of cards were falling, and our time was up. It was time to stop running and just get right with the Lord. Just be real. He didn't want to do that. I told him, "Hey bro, God is going to cut you down sooner or later. Nobody can beat sin. It doesn't mean that I don't love you, but this type of thing, I can't back you up." Where I'm from, anybody in my family will tell you if they are honest, you don't back up the thing that has to do with young kids. You could be a murderer, you could be a stealer, a liar, but our code where we are from, that don't fly. So, I didn't strangle him and beat him up. I said, "I'm outta here."

It was rough for me and my dad, because we were already on shaky ground. I know my dad was hurt. I get it. I'm his son, and I was loyal. I believed I still was loyal. I just think me and him together at that time were toxic. It was a bad. We weren't good together. So when I went to Virginia, I thought that was a time to change my life, and I really wanted to get closer to God, which I did. Through it all, it made it very hard though with my mother, who I love dearly, my family. It was hard, because when there is no communication, the enemy gets in there and can really mess it up.

Geronimo was like, "Oh, I love you even if they don't." He would put stuff in my ear. I knew he didn't love me. I knew he was just playing, trying to get me on his side. Because he figured if he got me on his side, then we are unstoppable. Then I did music there, and a big thing happened with the music. We started having revivals. People started falling out and getting saved. We had like a thousand people show up for worship nights I was doing. That bothered Geronimo, too, because he was prideful. "I don't want you taking my people." So I really felt like I had no place to call home.

I met some great people in Virginia that I loved, but I knew I had to go. So my dad was initially mad, because he didn't know the whole story or what was going on. He didn't know - my dad didn't know what really happened there. I told my dad, and my dad told me one day Geronimo will thank you for warning him. But Geronimo cried to my dad, and unfortunately, a lot of ugliness happened. My dad had to - was trying to be there for both sons, but I was mad at my dad. "You don't believe me. I can't stand you."

Geronimo and me probably have the worst relationship out of everybody, because I'm a realist and I call them out. I said the truth. I did some things, not the Jesus way that I could have because I was angry and upset. But I still believe that I made the right stand against him. We haven't talked in years. I saw him before he got - before all the stuff, his big church went down. But yeah, me and him probably have the worst relationship, because I never respected him as a man. I didn't think he ever had any integrity. I don't respect people that leave their kids. It doesn't mean I don't love him. I just have no respect for him. So for me, it a was a hard one. Geronimo and my story still isn't finished, and I believe God will bring closure one day and peace. But for now, I don't got too many good things to say about Geronimo unfortunately.

I moved back to Orange County, and me and my dad didn't talk for years. A lot of it was my pride, but a lot of it was just learning. Families do this, and people always want to put it off like, "Set Free is weird," or, "The Aguilars are just crazy." It's like we are nutty, but normal families that I talk to everyday, dads and sons they haven't talked in 20 years. It takes time. God worked on our relationship.

Once Geronimo was put in prison for 40 years, me and my dad we came to have a great relationship. So maybe God used all this to test us and see what we are really about. I love Geronimo. It never was coming from a place of hate. But if you love somebody, you tell them the truth. I loved him, and I did what the Bible said. I tried to warn him. I tried to help him. I love him. He's my brother still. I wanted to see him be okay, but there is still a price you have to pay. All of us - we all have to pay a price when you do something terrible.

BILLY AGUILAR: The broken heart on my brother's face was enough for me. Nothing was going to change what happened. The devastation in my brother's life was heavy. As a parent, that's the last thing you want to hear go down with your oldest boy. Especially a boy that you found after so many years that was lost, because people didn't want you to see him. I've never talked to my brother one iota about the Geronimo situation. My situation with my brother with Geronimo is I just pray for him. Because talking to him is not going to change a thing. I don't want to stand judgmental. By the grace of God, there go I. I learned that through Set Free Ministries, and I apply it. I wish the best for Geronimo. Hey, choices. He screwed up. Do your time. Get out. But you got to do your time now. But to see his dad's face was enough for me to keep my mouth shut and just love him where he is at.

A lot of people say, "That's easy to do." No it's not. It's not easy to do. A lot of people want to hear the gossip. That's what they want to hear. They want to hear, "What did he really do?" "I don't know, I haven't talked to Geronimo probably in 10 years." The fastest growing church on the east coast at one time - that rocked that church. I heard people telling me about that church. "Are you affiliated with the church?" I go, "No, I'm not affiliated. It's my nephew. Geronimo is my nephew, but Geronimo screwed up big time, and according to Texas, he'll do most of that time." Texas is like doing federal time. In Texas, you get seven years, you are doing seven years. In Texas, you get the death penalty, you are going to die. Welcome to Texas. That's where he was tried and convicted.

I believe I heard my brother tell somebody, "At least he'll get the opportunity to get closer to God." Wow, is that cool? It's like I'd be in the fetal position at home if one of my sons had to go do that kind of time. My wife would be devastated, you know? But he handles it well. He carries a lot, and he doesn't tell nobody. That is just the kind of guy he is.

SANDRA "SAINT SANDRA" AGUILAR

PASTOR PHIL: Sandra is the epitome of what Proverbs 31 talks about, the virtuous woman. First off, she's meek, a quiet spirit. She is a very prayerful woman. She is funny as can be. She's blind as can be. She still thinks I'm a good looking cool guy. She is a great mother. A great friend. She's a party animal with me. She is a soldier. She is there with me through the good, bad, and ugly. She doesn't hesitate. She is ready to move in and do what I'm go-

Pastor Phil and Sandra

ing to do, go where I'm going to go. She has been on this roller coaster ride with me now for 39 years. It's just amazing. It blows my mind. I would have left me a long, long time ago. But she stuck in there when people said, "You are stupid. You are a fool." I tell you - God saved the best wine for last, because I love her more now today then I ever loved her. God saved the latter glory more than the former glory, because right now it's the best time of our life - the funniest time of our life. Watching things that are happening in our lives. She's just so easy to love. She is so easy to love. When I wake up in the morning hearing her say, "Good morning." That's the sweetest sound in the world.

TRINA: My mom is definitely - her nickname she lives up to it for sure, Saint Sandra. She has put up with a lot of stuff. I don't care what anybody says. I know when we were younger, people would call her 'doormat' and stuff like that. Weird, right? I used to feel so bad. But now that I'm older and I have my own kids and family, I totally understand why she did lots of the things she did. If you see them now, it's hilarious because my dad takes her on dates, and they do all this stuff that I've never seen before. So that's pretty funny.

My mom is like really funny and has a sense of humor. She is a whole different person now, too. She is like a real example of what a wife and what the Bible tells you to be. People don't know what she told him behind closed doors. Everybody just assumes that she went along with whatever he did, but that's not true at all. She's just not the type to go tell his business out on the street. She'll just deal with it at her house. So people don't know that side of her. She's amazing. She's the backbone of our family for sure. Everybody talks to her. Nobody doesn't talk to her. And a lot of times we'd have to go to her, because everybody would be too scared to talk to him. So she would be the one to ask stuff for us or something. She's amazing.

CHILL: In my eyes, she is what grace looks like. She is what love looks like. She is what long-suffering looks like. She is all these things to me. She is the glue that kept the Aguilar family together all these years and still keeping us all together. Without her, we'd either be dead or locked up in a prison cell somewhere. When I think of my mother, what I admire about her is that she really does love people with the heart of Jesus and that is very hard to find these days in Christians and people. She really believes in forgiveness and turning the other cheek and loving people where they are at. That always inspired me to be better. She is a life coach to all the Aguilars. She takes time and counsels with all of her kids. She's been a strength and refuge for all of her kids - all of us. When we couldn't talk to my dad most of our lives growing up and have conversations, she was the middle woman.

So when I think of my mother, I just think of grace. I think of love, compassion, kindness. So many things to describe her, how beautiful she is inside and out. But one thing is she keeps everybody together, and if one side isn't talking, she is the negotiator in between. She brings everybody back together. I think that was probably the strongest asset in the Aguilar life.

In all the ministry and all the years of doing cool stuff, she was the backbone behind it. So that's what I admire about her - just being strong. It takes a strong woman to love a broken-hearted man or a broken-hearted son. So that to me is very, very cool that God made her just stand with us and have our backs. She doesn't need the spotlight. She doesn't need the glory.

MJ: I definitely feel like - when you talk about people's gifts, we all kind of know the standard gifts or maybe the ones we kind of hope to have. She has gifts besides obviously being a wonderful person, great singer. She did that for many years. I still hear her singing as a young boy. Just that voice, I found a lot of comfort in that. But she has these other gifts and qualities starting with obviously her and her husband that are just one of a kind when it comes to her patience and faithfulness. And even when I didn't know how to spell faithfulness, I knew that she was faithful. I knew how caring and concerned she was just as a mother, as a wife, and as an all around human being.

Over the years I was getting my own family and growing up, I just more and more admired the way she saw things - the way she chose to use that gift. She would kind of just walk like she was on her own little planet while all this stuff was happening. Ups and downs and highs and lows. She was just a constant, that thread. In a lot of ways - obviously my dad was apart of that, but she really kept me together. I can really only speak for me, so I will. But she kept me together when there wasn't much being explained or offered. I was confused in different areas of my life, not just as a child but even years. She was that person. She was just like a rock. She was my Peter. She was and is in a lot of ways - just that constant love and just being there. Even when I know she didn't want to be there, even though I know she was going through her own stuff, she would always be there for me and love her children. Sometimes maybe love them too much, but just always there, always available. So thoughtful, so selfless. Probably more today than any other day in my life, I admire that, because that's something I'm trying to work on being. So, she was a great example and is.

PASTOR PHIL AGUILAR

SANDRA: Phil's changed. Every time God has to get his attention - He has to do it through a fire, a raid, an arrest. It takes awhile to get his attention but when he does, he immediately knows its God, and he immediately humbles himself and gets back on track. I don't know how someone lives with a mind and a character that you've developed as a child for whatever reasons and become a Christian and stay on track. I didn't have that problem. I was very loved, and I felt very loved and secured. So for him, whenever there is a challenge or he's being challenged or someone is attacking him, he has this tendency to do something that makes every-body's world blow up around them. So now he's just passive, humble. Nothing bothers him. Nothing phases him anymore. He's just going to do what he does until he dies for sure. What I love about Phil Aguilar is what I've loved about him the first time I was around him - his compassion for other people.

Sandra and Pastor Phil

His love for other people. His desire to help other people. Even when I think he overdoes it. Even when I don't agree with him. No matter what anyone says about him bad or negative, you'll hear a thousand more people say the wonderful things about him. It's the same thing. He's very caring. He's very loving.

I think he was the hardest on his children in the sense of not being as loving towards them in their mistakes and things like that. He'd be harder on them, and they would always say to me, "I don't understand. He loves them more than he loves me. He takes care of them more than he takes care of me." No, he knows they don't have love. It was hard for them to understand that, but it was because he knew they were okay.

He's grandfather of the year - every year. He loves his grandkids - every one of them. He didn't get to spend time with his own children when they were young and do the things with them, so he missed out a lot and he realizes he missed out on a lot, and he doesn't want to miss out on his

TRINA: What I love about Pastor Phil is the heart he has for people and how he seriously gives up his time. I wouldn't say gives up stuff he loves to do, because this is what he loves to do is help people. But, he'll give his last dollar. He'll move them in if my mom will let people live in the house right now it would be full, but she won't. So I love that about him, because that's what I love. And if my husband would let me, I'd have my house full, too. There is certain stuff he does that is embarrassing to me for sure. But now, I just learn to take the good and try to overlook the bad stuff, because me and him we definitely work together. We are so much alike, but we are so different in a lot of ways too. So I don't really know how to explain it well, but we have the same goal. But the way we reach is not the same. So I have to respect the way he does it, and he is learning to respect the way I do it. It's interesting. I never thought we would work on this kind of level together.

CHILL: For years, I was so mad at my dad, because I felt like he could have done more. I had all these high expectations and the reality is the dude has to look at himself in the mirror every morning and deal with the stuff he's been through or done. He don't need nobody to kick him or the bad he's done. He knows what he's done. I just started looking at my dad with the eyes of love. If it wasn't for my beautiful mother, I said I would never talk to my dad again. My beautiful mother - she prayed and prayed and this is me as a Christian. I'm taking a stand against my brother and Jesus and I'm about Jesus, but I hate my father?

The phony friends came along that liked seeing me and him fighting. At the time, I was just out of my mind. I was so mad at my dad for not doing what I thought he should do as a father and never looked at that is his son, too. I remember telling my mom, "I'll never talk to you guys again. I'll never talk to you. I hate my dad," at that time for not being the dad he should be. Remember, we are adding a lot of stuff from the past into these feelings. We never dealt with that. So my beautiful mother I told her, "Don't call me. Don't talk to me. You'll never see your granddaughters." I said some very harsh things because I was hurt. Families say bad stuff when they are hurt that they don't mean. My beautiful mother never stopped praying. The mother who they are going to protect their kid from anything.

We didn't get to talk much, because she was one side and I was on the other, which I get. I've been there, so I know how it rolls. Out of sight, out of mind. Love the ones you are with. I grew up on that, so we probably could have ended it quicker, but my pride and my dad's pride. Here's what happened, my wife's brother 38 years old went to the hospital one week and six months later he's dead. He died of cancer, my brother-in-law. My wife says, "You should probably call your dad." Life was just going terrible, too. Let's be honest. For me, every door was closing. I hear God, "You need to forgive." I had people in my ear, "You don't need to forgive. Your dad is this. Your dad is that." They loved that I wasn't cool with my dad, and that's sad if you think about it. I would never want any kid not to be cool with their dad. Even if their dad did wrong or did bad, the past is the past. My beautiful mother - she kept praying and one year ago - literally one year ago, my mother said, "I don't care what any of your brothers or sisters think about it. I don't care what your dad thinks about it. You are my son, and I love you." That's powerful. When a mother tells you that - especially after what I'd been through and what I had said. Everybody gets hurt in it.

My brother Geronimo had daughters. I'm sure I hurt them by things I said, right? I was just trying to do what was right. One day maybe they will understand that I was never trying to hurt them. So I get when stuff starts flying, innocent bystanders get hit. In this, my mother got hit, and my wife got hit. People got hit and feelings were hurt. Me and my dad slowly started talking. We met for dinner and my mom says, "You got to see him now. He's different." This guy is never going to be different. I never seen my dad cry. I never seen my dad - he said, "Son, I love you. I love you. I'm proud of you." "What you are proud? I've never heard that in my whole life."

So I knew that God did a supernatural thing in my dad's life. I lost a few friends, but I don't care. It's my dad. My dad, like any dad - they have stuff they go through. I always tell people this. For my dad - everybody else says, "Oh, Phil Aguilar fell from grace. Phil Aguilar fell from grace." I always say, "No, he fell to grace, because God is love, and God is grace." You don't fall from grace. That was the thing, for me, I started seeing that my dad really changed. That you were talking about, "Hey, have you seen your dad change?"

No, I didn't see him change in the years back, but once I saw him with the eyes of Jesus, I saw he's just a man just like me and you. Getting out of bed every morning and having to put on the good man or the old man. It's a choice he has to make. For a long time, he put on the old man. That lead to pride and fighting and arguing. Then, he puts on the Jesus side, and we click. When he talks about Jesus and I talk about Jesus, we click. When we talk about anything that has to do with family, it could be drama, but we know we love each other now. We know each other. You have to go through some stuff. Confrontation is good. It was good for us. It hurt, but it was good. Because now we are at a place with the Church of God and him doing that. He brought me under the Church of God's wing and helped me plant a church in Burbank. Now we are ministering to hundreds of people a week there.

Me and him now together are doing ministry like I always wanted. There is nothing in between. There is no bike talk. We laugh. We can't even stand talking about the old days. It was so old. It was so long. There were some great memories, but it's so old. Now, we are here. What God is doing now is so much more great. The Church of God has just embraced us and helped us. The bishop and everybody has just been a blessing. Eddie Banales, all these guys have poured into us, and they took once what was broken and lost, is now found. They put us together. It was weird how God worked it out. The same thing that tried to destroy our family, which is religion and church and ministry, is now the same thing that brought us back together. So me and my dad, we have a great relationship. I'm so glad this stuff happened, because we would never have had this relationship if we didn't go through this.

AGUILAR LOVE

MJ: Well, man, I love and admire him a lot. I remember we didn't have a lot of moments me and him where it was just me and him as a kid. I have a lot of moments where I was around him. We were at the same places and sharing the same good news on the same plane and the same bus and same building, but there is a few moments that I really remember where it was just me and him like a face to face - almost like a father and son. Just because of the work we did and the style that he was as a parent or just as a person, I don't know.

I really felt his passion, his love, his dedication for servanthood and for loving Jesus when he just told me, "Son, I don't care what you do as long as you just love Jesus with everything you've got, you are going to be alright. I'm going to make sure that you are alright. I'll give you whatever you need as long as you just keep loving Jesus." I was maybe 10 or 12 years old. So I'm trying to even at that young age trying to comprehend, but I understood it then, and I remember it now. I'll never forget it. It was a moment we had, and it was a moment that I definitely now in my older years admire more as someone who is trying to be that servant, who is trying to stay servant minded, and trying to be a leader. But probably make sure I'm a servant before I'm a leader, and he showed me that over and over again through his actions.

In so many ways to me, he is more like a character in the Bible than anybody that I have ever encountered. That's not because he is my dad. That is just to me because how I feel the truth - because of what he has been through and knocked down, get back up. Fell down, get back up. Tripped and fell forward, persevered. Just continued to evolve in his faith and his trust in God. He showed that. Even when he wasn't showing what I thought were maybe the strongest father qualities, he was showing godly qualities that I couldn't help but to admire and look up to. I always tried to focus on that rather than maybe some of the other things. He always offered that. Obviously, he was always there as far as making sure a roof was over our head and we were fed. Whether it was filet mignon or chow mein, that just kind of speaks to the highs and lows that we've all been through in life. He just kept it God. He just kept it Jesus. He kept us focused on what matters most and I always loved that about him.

He's a little nutty and crazy and different and special and weird and wild and famous and infamous and all of the above. He is probably the most inconsistent, consistent guy I know. I don't know if that makes sense. It's just because he's so all over the place, but he is so focused at the same time. His feeling will take him here, but then he knows exactly what he's called to do on this earth. Because I get to serve with him every single day now, I really just try to stop and pause and appreciate the moment and learn from him and work side by side. Which to me is just a blessing and more of the Word coming to life in the things he told me and get to see play out now. I get to see that in the flesh, and I get to see that as I'm doing it with him.

Keep serving Jesus and hope in God. He's going to work it out. Even if it's through our troubles or our difficult times or our anguish, He is going to accomplish what He is going to accomplish. We might be the ones used for that. I got to trust Him. So to see him go through it all and being there for it all, man, I just have so much respect on a whole other level. I like it again, because I just try to make the Bible real, and I feel like God gave me someone who I needed in my life growing up and to this day. Where I needed someone like him who just went through it, struggled, heart after God but stumbled maybe in this area or fell short here and didn't just throw in the towel, but kind of used the towel to wipe the tears and get back in on the fight. He is a fighter. It's just so cool to see that happening. God used him. So I just admire his fight. I really do.

AGUILAR GRANDCHILDREN

PASTOR PHIL: I have 23 grandchildren from five children. We are blended families, his, hers, theirs and ours, but I know all of them personally. Most of them I get to see quite often. I've got them from two years old to 25 years old. I take them to the parks. I take them to the playgrounds. I take them to contents. I take them out dancing, swimming, pool parties. I love my grandchildren. I believe God gives us grandchildren, because we were so blessed and behaved by not killing our children, so he gives us grandchildren, because they are better than children. It's another generation that I get to share the love of Jesus with. I teach them the finger and how to tell people

Scarlette Aguilar and Pastor Phil

to go to heaven. Love on people. Forgive people. It's another chance, because when I was in the ministry with all my children, I was doing 18 hours a day as a ministry. A lot of times I didn't get to spend time with my children that I get to spend with my grandchildren now. I get to do a little time with them, a little makeover with them, and realize what's really important. That's why I love spending time with my grandchildren.

PASTOR PHIL AGUILAR

CONFERENCE KEYNOTE
Pastor Phil is a sought after speaker for conferences on pastoral ministry, leadership, and drug treatment.

GUEST SPEAKER
With over forty years of ministry experience, Pastor Phil is an excellent guest speaker to book for your weekend or mid-week church service.

EVANGELIST
Whether it's on outreach to skid row or a youth rally in the suburbs, Pastor Phil can bring the Word like no one else.

DRUG TREATMENT CONSULTANT
With over forty years in addiction treatment, Pastor Phil is known as a miracle worker when it comes to helping people find freedom.

MORE INFO: www.SetFree.org
www.BlackSheepRecovery.com

BOOK PASTOR PHIL:
714.400.4573 or setfreephil@aol.com

RESOURCES

DOCUMENTARY FILM
Set Free Posse: Jesus Freaks,
Biker Gang, or Christian Cult?

More info at www.SetFreeFilm.com.

BOOKS
Trained to Serve Jesus: The Heart and History of
Set Free Church and Its Founder Phil Aguilar

Go To Heaven: Chiefisms That Shaped
The Ministry of Pastor Phil Aguilar

Available on www.Amazon.com.

MUSIC ALBUMS
Giving the Glory
Start Me Up Jesus
Goin' God's Way
We Need Peace
Set Free Tribe Greatest Hits
West Coast Flava

*All albums and songs are available individually on
iTunes, Amazon Music, Google Play, and other platforms.*

MORE INFO: www.SetFreeFilm.com